TABLE OF CONTENTS

FREEDOM OF TESTATION AND INTESTATE SUCCESSION

PROTECTION OF THE FAMILY

EXECUTION, VALIDITY AND COMPONENTS OF WILLS

Wills, Trusts, Probate, Administration and the Fiduciary

by
MYRON G. HILL, JR.
Adjunct Professor of Law, Antioch School of Law
Member of Bars of: District of Columbia, Ohio, U.S. Court of Federal Claims, U.S. Court of Appeals for the Federal Circuit and U.S. Supreme Court

HOWARD M. ROSSEN
Director, Ohio Bar Review & BAR/BRI
Member of Ohio, District of Columbia, Florida, Pennsylvania and U.S. Supreme Court Bars

and

WILTON S. SOGG
Adjunct Professor of Law, Cleveland-Marshall College of Law, Cleveland State University
Lecturer on Law, Harvard Law School
Member of Ohio, District of Columbia, Florida, N.Y., U.S. Tax Court and U.S. Supreme Court Bars

SMITH'S REVIEW
published by
Emanuel Law Outlines, Inc.

Emanuel Law Outlines, Inc. • 1865 Palmer Avenue • Larchmont, NY 10538

Abbreviations Used in Text

Bogert—George J. Bogert, *Trusts*
(West Publ., Hornbook Series, 6th Ed. 1987)

Clark—Clark, Lusky and Murphy, *Cases and Materials on Gratuitous Transfers* (West Publ., 3rd Ed. 1985)

Dukeminier—Dukeminier and Johanson, *Wills, Trusts and Estates*
(Little, Brown, 4th Ed. 1990 w/ 1992 Supp.)

Haskell—Paul G. Haskell, *Preface to Wills, Trusts and Administration* (Foundation Press, 1987)

McGovern—McGovern, Kurtz, and Rein, *Wills, Trusts and Estates*
(West Publ., 1988)

Rest. of Trusts, 2d—American Law Institute, *Restatement Second of Trusts*
(Student Edition, 1959)

Ritchie—Ritchie, Alford, Jr., and Effland, *Cases and Materials on Decedents' Estates and Trusts*
(Foundation Press, 6th Ed. 1982)

Simes—Lewis M. Simes, *Law Of Future Interests*,
(West Publ., Hornbook Series, 2nd Ed. 1966)

UPC—*Uniform Probate Code; Official 1991 Text with Comments*
(West Publ., 10th Ed. 1991)

Waggoner—Waggoner, Wellman, Alexander, and Fellows, *Family Property Law*
(Foundation Press, 1991)

ISBN#1-56542-181-7

CONSTRUCTION OF WILLS

REVOCATION AND REPUBLICATION OF WILLS

NATURE OF TRUSTS

PRIVATE EXPRESS TRUSTS

CHARITABLE TRUSTS

RESULTING TRUSTS

CONSTRUCTIVE TRUSTS

CREATION, MODIFICATION AND TERMINATION OF TRUSTS

LIMITATIONS ON CREATIONS AND DURATION OF INTERESTS IN TRUSTS

JURISDICTION OVER ADMINISTRATION

PROBATE, APPOINTMENT OF THE PERSONAL REPRESENTATIVE AND MANAGEMENT OF THE ESTATE

THE TRUSTEE AS FIDUCIARY

FREEDOM OF TESTATION AND INTESTATE SUCCESSION

I. TRANSFERS ON DEATH — INTRODUCTION

A. **Ability to transfer:** The ability to ***transfer property at death*** is one of the bundle of rights included in the concept of private property.

1. **Two theories:** Two major theories exist as to the nature of the right to make transfers at death:

   a. **"Natural right":** That it is a "natural right" inherent in the people. *Nunnemacher v. State,* 108 N.W. 627 (Wisc. 1906).

   b. **Granted by state:** That it is a right ***granted by the state*** and as such can be ***taken away*** or ***regulated*** by the state. This is the more widely held view.

2. **Differing results:** The result in a succession case may depend on which theory (a or b above) is accepted. If theory (a) is accepted, the state's ability to put limits on death transfers is restricted. If theory (b) is accepted, by contrast, the state has the ***absolute power*** to grant or deny death transfer rights, or to place on them whatever limitations it desires. The following example illustrates the effect of theory (b).

   Example: D dies intestate, domiciled in California. D's intestate successors are citizens and residents of the Soviet Union. A California statute provides that all non-resident aliens must demand their intestacy interests within five years from the date of succession, or the interests escheat to the state. Resident aliens, by contrast, need only demand their interests within five years from the date of a decree of distribution. The non-resident alien claimants do not demand their interests within five years of D's death, but do appear before the expiration of five years from the distribution decree. The state claims escheat, and the claimants claim that the statutory scheme discriminates against them in violation of due process.

   Held, for the state. A state has full power to regulate the descent and distribution of decedents' estates and may, if it sees fit, give non-resident aliens merely a conditional interest in the estate. Since the state has full power to prohibit any succession at all, it may alternatively impose any conditions it wants on the succession. *In re Estate of Herman*, 485 P.2d 785 (Cal. 1971).

3. **Arguments pro and con:** Should states give their citizens wide latitude in the disposition of property at death? Arguments can be made on either side of this question.

   a. **Against latitude:** Arguments against giving the decedent wide latitude in disposition are:

      i. **Undemocratic:** Inheritance violates the basic democratic ideal of ***equality of opportunity***;

      ii. **Control from grave:** The dead cannot wisely ***dictate*** the best uses of property for long periods of time ***after their death***;

      iii. **Poor use:** People who inherit large amounts of wealth may not use it in the ***best interests of society***; and

      iv. **Sloth:** Inheritance causes its recipients to be ***self indulgent*** and ***unproductive***.

   b. **In favor of latitude:** The following arguments can be made in favor of giving an owner wide latitude in disposing of his holdings at death:

      i. **Incentive:** A broad right of disposition gives a person an ***incentive*** to engage in productive (and wealth-building) activity while he is still alive;

      ii. **Capital:** Inherited wealth is necessary to the economy as a source of ***capital***;

      iii. **Source of support:** Inheritance provides a source of ***support*** for ***dependents*** of the decedent;

      iv. **Philanthropy:** Inherited wealth is a key method of supporting ***philanthropy***;

      v. **Justice:** Inheritance is just, because its usual recipients have ***indirectly contributed*** to its production; and

      vi. **Socialism:** Abolition of inheritance is a first step to state socialism.

   See Clark, pp. 3-4.

4. **Constitutional limitation:** The federal government may not enact a complete prohibition on the passing of land by will or intestate succession. To do so would violate the Just Compensation Clause of the Fifth Amendment.

   Example: In the late 1800s Congress enacted a series of land Acts which divided certain Indian reservations into individual allotments, which were held in trust for Indians by the federal government. As the allottees died, the land passed to their heirs according to state intestate succession law. After 1910 the allottees could dispose of their land by will. This plan was approved by the Indians affected. The purpose of the law was to protect Indian ownership of the lands. However, as successive generations came to hold the land, the parcels became splintered among hundreds of owners, resulting in unproductive use of the land.

In 1983, Congress provided that no interest in the land could be passed after death by an owner who had received less than $100 from the land in the year preceding his death. Instead, the land would escheat to the Indian tribe in that reservation. No provision for payment to the heirs was made.

Heirs who would have taken the land by will or intestate succession if the land had not escheated to their tribe, filed suit against the federal government, claiming the 1983 statute was a taking of property without just compensation in violation of the Fifth Amendment.

Held (by the U.S. Supreme Court), the statute is unconstitutional because it is taking of property without compensation. Although the owner had the use of the land during his life and could convey it *inter vivos*, the right to pass title to one's heirs is itself a valuable right. The 1983 statute effectively abolished disposition of property in intestacy or by will. The destruction of these rights is a taking without just compensation under the Fifth Amendment. *Hodel v. Irving*, 481 U.S. 704 (1987).

II. INTESTACY — TERMINOLOGY

A. Terminology in general: In this section, we introduce some of the terminology that is used in connection with ***intestate succession***, i.e., the distribution of property when there is no will.

1. **Intestate:** If a person dies without a will, he is said to die ***"intestate."*** Conversely, a person who dies leaving a valid will is said to die ***"testate."***

2. **Testator:** Traditionally, the person who made the will was called the ***"testator"*** if a man, and the ***"testatrix"*** if a woman. The modern practice, followed in the Uniform Probate Code, uses ***"testator"*** for both men and women.

3. **Real vs. personal property:** Different terms are used to distinguish the passage of ***real property*** from the passage of ***personal property***.

   a. **Descent:** When the property is ***real estate***, that property is said to pass by ***"descent."*** The statute that provides for the handling of an intestate decedent's real property is typically called the ***"statute of descent."***

b. **Distribution:** When ***personal property*** passes, the person receiving it is generally called the ***"distributee"*** or "next of kin." The statute governing passage of personal property in intestacy is usually called the "statute of ***distribution."***

c. **Significance of distinction:** Under early English law, the distinction between real and personal property was of great significance. One given land was a ***"devisee"*** and one who received personal property was a ***"legatee."*** Modern legislation, for the most part, has abolished the practical distinction between real estate and personalty in intestate situations, although the terminology is still in common use.

Example: The Uniform Probate Code makes no distinction between real and personal property; UPC §1-201(10) defines "devise" to include the disposition of real and personal property by a will. An intestate's property, whether real or personal, passes by intestate success to his heirs.

4. **Consanguinity: *"Consanguinity"*** means a blood relationship between two people. Consanguinity is either ***"lineal"*** or ***"collateral."***

a. **Lineal:** A ***"lineal"*** relationship between two persons means that the two are ***directly related*** to each other, in either a descending or ascending line. Thus, father-son, grandfather-granddaughter, great grandmother-great grandson, are lineal relationships.

b. **Collateral:** A ***"collateral"*** relationship between two people means that they have a ***common ancestor***. Here are some examples:

i. ***Brothers*** (if A and B are brothers, they have a common ancestor, namely a father and/or mother);

ii. ***Cousins*** (first cousins have a common ancestor, the grandparent);

iii. ***Uncles and aunts*** to nephews and nieces (if E is F's uncle, the common ancestor is E's parent and F's grandparent).

B. **Intestacy statutes:** Statutes in every state set out the order in which persons succeed to an intestate's property. See, e.g., §§2-101 through 2-114 of the Uniform Probate Code (UPC).

1. **Rationale:** Intestacy statutes provide for orderly administration, by identifying successors to an intestate's estate. These statutes attempt to carry out the distribution that most intestates would have provided had they made wills. They operate on the theory that

most persons prefer near relatives to more remote relatives.

2. **Order of preference:** Intestacy statutes generally establish an order of preference among certain named relatives of the deceased.

   Example: A typical statutory pattern provides for the following line of succession: (1) surviving spouse; (2) children; (3) parents; (4) brothers and sisters and their lineal descendants; (5) grandparents and their lineal descendants; (6) next of kin, (7) if no next of kin, then escheat to the state. See UPC §§2-102 through 2-103, 2-105, implementing the above order of preference.

3. **"Next of kin":** Many statutes use the term ***"next of kin"*** to control the order of preference. That is, the statute may say that the property goes to the decedent's next of kin. A person's next of kin are all those living persons standing at the ***same closest degree of consanguinity*** (blood relationship) to the person.

   a. **Two methods:** Two methods have developed for computing degrees of consanguinity for purposes of determining next of kin: (1) the civil law method and (2) the common law method. In the U.S., the ***civil law*** method is used almost exclusively.

   b. **Civil law method:** Under the civil law method, the degree of blood relationship is computed differently for ***collateral*** relatives than for ***lineal*** relatives:

      i. **Collateral relatives:** For a collateral relative, one ***counts the generations*** from the ***decedent*** up to the ***common ancestor***, and then the generations from that ancestor down to the claimant.

      Example: Assume we need to determine the degree of relationship between Decedent and her First Cousin. The common ancestor is the grandparent. Therefore, there are two generations from Decedent to the grandparent, and another two generations from the grandparent down to the First Cousin. Thus Decedent and the First Cousin are said to be "related in the fourth degree" under the prevailing civil law method. See Chart I, *infra*, p. 6.

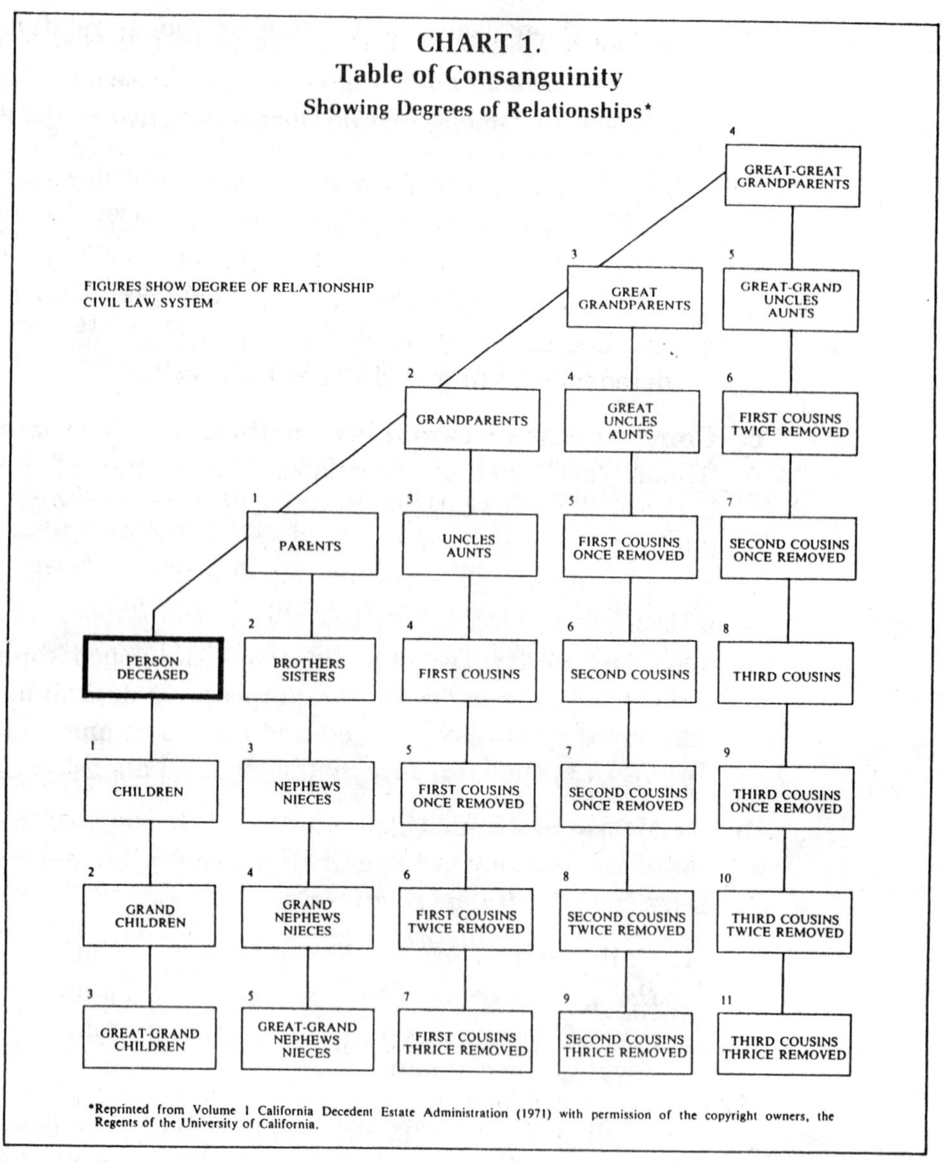

CHART 1.
Table of Consanguinity
Showing Degrees of Relationships*

*Reprinted from Volume 1 California Decedent Estate Administration (1971) with permission of the copyright owners, the Regents of the University of California.

ii. Lineal line: Under the civil law method, to determine the degree of relationship between two ***lineal*** relatives, it is not necessary to find the common ancestor — it is only necessary to count generations, either in the ascending or descending line.

Example: We need to find the degree of relation between the decedent and his great grandson. Counting down from the decedent, there are three generations (child, grandchild, and great grandchild). Therefore, the two are related in the third degree. See Chart I, *supra.*

iii. Tie breaking: Normally, in the civil law system, two claimants of equal degree will ***share***. (For instance, as shown in Chart I, a first cousin twice removed would share with a second cousin, since each is in the sixth degree of relation to the decedent.) Some states modified the civil law method by providing if two claimants are in the same degree of relation to the decedent, the claimant with the ***nearer common ancestor*** prevails. (In such a system, the first cousin twice removed would win out over the second cousin, since the former is related to the decedent through the decedent's grandparent, the latter only through the decedent's great grandparent.) Haskell p. 15.

c. **Common-law or canon law method:** The ***"common law"*** or "canon law" method calculates the degree of relationship between lineal relations in the same way as the civil law method. But the common law method computes the relation between collateral relatives differently from the civil law method: instead of taking the ***sum*** of the steps to the ancestor and down to the claimant, the common law method takes the steps up to the ancestor ***or*** the steps down to the claimant, ***whichever is larger***.

Example: We need to determine the degree of relation between decedent and his Uncle. Under the civil law method, they are related in the third degree (two steps up from decedent to his grandparent, plus one step down to the Uncle). Under the canon law method, they are related in the ***second*** degree, because we take the ***greater*** of the two steps up to the grandparent or the one step down to the Uncle — the greater of two steps and one step is two steps.

d. **A complicated example:** To practice computing under the two methods, let's take a complicated example drawn from Chart II, *infra*. Our problem is to determine the degree of relationship between E (the child of X) and S (the child of G). (As shown on the chart, X, Y, and Z are all children of C; D and E are children of X, and so on.)

CHART II. Kinship—Civil and Canon Law Methods Compared

The following example demonstrates the method of determining kinship under the civil and canon law systems:

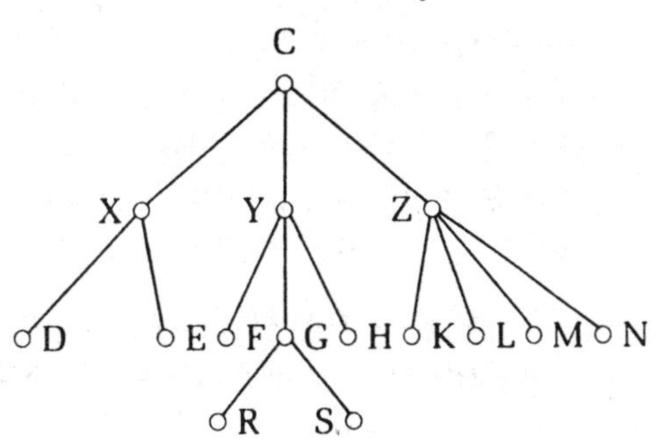

i. **Civil law method:** Under the civil law method, E and S are related in the fifth degree. Starting with E, it is: (1) up to X; (2) up to C; (3) down to Y; (4) down to F; (5) down to S.

ii. **Common law method:** Under the common law method, E and S are related in the ***third*** degree. It is the greater of: (1) the number of steps from E up to the common ancestor, C (two steps) or (2) the number of steps from C down to S (three steps: C-Y, Y-F and F-S).

e. **Effect of difference:** The choice of method (civil vs. common law) will usually not make a difference as to who takes the estate (though the civil law method will usually produce numbers in a higher degree).

f. **Parentelic system:** In a few states, the system of determining takers does not involve the computation of degrees at all. Instead, the ***parentelic*** system is used, in which all descendants of the ***nearest ancestor*** are preferred over descendants of more remote ancestors. See Haskell, pp. 15-16.

Example 1: Under a parentelic system, all descendants of the decedent's parents would take before any descendant of the decedent's grandparents, even though the latter might have a closer degree of kinship.

Example 2: In the family shown in Chart II, *supra*, assume that F dies, and S and Z are the only living survivors. Under the parentelic system, S would take the whole estate, because the common ancestor that she shares with F (Y, who is the decedent's father) is closer to the decedent than the common ancestor that Z shares with the decedent (C, who is the decedent's grandfather). Yet under a civil law system, they would share, since each is in the third degree of relationship to the decedent (assuming that the civil law has not been modified to ***"break ties"*** as discussed *supra*, pp. 6).

4. **Escheat:** Statutes vary as to the number of relationships they specify — some go only to grandparents and their issue, others to great-grandparents or beyond. No matter how far out the statute goes, however, it may not go far enough to find any living descendants of a particular decedent. Therefore, every statute provides that ***if no next of kin can be found*** (going to the furthest class of relatives defined in the statute), the ***intestate estate passes to the state***. This passage to the state is known as the ***doctrine of escheat***.

5. **Renunciation:** When a gift is made by a living person or by a will, the ***recipient cannot be forced to accept it*** — the donee or

legatee may ***renounce*** the gift or bequest. This is sometimes called a ***disclaimer***. In the case of intestate succession, however, this has not always been true.

a. **Traditional view:** Traditionally, the vesting of title in the heir has been deemed to occur by operation of law rather than volitionally. The heir has ***no ability to renounce***. This deprives the heir of the ability to avoid ***creditors***, or ***estate taxes***, by ***renouncing in favor of someone else*** (e.g., a child who has no creditors and is younger, with less of an estate-tax burden). See Haskell, p. 22; Waggoner, p. 96.

   Example: D obtains a judgment against X. Subsequently, X inherits land from her mother, who dies intestate. X renounces her inheritance. *Held*, the land passed to X the instant that her mother died, and D's lien attached to X's interest at that moment. Thus the renunciation does not defeat D's lien. *Coomes v. Finegan*, 233 Iowa 448, 7 N.W. 2d 729 (1943).

b. **Modern solution:** Most states now allow heirs to ***renounce*** and thereby defeat claims of creditors. Where an heir renounces an inheritance, the property passes as though the heir had predeceased the decedent. See UPC §2-801, which allows the heir to ***file an instrument of renunciation*** within nine months after the death of the decedent.

C. **Division of shares:** Suppose that there is more than one descendant of the intestate decedent. How do they divide the property? They don't necessarily divide it equally.

1. **Some terminology:** Before we can examine how states commonly solve the problem of dividing the estate among multiple descendants, we must first understand the meaning of two important terms: (1) ***"per capita"*** and (2) ***"per stirpes."*** The following chart (Chart III) will help us in our analysis.

CHART III.

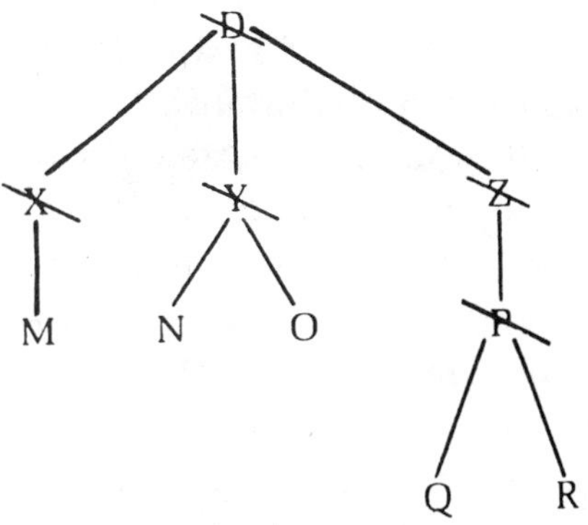

(A line through the party indicates deceased)

a. **Per capita:** Taking ***per capita*** means taking ***equally***, divided among the number of takers.

Example: M, N, O, Q, and R, share in D's estate as shown in Chart III. If they take ***"per capita,"*** each will take a fifth, since there are five of them.

b. **Per stirpes:** Taking ***per stirpes*** (Latin for "by the root") means taking ***"by right of representation."*** If an estate is distributed per stirpes, a taker's share is determined by the share his ***ancestor*** would have had. The most common application of a per stirpes distribution occurs when the ***living descendants are not all from the same generation***.

Example: If the five living descendants in Chart III take ***per stirpes***, Q and R will share ***by representation*** what their now-deceased parent (P) would have taken had he been the survivor; they will thus each get one-eighth. M, N and O will each get one-fourth, under the ***majority approach*** to ***per stirpes***. (See *infra*, p. 11.) Observe that if P's spouse is still alive, the distribution will not change. P's living spouse takes nothing because there is no blood relationship between P's spouse and D.

2. **All same generation:** In a situation where ***all of the living descendants*** are members of the ***same generation***, most American statutes give (or are interpreted to give) a ***per capita*** distribution.

Example: D dies intestate, leaving grandchildren A, B and C as next of kin. A is the daughter of D's deceased son, M. B and C are the sons of D's deceased son, O. (The situation is diagrammed in Chart IV, *infra*.) The relevant statute provides property is to pass "in equal shares to the children of said deceased person or the legal representatives of deceased's children." A claims she is entitled to one-half of the estate (i.e., B and C should each get one-fourth because they take through their parent, O who would get one-half); A claims the distribution should be per stirpes. B and C claim that all three take directly as heirs per capita.

Held, for B and C. The estate should be divided one third to each of A, B and C. Most American statutes concerning descent and distribution (including the one here) are derived from the English Statute of Distributions. Under the English statute, per stirpes distribution occurs only when the claimants are from different generations. American jurisdictions have adopted the same approach; when all claimants are part of the same generation (i.e., equally related to the decedent), they take per capita. This rule is clearly just and is in harmony with other provisions of the statute under which father and mother share equally, brothers and sisters share equally, and next-of-kin share equally. *In re Martin's Estate*, 120 A. 862 (Vt. 1923).

CHART IV.

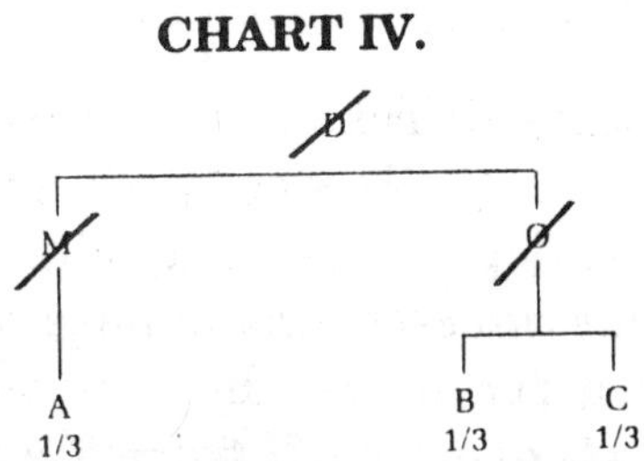

(A line through the party indicates deceased)

3. **Different generations:** When the survivors are ***not of the same generation***, nearly all states distribute the estate ***per stirpes***.

    Example: D dies, leaving two children (X and Y) and two grandchildren (M and N, who are the children of D's deceased child Z). In nearly all states, X will get one-third, Y will get one-third, and M and N will each get one-sixth — that is, M and N will take per stirpes, by splitting the one-third interest that their parent Z would have gotten had he been alive.

    a. **Root level:** When all the decedent's children are dead, the states vary as to which level should be used as the ***"root level"*** in computing the ***per stirpes*** distribution. The choices for root level are: (1) the first level in which there is a survivor (the ***majority approach***) and (2) the level nearest the decedent, even though there are no survivors at that level (the ***minority approach***).

    b. **Majority "first survivor" approach:** Under the majority approach, the root level is the ***first level at which there is at least one survivor***. The estate is then divided into the number of shares equal to the number of persons who survive at that level, or who have issue who survive.

    Example: Using the family shown in Chart III, *supra*, p. 9. the root level is the level of the grandchildren. At that level, there are three living descendants and one who has died but has living issue. Therefore, the estate is divided into fourths, with M, N and O each getting a fourth and P's fourth being split between his living children Q and R, each of whom gets one-eighth. See Chart V(A), *infra*. Chart V(B) illustrates the minority view which treats the level nearest the decedent as the root level ***whether or not there is a survivor at that***

level; this minority approach is discussed more fully *infra*, p. 13.

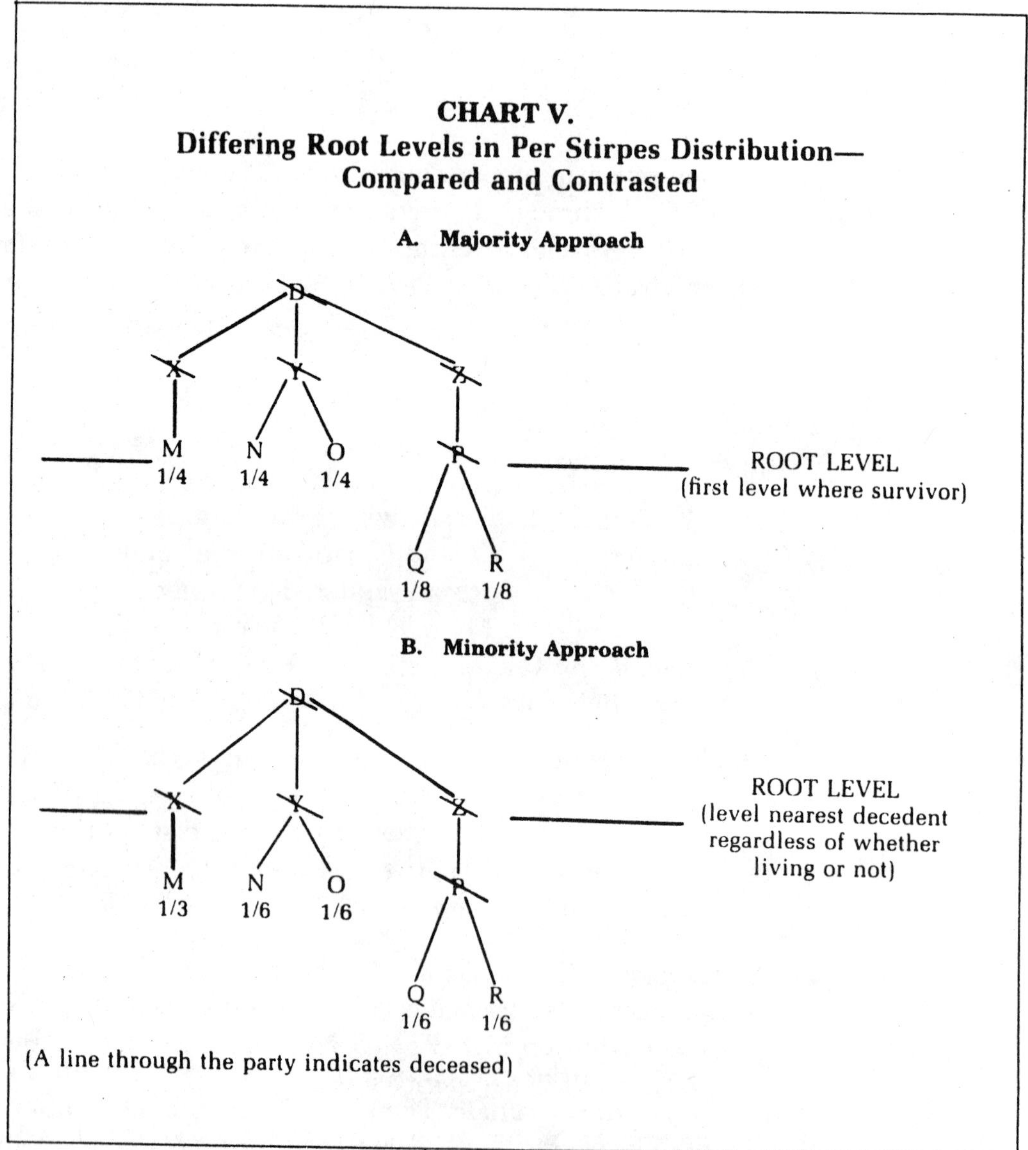

Example: The deceased, D, dies intestate, leaving the following surviving relatives only: (1) two nephews, A and B, sons of D's deceased brother, James; (2) four nieces, E, F, G and H, surviving daughters of D's deceased sister, Mary; and (3) five grand-nephews, K, L, M, N and P, sons of Mary's deceased daughter, Julia (diagrammed in Chart VI, *infra*). The applicable statute provides that the relatives of the deceased intestate standing in the same degree shall take per capita, and when some in such same degree are dead leaving issue, the issue shall take per stirpes.

Under the majority approach (applicable here), the root level for determining per stirpes distribution is the grandchildren of C (the oldest generation that has some living survivors). With six living members of that generation (A through H), plus one dead member (Julia), who has living issue, the estate must be divided into seven parts. Each of the five living children of Julia (K through P) takes one-fifth of one-seventh, or one-thirty-fifth. (The six living grandchildren of C, A through H, take per capita according to the statute; each gets one-seventh, leaving the final seventh for Julia's children.) *Kincaid v. Cronin*, 22 N.E.2d 576 (Ohio App. 1939).

CHART VI.

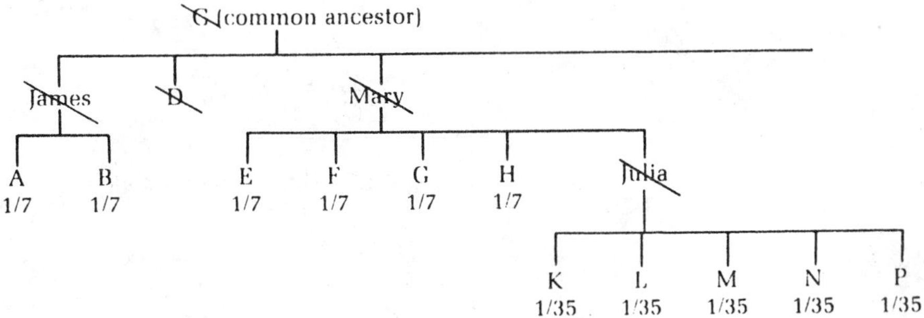

(A line through the party indicates deceased)

c. **Minority "first generation" approach:** Under the minority approach, the root level is the ***generation closest to the decedent***, even if that generation has no members surviving at the time of the decedent's death.

Example 1: Again, assume the family shown in Chart III (*supra*, p. 9). Under the minority approach, the root level is the generation of D's children, even though all of them (X, Y and Z) have predeceased D. Thus, the estate is divided into three equal portions, one for the line of each of the now-deceased children of D. Therefore, M (X's child) gets one-third; O and N (Y's children) each gets one-sixth; and Q and R (D's greatgrandchildren) each gets one-sixth. See also Chart V(B), *supra*, p. 12.

Example 2: D dies, leaving a trust to be divided on the death of the last of his seven children. The trust agreement states that the property should be distributed at the death of the surviving child, to D's descendants as they would have been entitled as his heirs at law had D died at the time of distribution. D is survived by four grandchildren and two great-grandchildren, as shown in Chart VII, *infra*. The applicable statute provides that if all of the descendants are of the same degree they take per capita, and that otherwise they take per stirpes.

Held, the root level is the generation of D's children, even though all of them predeceased D. Since there are four children who have left issue that survived D, the estate is divided into fourths. Louise and Joseph take one-eighth each (dividing the one-fourth share of Clara). Jan takes the one-fourth share of Flora. Ethel takes the one-fourth share of Charles. Harry and Elizabeth take one-eighth each (dividing the one-fourth share of Robert). *Maud v. Catherwood*, 155 P.2d 111 (Cal. 1945).

CHART VII.

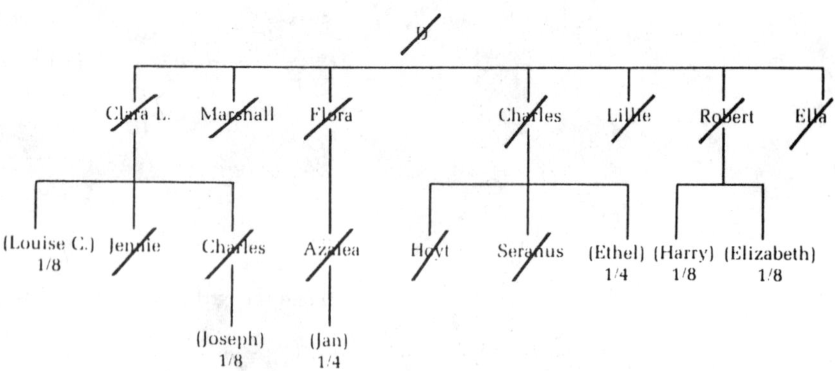

(A line through the party indicates deceased)

Note: Under the majority approach in the "root level" per stirpes problem, the number of shares in *Maud* would have been determined at the level of the grandchildren (i.e., the first level where there are survivors). The result would have been that each of the survivors would have taken one-sixth: Louise, Ethel, Harry and Elizabeth taking in their own rights; Joseph taking the share of Charles, and Jan taking the share of Azalea, *supra*, p. 11.

d. Uniform Probate Code: UPC §2-106 as revised in 1990 adopts the system of representation called ***per capita at each generation***. This always results in ***equal shares to those***

equally related. This method usually results in the same distribution as under the majority "first survivor" approach, but there is an exception illustrated in the Comment after UPC §2-106.

CHART VIII.

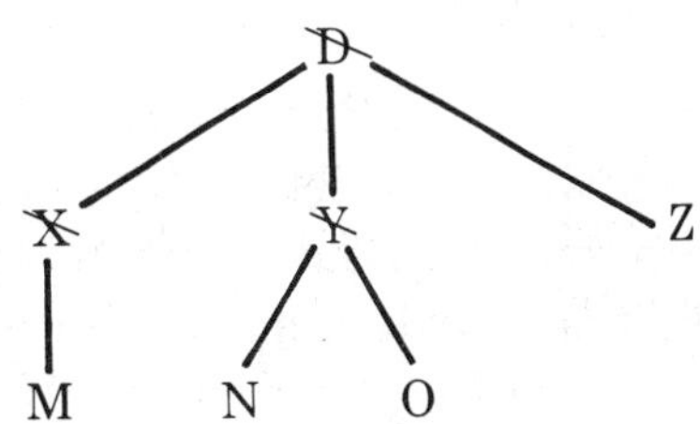

(A line through the party indicates deceased)

Example: D dies intestate leaving one child, Z, and three grandchildren (M, the child of X, and N and O, the children of Y). X and Y predeceased D. The situation is as shown in Chart VIII above.

Under the UPC *per capita at each generation* system, Z receives one-third. The remaining two-thirds of the estate is ***combined*** and divided equally among M, N and O, so that each receives two-ninths.

Under the majority approach (see **(b.)** *supra* p. 11), M, N and O take by representation from their parents, so M receives one-third and N and O receive one-sixth each.

Note: The UPC method, which assures equal distribution among descendents of the same generation, has been adopted by two states: North Carolina and Maine. See Waggoner, p. 85.

D. Half-bloods, illegitimates, and adopted children: Several relationships can pose special problems in intestacy: (1) half-bloods (especially step-siblings); (2) illegitimate children; and (3) adopted children.

1. **Half-bloods (including step-siblings):** The most common illustration are ***step-siblings*** — if H marries W1 and they have child A, and H then marries W2 and they have child B, A and B are relatives of the half-blood because they share only ***one common ancestor*** (H) rather than two.

   a. **General descendants:** The term ***"relative of the half-blood"*** also refers to any more-distant relationships, that involve only one common ancestor. For instance, suppose that

B in the prior paragraph had a child, C. C would be a half-blood relative of A, since the two of them have only one common ancestor (H, who is A's father and C's grandfather).

b. **General rule:** States vary as to how they treat relatives of the half-blood for intestacy purposes. In most states today the half-blood inherits the same way as would a relative of the whole-blood in the same relationship. UPC §2-107.

Example: H, while married to W1, has a son, A. H then marries W2, and has two daughters, B and C. B dies intestate. In most jurisdictions, A and C will split the estate equally, even though A is only a half-sibling to B, whereas C is B's full sibling.

c. **Minority rule:** In a few states, the half-blood takes only ***one-half*** what a full-blood in the same relationship would take. In such a state, using the previous example, A would take one-third and C would take two-thirds. In these ***minority jurisdictions***, if there are only half-bloods, they take ***all***. (Thus if C died before B, A would take B's entire estate.)

d. **"Ancestral" property:** Some states have special rules for ***"ancestral"*** property. Ancestral property is ***property that has come to the decedent by gift, bequest or intestacy from some ancestor***. These special rules provide that when a half-blood and a whole-blood are of equal degree, but the half-blood is not a blood relative of the ancestor from whom the property derives, the half-blood does not take anything.

Example: Decedent dies intestate, leaving an estate consisting solely of Blackacre, which decedent received previously by bequest from his paternal uncle. Decedent leaves a half-brother (the child of the same mother as Decedent, but not the same father) and a full sister. In a state that treats ancestral properties specially, the half-brother will probably not inherit anything, as he is related to Decedent through their mother and Blackacre comes to Decedent via his father. Decedent's sister would get all of Blackacre.

e. **Only for breaking ties:** This special treatment for ancestral property, when it exists, often applies only to break ***"ties,"*** not to favor ***more remote*** full-bloods over closer half-bloods.

Example: Decedent's only surviving relatives, in addition to a maternal half-brother, are children of some maternal siblings and some paternal cousins. Part of Decedent's estate is real estate left to her by a paternal uncle. The relevant statute provides that "kindred of the half-blood inherit equally with those of the whole blood in the same degree, unless the inheritance comes to the intestate by descent, devise or gift of some one of his ancestors, in which case all those who are not of the blood of such ancestors must be excluded from such inheritance."

Held, the special treatment for ancestral property does ***not*** apply here — it applies only where the half-bloods are of the same degree of relationship as the whole-bloods. Here, the half-bloods (Decedent's siblings and children of siblings) are in a closer degree of relationship than the full bloods (who are merely cousins). Therefore, the special ancestral property provision does not apply, and the half-siblings and their children, not the paternal cousins, take. *In re Estate of Robbs*, 504 P.2d 1228 (Ok. 1972).

2. **Illegitimate children:** We turn now to the rights in intestacy of ***illegitimate*** children, termed ***nonmarital children*** by some authorities today.

   a. **Common law:** At common law, an illegitimate child is treated as being a child of no one and has ***no right to inherit***. Similarly, no one has the right to inherit ***from*** an illegitimate child except his own issue.

   b. **Modern rules:** Today, these restrictive common law rules have been ***abolished*** by statute in every state. However, the precise terms of these statutes vary from state to state.

      i. **Inheritance from mother:** In nearly all states, an illegitimate child is treated as the child of at least his ***mother***, and may inherit from her and from her relatives. Also, the mother's relatives may inherit from the illegitimate child.

      ii. **Inheritance from father:** In most state, an illegitimate child is ***not*** treated as the child of the ***father***, unless the father ***legitimated*** him by marrying the child's mother, or ***acknowledged*** him.

   c. **Effect of legitimation:** Once a child is legitimated by the subsequent marriage of his parents, he or she is treated in the ***same*** way for inheritance purposes as a child born in wedlock.

   d. **Effect of null marriage:** Suppose the parents have gone through a purported marriage ceremony, but for legal reasons the marriage is void (e.g., one parent was previously married and not validly divorced.) In this situation, the children of the invalid marriage are nonetheless treated as ***legitimate***.

   Example: H marries W1, by whom he has children A and B. H then enters into a bigamous "marriage" with W2, by whom he has children C & D. A, B, C and D are all treated as legitimate, even though the marriage to W2 is void.

e. **Constitutional limits:** The ***United States Constitution*** places limits on the extent to which states may disadvantage illegitimate children in the intestacy area. The Court will give fairly close scrutiny to intestacy schemes that disadvantage illegitimates, and may strike down those schemes that cut off illegitimates without a fairly important reason for doing so.

   i. **Complete ban on illegitimate succession struck down:** For example, if the state completely ***bars*** unacknowledged illegitimate children from intestate succession, this is a violation of the ***Equal Protection Clause***. Thus in *Trimble v. Gordon*, 43 U.S. 762 (1977), the Supreme Court struck down the Illinois intestate succession scheme insofar as it prevented illegitimate children from inheriting from their fathers. Even though the state had a legitimate interest in ***preventing false claims*** of paternity, a complete exclusion of illegitimates from the intestate scheme was not an appropriate way to achieve that objective, the Court held.

   ii. **Tough proof requirements:** Although the state may not completely cut off illegitimates from intestate succession, it ***may*** impose special ***procedural rules*** for proving paternity. For instance, a New York statute prevented illegitimate children from inheriting by intestacy from their fathers unless a court made a ***finding of paternity during the father's lifetime***. This statute was ***upheld*** by the Supreme Court, even though it was fairly similar to the statute struck down in *Trimble*, *supra*, *Lalli v. Lalli*, 439 U.S. 259 (1978).

   iii. **Rationale:** The difference between *Trimble* and *Lalli* was that the *Trimble* statute ***completely*** barred illegitimate children from inheriting from the father (unless the parents married at some later date), whereas the New York statute, by contrast, accepted a judicial finding of paternity as a substitute for legitimation. The *Lalli* court held that the state's interest in barring spurious claims, and in achieving finality in the disposition of estates, justified the requirement of a paternity finding during life.

   iv. **Summary of constitutional rules:** Therefore, the constitutional rule seems to be: The states ***may not completely bar*** illegitimate children from inheriting from their parents, but they may impose ***procedural requirements*** for proving paternity (e.g., that paternity be judicially established during a father's life).

f. **Recent liberalization:** Partly in response to the Supreme Court's constitutional rulings, most states have broadened the rights of illegitimates to take by intestacy.

i. **Uniform Probate Code:** UPC §2-114 provides that a person is the child of his or her natural parents, regardless of their marital status. So long as the parent-child relationship is established, the child may inherit from or through them.

3. **Adopted children:** The right of ***adopted children*** to take by intestacy is handled entirely by statute in all states.

a. **Inheritance from adoptive parent:** In all states, the adopted child is the child of the ***adoptive*** parents for purposes of intestacy. In most states, the adopted child also can inherit "through" the adoptive parent; thus if A adopts B, and predeceases B, B can inherit from A's mother. Haskell, p. 16.

b. **Inheritance from natural parent:** Most states ***cut off*** the adopted child from intestate succession from his ***natural*** parents. Thus if A gives birth to B, and C adopts B, B will not take by intestate succession from A.

i. **Strict application of rule:** This rule has led to harsh results in some states.

Example: H1 and W are married and have a child, C. H1 dies and W marries H2. H2 adopts C. The adoption cuts off intestate inheritance rights of C through H1. Therefore, C may not inherit from H1's parents, *Estates of Donnelly*, 502 P.2d 1163 (Wash. 1972); or from H1's brother, *Hall v. Vallandingham*, 540 A.2d 1162 (Md. 1988).

ii. **Exception for adoption by spouse of natural parent:** Many states follow a different rule from that relied on in the example above. If a natural parent ***remarries*** and the new spouse adopts the child, the child may still take by intestacy from or through both natural parents. The Uniform Probate Code follows this approach; under §2-114(b): "Adoption of a child by the spouse of either natural parent has no effect on (i) the relationship between the child and that natural parent or (ii) the right of the child or a descendant of the child to inherit from or through the other natural parent."

Example: C is the natural child of H1 and W, who are then divorced. W marries H2, who adopts C. C can still take by intestacy from H1 (as well as from W and H2) under the modern and UPC approach. Also, if H1 dies, and H1's parent or sibling then dies, C can inherit through H1, reversing the results cited in the previous example.

c. **Adoption solely for intestacy purposes:** Some states recognize the effectiveness for inheritance even of adoptions that are in essence ***shams*** carried out solely for inheritance purposes.

Example: H is the life-income beneficiary of an irrevocable trust. The trust provides that upon H's death, the trust corpus shall go to H's heirs. H has no children. H "adopts" W, his wife, as his "heir" solely for the purposes of enabling her to receive the trust corpus on his death. Some (but by no means all) courts would allow W to inherit the trust corpus as if she had been H's child. UPC §2-705(c) is contrary and prevents that result.

E. **Advancements:** An ***advancement*** is a gift made by an intestate during his life to a relative, with the intent that it be applied ***against any share*** in the intestate's estate to which the recipient may later be entitled.

1. **Computation:** To compute the distribution of the decedent's estate when there has been an advancement, the amount of the advancement must be in effect ***"added back"*** into the estate. The statutory distribution is then computed, and the amount of the advancement is deducted from the recipient's share.

Example: T dies intestate leaving three children, A, B and C, as his sole statutory heirs. He leaves a net estate of $1400. During T's lifetime, he gave A $300 and B $100, accompanied by a letter stating that these gifts were an advance against their inheritance. The net estate would be treated as if it were $1800 ($1400 plus the two gifts). A would receive $300 (his one-third share of the $1800 less the $300 he had already received); B would receive $500 by a similar computation, and C would receive $600.

2. **Absolute gift:** The doctrine of advancement does not disturb the ***absolute finality*** of gifts made by the intestate during his life. That is, a person who has received advancements that total more than his statutory share need not return the excess.

Example: T dies leaving his children, A and B, as his sole statutory heirs. He leaves an estate of $1000. During his lifetime, he made a $2000 gift to A "as an advance against your inheritance." Under the computation described above, A has already received $500 more than he "should" have. He will receive nothing from the estate (and B will receive the entire $1000), but A does not have to return anything to the estate. Haskell, p. 19.

3. **Interpretation:** Not all inter vivos gifts are treated as advancements when the donor dies intestate. The issue of whether an advancement was intended rather than an absolute gift is always a question of the ***donor's intent.***

   a. **Up to three possibilities:** Thus a payment made by a donor may have been intended by him to be any of the three following things: (1) ***an outright gift*** (which would not reduce the recipient's share of the subsequent intestate estate); (2) a loan (in which case any excess over what would be the ***"borrower's"*** statutory share must be repaid to the estate); or (3) ***an advancement.***

   b. **Evidence of intent:** Traditionally, a substantial inter vivos gift to a child or other descendant was ***rebuttably presumed*** to be an advancement — the recipient had the burden of proving that the intestate intended an outright gift that would not reduce the recipient's share of the estate. Haskell, p. 19.

   c. **Modern statutes:** But many states today have enacted statutes that ***abolish*** this presumption. In fact, the modern statutory trend is to provide that even substantial inter vivos gifts to children are ***not*** advancements unless either (1) there is a ***writing*** signed by the donor stating that the gift is an advancement; or (2) the recipient has ***acknowledged*** that the gift is an advancement. Haskell, pp. 19-20.

      i. **UPC:** The Uniform Probate Code follows this approach: Under UPC §2-109, property given during his lifetime by one who dies intestate is treated as an advancement against the recipient's share of the estate only if declared in a contemporaneous writing by the decedent or acknowledged by the heir in writing to be an advancement.

4. **Valuation date:** To apply the advancement doctrine, the inter vivos gift must of course be ***valued.*** The general rule is that the gift should be valued as of the date on which it was ***received,*** not the date of death. See UPC §2-109(b).

5. **Recipient of advancement predeceases decedent:** Suppose that T gives an advancement to his son, A, and that A ***predeceases*** T. Suppose further that T's other child, B, survives T, and that A is survived by his son S. Must the advancement doctrine be applied, so that S's share of T's estate is reduced? In most states, the answer is ***"yes,"*** even if S never obtained any benefit from the bequest. Haskell, p. 21.

   a. **UPC:** But the Uniform Probate Code does ***not*** follow this majority rule. UPC §2-109(c) provides that "if the recipient of the property fails to survive the decedent, the property is not taken into account in computing the division and distribution of the decedent's intestate estate, unless the decedent's contemporaneous writing provides otherwise."

6. **Compare to doctrine of satisfaction:** The doctrine of advancement is very similar to the doctrine of ***ademption by satisfaction***, in the context of wills. Under the latter, bequests are reduced by the amount of inter vivos gifts to the same person in certain circumstances. See *infra*, pp. 57.

F. **Qualifications on the right to inherit:** A person who would otherwise be entitled to inherit may lose that right because of wrongdoing, alienage, his own prior death, or other reason. We consider a number of these special circumstances that may result in loss of the right to inherit:

1. **Must be alive:** A person must be ***"in being"*** (that is, either ***alive*** or in ***embryo***) at the time the intestate dies, in order to inherit.

   a. **Conceived by time of death:** A person who has been conceived at the time of the intestate's death and who is born alive thereafter inherits ***as if he had been born in the intestate's lifetime***.

   b. **Presumption of survival:** It may be unclear whether or not A has survived B (e.g., because they both die in the same accident). In this situation, many states provide that if there is no evidence of the order of death, ***neither*** shall be presumed to have died first, and the estate of each passes and descends ***as if he had survived the other***. See Waggoner, p.71.

      Example: H and W are married and have no children as a couple. However, H has a son, S, by his first marriage, and W has a daughter, D, by her first marriage. H and W are killed in a car crash, and there is no evidence who died first. Under the law of many states, neither is presumed to have died first. Therefore, H's estate will go entirely to S and W's estate will go entirely to D.

   c. **Survival requirement:** Many modern statutes provide that any person who fails to survive the decedent for a ***fixed period*** is deemed to have predeceased him for purposes of intestate succession. For instance, §2-104 of the UPC requires that the heir survive the decedent by ***five days*** in order to inherit.

      Note: The requirement of survival for five days has also been applied to other gifts, to life insurance, and to joint tenancies and joint accounts with a survivorship feature. UPC §2-702.

2. **Intent to kill:** A person who ***intentionally kills*** the decedent will, in most states, ***not*** be allowed to inherit from him. Most states

accomplish this result by statutes expressly denying the intentional killer the right of intestate succession.

a. **Manslaughter vs. murder:** All states bar a convicted ***murderer*** from inheriting. Some but not all also bar a person convicted of ***voluntary manslaughter***, on the theory that this kind of killing is intentional even though committed under somewhat mitigating circumstances. See, e.g., *Estate of Mahoney*, 220 A.2d 475 (Vt. 1956), where even without a statute, the court prevented a spouse convicted of voluntary manslaughter from inheriting, by imposing a constructive trust on the estate for the benefit of the other heirs (see *infra*, p. 125).

i. **UPC:** The Uniform Probate Code, §2-803, bars one who has ***"feloniously and intentionally"*** killed the decedent from inheriting. Thus one who is guilty of *in*voluntary manslaughter would still be allowed to inherit under the UPC.

b. **Standard of proof:** Clearly the ***conviction*** of a person for murder or other intentional wrongful killing, is sufficient proof for the civil court to bar the inheritance. But even where there has been no trial, or the person has been ***acquitted***, some states allow the civil court to bar the inheritance. For instance, UPC §2-803 bars inheritance either upon a conviction for the felonious and intentional killing, or upon the civil court's own determination ***"by a preponderance of the evidence"*** that the killing was felonious and intentional. Other states will allow the civil court to make this finding, but require a stricter standard of evidence than a preponderance (e.g., "clear and convincing" evidence), because of the stigma attached to such a finding.

3. **Other wrongdoing:** In some states, parents or spouses can be deprived of the right to inherit if they are ***"unworthy"*** in some specified way. For example, in many states a parent may not share in the estate of a child whom he has ***abandoned*** or ***neglected***. Similarly, in some states a spouse who has ***abandoned*** the decedent or committed adultery is deprived of the right to inherit. Dukeminier, p. 121.

4. **Aliens:** At common law, ***aliens*** were not permitted to inherit real property or, in some instances, personal property.

a. **Complete ban abolished:** This complete ban has been ***abolished*** in virtually all states.

b. **Restrictions on amount:** On the other hand, a sizable minority of states have now enacted broader provisions (covering both purchases and inheritance) that limit the ***amount*** of ***land*** that may be held by an alien, limit the ***time*** for which he may hold it, or even in a few instances bar him completely from holding it.

c. **Reciprocal statutes:** Also, an additional minority of states have enacted so-called ***reciprocal*** statutes, whereby an alien is permitted to inherit real or personal property in the state only if the alien's own country extends a similar inheritance right to Americans. Such statutes were frequently used in the past to deny legacies to residents of Iron Curtain countries.

d. **Constitutional problems:** However, the various state statutes that restrict inheritance by aliens pose potential ***constitutional*** problems. For instance, such statutes may violate the Equal Protection Clause of the Fourteenth Amendment, or the federal government's monopoly in foreign affairs. See, e.g., *Zscherning v. Miller*, 389 U.S. 429 (1968), in which the Supreme Court held that an Oregon statute which required the withholding of legacies from Iron Curtain residents, violated, at least as applied in that case, the federal government's monopoly of the field of foreign affairs.

5. **Renunciation:** An heir may ***voluntarily renounce*** (disclaim) the right of intestate succession. Most frequently, this is done to route the legacy to a different family member, in order to achieve tax savings.

> **Example:** D dies survived by her son, S. S has two children, G1 and G2. If S had not been alive at D's death, G1 and G2 would have been D's heirs. After D's death intestate, S could "renounce" or "disclaim" his inheritance. This would have the effect of making the inheritance go to G1 and G2. This might produce tax savings, since the income earned by the inheritance might be taxed at lower rates in the hands of G1 and G2 (who, let us assume, are low-scale employees) than in the hands of S (who, let us assume, earns a high salary). Use of this renunciation technique is also more beneficial than S's receiving the bequest and re-gifting to G1 and G2, since the re-gifting approach might cause a gift tax to be payable. See Waggoner, p. 96

a. **Common law:** At common law, the device of renunciation ***was not allowed***. Thus on the facts of the above example, S would be deemed to have received the inheritance, and it would have been necessary for him to re-gift to G1 and G2.

b. **Modern trend:** But today, virtually all states allow an heir (as well as a legatee or devisee under a will) to renounce. The effect of this renunciation is that the inheritance ***never passes*** to the heir at all, but goes ***directly to the next-in-line***.

i. **Formal requirements:** States vary with respect to the formal requirements required for a renunciation. UPC §2-801 is reasonably typical: The renunciation must be in ***writing***, be ***signed*** by the person renouncing, ***describe*** the property or interest renounced, and be ***filed*** with the probate court not more than nine months after the decedent's death. The federal estate and gift tax consequences of a renunciation are governed by the Internal Revenue Code, §2518(c)(3), which imposes similar formal requirements for a valid renunciation.

PROTECTION OF THE FAMILY

I. PROTECTION AGAINST DISINHERITANCE

A. **Introduction:** The balance between allowing freedom of testation and imposing certain limits on disposition is reflected in the rules relating to mandatory shares of the estate provided for the surviving spouse and children. Provision for the spouse and children of a decedent is a major reason both for allowing testamentary disposition of property and for placing limitations upon the freedom of testation.

B. **Protection of the spouse:** Our two basic legal systems both protect the surviving spouse against disinheritance. One is based on ***community property*** principles; the other is rooted in ***common law***.

1. **Issues:** The ***issues*** addressed by both bodies of law include:

   a. the ***portion*** of the decedent's estate to which a ***surviving spouse*** is entitled;

   b. the extent to which rights of the spouse may be ***defeated by lifetime transfers*** or other actions of decedent; and

   c. the extent to which a spouse may take ***priority over creditor's claims***.

2. **Community property system:** The community property system generally treats the husband and wife as ***co-owners*** of property acquired by either during the marriage. On the death of one, the survivor is entitled to one-half the property and the remainder (along with property not part of the community) goes according to the will of the decedent or under the relevant statute, if the decedent is intestate.

   a. **Separate property:** Property acquired by gift, bequest, descent or devise and property acquired by the decedent prior to the marriage are not part of the community.

      Example: H, a domiciliary of a community property state, takes out two life insurance policies before his marriage to W. The policies name H's estate as beneficiary. Upon H's death, the executor of his estate claims that all of the proceeds of the policies belong to H's separate estate. W argues that only that part of the proceeds found to be in proportion to the amount of premiums paid by H before his marriage belongs to his separate estate.

      Held, for the estate. The general rule is that "[i]f either spouse before marriage procures a policy of life insurance on his own or another's life, in his favor or in favor of his estate, the policy and its proceeds are his separate property. His rights to the proceeds date from the policy." Such a ruling is consistent with Texas community property law as applied to other types of property. *McCurdy v. McCurdy*, 372 S.W.2d 321 (Tex. Ct. Civ. App. 1963).

Note: The decision in *McCurdy* included provision for the reimbursement to the community estate of the premiums paid with community funds.

i. **California rule:** Unlike Texas, California has adopted the apportionment method for life insurance proceeds. As noted by the *McCurdy* court, such an approach is consistent with California's laws on other community property, such as realty.

b. **Variations: There are *eight states*** which have some form of community property: Arizona, California, Idaho, Louisiana, New Mexico, Nevada, Texas and Washington. There are substantial differences among them with respect to the right to manage, control and alienate the property.

i. **Gifts:** Where a gift is made from community property, the relationship of the donee to the donor is important. If the donee is a close relative, the gift will probably be upheld. If the donee is not related, there is a presumption that the gift is ***"constructive fraud."***

Example: H holds a life insurance policy obtained while H and W were married and living together. H is separated from W for ten years before his death, and during that time changes the beneficiary to an unrelated person.

Held, W is awarded one-half of the value of the policy. W is not required to show actual fraudulent intent by H. Constructive fraud is shown by the fact that the insurance was purchased with community funds for an unrelated person. Then the beneficiary has the burden, not met in this case, to justify such use of community funds. *Givens v. Girard Life Insurance Co.*, 480 S.W.2d 421 (Tex. Ct. Civ. App. 1972).

ii. **California:** Under recent California legislation both spouses have equal management and control over the marital property. However, each spouse must "act in good faith with respect to the other spouse in the management and control of the community property," and gifts by one without the consent of the other spouse are prohibited. Calif. Civ. Code §5125; McGovern, p. 142.

3. **"Common Law" system:** In most states, the surviving spouse is protected by some form of ***elective share*** legislation. Such a system

evolved out of the common law concepts of ***dower*** and ***curtesy***.

a. **Common law dower and curtesy:** At common law the wife was entitled to ***dower***, a life interest in ***one-third*** of the land owned by her husband in fee simple or fee tail during the marriage. ***Curtesy*** was the right of a husband, if there were issue born of the marriage, to a life interest in all of his wife's lands held in fee simple or fee tail.

   i. **Fixed interest in land:** Dower or curtesy gives a ***fixed interest*** to one spouse in all land owned during the marriage. Unless released by the holder thereof, a dower or curtesy interest cannot be defeated by transfer to a bona fide purchaser and is not subject to creditors' claims.

   ii. **Interest is inchoate:** The dower interest in lands of a spouse is "***inchoate***" during the life of that spouse; i.e., the dower holder must survive his or her spouse to take a possessory interest. On survival the inchoate interest becomes "***consummate***", i.e., vested in possession.

   iii. **Pure dower and curtesy generally abolished:** Most states have ***abolished*** common law dower and curtesy. Many have established similar ***statutory schemes***, usually treating husband and wife identically. Some states subject dower to debts of the decedent and some extend such rights to personalty as well as to land. Some allow dower in addition to testamentary provisions; others, in lieu of testamentary provisions.

b. **Elective share:** Most states have statutes allowing a surviving spouse to ***elect*** either a forced share (usually one-third or what would have gone to such spouse by intestacy) or the provision made in the spouse's will. This election must be exercised in the manner and within the time provided in the ***statute***. In some states such provision is in lieu of dower. In others dower still attaches to property transferred by a decedent during life without consent or waiver, and in still others one may choose between several alternatives. Election provisions usually attach to the net probate estate and the statutory interests are therefore subject to creditors' claims.

   i. **Uniform Probate Code:** Under the UPC, the surviving spouse gets an elective share, which depends on the ***length of the marriage***. For example, if the marriage has been five to six years, the surviving spouse receives 15%; if the marriage has been fifteen years or longer the surviving spouse is entitled to 50% of the estate. UPC §2-201.

ii. **Effect of inter vivos transfer:** To determine whether an ***inter vivos transfer*** during marriage is ***effective*** to deprive a surviving spouse of an elective share, courts generally follow one of two approaches. The first inquires whether the transfer was made with intent to deter the election; the other considers whether the transfer is real or illusory. Where one spouse transfers property to a trust with a third person (not the other spouse) as beneficiary, that fact that the settlor reserves power to change the beneficiary or receive the income will often persuade the court that the elective share should apply to the trust corpus, regardless of which approach is used.

Example 1: W dies intestate. During her lifetime she had created savings-account trusts, or "Totten Trusts," for the benefit of her two children from a prior marriage. The trusts named W as the trustee and provided that the accounts were to be paid to the beneficiaries on W's death. Under the law applicable to Totten Trusts, while alive W "retained absolute, unqualified control over the bank accounts and possessed and exercised all incidents of complete ownership, including the right to receive interest payable thereon and withdraw the principal thereof." At issue is whether the trust is effective to defeat the statutory share of H, her surviving spouse, in her estate.

Held, for H. The extent of W's control over the trusts during her lifetime rendered the transfer of the property to the trust *illusory and invalid* as against H. The balances in the savings-account trusts should be treated as the property of W for the purpose of determining H's statutory share in W's estate. *Montgomery v. Michaels*, 54 Ill.2d 532, 301 N.E.2d 465 (1973).

Note: The court in *Montgomery* found W's *intent* to be an unsatisfactory test of the validity of a challenged transfer of property — what mattered was the practical effect of W's control over the property after it was transferred to the trust.

Example 2: During his marriage H transfers real estate to himself as sole trustee. All income is payable to H, who has power to revoke the trust at any time. On H's death a successor trustee is directed to pay income to third parties. H has been separated from his wife, W, for many years. H's will states that he intentionally made no provision for W. W contends that the trust assets should be part of H's estate, and that she should receive her statutory share.

Held, H created a valid inter vivos trust and W may not claim against the trust assets. The fact that H retained broad power over the trust does not make it invalid. The trust was valid under the law in effect when it was created, so the trust assets cannot be applied to H's estate. *Sullivan v. Burkin*, 390 Mass. 864, 460 N.E.2d 571 (1984).

Note: But the court in *Sullivan* stated that with respect to any inter vivos trust created or amended *following* its decision, if the deceased spouse who created the trust retained sole power during his life to direct the disposition of the trust assets for his benefit, the trust assets would be included in the value of the estate. So the next person in W's position would win in Massachusetts.

c. **Control of trust:** As the above two examples show, courts generally look to the amount of ***control*** one had over a trust in determining whether it is part of an estate. The UPC Comment after §2-202 states: "The general theory of revised Section 2-202(b)(2)(i) is that a decedent who, during life, alone had a power to make himself or herself the full technical owner of property was in substance the owner of that property for purposes of the elective share."

d. **Uniform Probate Code:** The ***Uniform Probate Code*** grants the surviving spouse the right to take an elective share of ***one-third*** of the decedent's "augmented estate." An "***augmented estate***" is one that has been adjusted to include certain lifetime transfers by the decedent. UPC §§2-113, 2-201 and 2-202.

e. **Protection against unintentional disinheritance:** Some states have statutes which protect a spouse against ***unintentional disinheritance*** by giving the spouse a share of the estate where a will was executed by decedent prior to the marriage and where it does not appear that the disinheritance was intentional. See UPC §2-301.

   i. **Provision outside will:** But if the testator makes a will before marriage, and then during the marriage provides for his spouse outside the will, a court may conclude that the survivor is ***not*** an "omitted spouse." The court so held where $230,000 was given to the surviving spouse before death, leaving only $100,000 in the estate, which testator had good reason to leave to other family members. *Estate of Bartell*, 776 P.2d 885 (Utah 1989).

f. **Waiver of rights:** A spouse may usually ***waive***, release or contract away dower or other statutory rights by either antenuptial or post-nuptial agreement if the agreement is fair and made with knowledge of all the relevant facts. See UPC §2-204.

C. **Protection of children:** The ***general rule*** is that ***children may be completely disinherited by their parents***.

1. **Limitations on right to disinherit children:** Children are nonetheless afforded certain ***protections*** against disinheritance.

a. **Pretermitted heir provisions:** Many states have pretermitted (omitted) heir statutes, which give children ***unintentionally omitted*** from a will an intestate share. Such statutes offer protection to children born or adopted after the execution of the will. In about half of the states, children living when the will is executed may also claim as a pretermitted heir. Such laws also generally apply to children believed to be dead, but who are in fact alive, at the time the will is executed.

Example: Testator's property is transferred to a testamentary trust for the benefit of designated beneficiaries, who include two grandchildren. A third grandchild, C, is not named in the will. All three are children of testator's deceased son. C claims as a pretermitted heir.

Held, C may recover. There is no affirmative indication on the face of the will that the testator intended to disinherit C. Further, the will was not ambiguous (it was silent as to C), so intent to exclude cannot be shown by parol evidence. C is entitled to her intestate share of the estate. *Crump's Estate v. Freeman*, 614 P.2d 1096 (Okl. 1980). See also UPC §2-302.

b. **Requirement that property be left to others:** A further limitation on the right to disinherit heirs is found in the requirement that a testator specifically ***leave*** his ***property to others***. To simply declare a desire to disinherit is insufficient if the property is not otherwise disposed of by will.

c. **Actionable right to support:** When there is a legal duty upon the parent to support a minor child, an ***action*** may be maintained against the deceased parent's estate for support payments.

D. **Gifts to charity:** At common law, laws commonly called ***Mortmain statutes***, limited the power of a testator to make testamentary gifts to a church. Later these statutes were expanded to include ***any charity***. The purpose of such statutes is to protect the family of a decedent from disinheritance by death-bed gifts to charity. Such limitations are usually operative only when near relatives (usually children, grandchildren, parents and surviving spouse) survive.

1. **Types of limitations:** Such statutes limit charitable gifts in one or both of the following ways: (1) limit the amount of the gift to a certain proportion of the estate and/or (2) invalidate gifts made within a specified period preceding death, (e.g., within six months).

2. **Modern trend:** Only three states have valid Mortmain statutes today. At least three courts have held such statutes unconstitutional as violative of the Equal Protection Clause. *In re Estate of Cavill*, 329 A.2d 503 (Pa. 1974); *Key v. Doyle*, 365 A.2d 621 (D.C. 1976); *Shriners' Hospital for Crippled Children v. Zrillic*, 563 S.2d 64 (Fla. 1990).

II. OTHER PROTECTIONS

A. **Generally:** Statutes providing for family allowance, homestead and exempt properties give a measure of protection to a family by providing property for them and exempting property from creditors' claims. These provisions vary from state to state.

B. **Homestead:** ***Homestead*** statutes allow the continuation of residence free from creditors' claims in the family home, usually during the minority of the children and/or life of the widow.

C. **Family allowance:** ***Family allowance*** statutes allow a certain amount for the support of the surviving spouse and children during the administration process.

D. **Exemptions:** ***Exempt property*** provisions usually allow specified chattels, such as wearing apparel, furniture and personal effects, to pass to the family of the decedent, not subject to general creditors' claims.

EXECUTION, VALIDITY AND COMPONENTS OF WILLS

I. GENERALLY

A. **Statutory right:** The right to make a will is wholly ***statutory***; there is no common law right to do so.

B. **Statutory compliance:** A will is not valid without statutory compliance.

C. **Historical basis:** All states have statutes enabling persons to make wills and prescribe the formalities for executing wills derived from the ***English Statute of Wills*** (1540) and the ***Statute of Frauds*** (1676).

D. **Requirements for a valid will:** A valid will requires: (1) a ***competent testator***; (2) ***physical compliance*** with the requirements of the statute; and (3) ***animus testandi***, the testator's intent that the instrument be a will (*infra*, p. 46.).

   1. **Validity affected:** ***Fraud and undue influence*** generally render a will invalid. In limited circumstances, ***mistake*** may also affect validity.

E. **Effectuating intent of testator:** The primary goal of the above principles is to ***effectuate the true desires of the testator***.

   1. **Other goals:** Other objectives include protecting the ***family***, facilitating ***judicial administration*** and preventing the ***unjust enrichment*** of those engaging in wrongful conduct.

II. DEFINITIONS OF WILL TERMS

A. **Will:** A will is a ***legal*** declaration of one's intention to dispose of his property after death.

B. **Common law will/testament distinction:** At common law an instrument disposing of personal property was called a "***testament***"; one disposing of real property, a "***will***." This distinction has been eliminated in modern times and an instrument conveying real and/or personal property is called a "will" or a "last will and testament."

C. **Ambulatory:** Every will is ***ambulatory*** — it can be changed or revoked at any moment before death by a competent testator.

D. **Testate/testator:** One who dies leaving a will dies ***testate***, and is called a ***testator***.

E. **Devise/legacy/bequest:** Gifts made by will are called:

1. if of land, a ***devise***;
2. if of money, a ***legacy***; and
3. if of personalty, a ***bequest***.

   Note: Modern statutes have abolished the distinction between real and personal property. For instance, UPC §1-201(10) defines a "devise" as the testamentary disposition of real or personal property by will.

F. **Personal representative:** The ***personal representative*** is the person authorized by the court to administer the estate.

G. **Executor:** An ***executor*** is a person named in a will to administer the estate.

H. **Administrator:** An ***administrator*** is a person appointed by the court to administer the estate of an intestate.

I. ***Administrator with the will annexed:*** When an executor cannot serve or will not serve, or when the will fails to appoint such, the court will appoint an ***administrator with the will annexed*** (or ***administrator cum testamento annexo***) to administer the will. For further discussion, see *infra*, p. 170. Compare with Intestate Succession, *supra*, pp. 3.

III. TESTAMENTARY CAPACITY:

A. **Competent testator defined:** A competent testator is a person with testamentary capacity; that is, one who is of ***sound mind*** and of a ***requisite age*** at the time of making the will.

B. **Minimum age:** All states have a ***minimum age*** (usually 18) below which a person lacks capacity to make a will. A person under the minimum age must necessarily die intestate UPC §2-501.

C. **Married women:** At common law, ***married women*** were unable to make wills. This rule has been abolished everywhere.

D. **Mental capacity or sound mind:** One has mental capacity, or sound mind, if he has sufficient mind:

1. ***to understand***
   a. the nature and extent of his ***property***,
   b. the ***persons*** who are the natural objects of his bounty,
   c. the nature of the ***testamentary*** act, and
   d. the foregoing elements in relation to each other; ***and***
2. ***to form an orderly desire*** as to the disposition of his property. See Waggoner, p. 214.

E. Mental incapacity: A testator may be incapacitated mentally because of ***mental deficiency*** (idiocy, imbecility) or ***mental derangement*** (having insane delusions such as those found in paranoia paresis, and senile dementia).

F. Insane delusion: An ***insane delusion*** is the belief in a state of facts when there is no ***evidence*** to support it and all evidence demonstrates the contrary. Before an insane delusion can invalidate a will, there must be the delusion and the will must be the ***product of such delusion***. In other words, the testator must have devised property in a way which, except for the delusion, he would not have done. *Kingdon v. Sybrant*, 158 N.W.2d 863 (N.D. 1968).

> **Example:** One month before his death, after nearly 40 years of a seemingly happy marriage, T executes a will that leaves W the minimum statutory share of his estate. W contests the will claiming that it is a result of T's unwarranted and insane delusion that W was unfaithful to him. To offset W's proof that T entertained an irrational obsession, the proponents offer evidence purporting to furnish a rational basis for T's belief. It is conceded that T was in all other respects normal and rational. The jury finds for W.
>
> *Held*, jury's verdict upheld. When an objectant submits "evidence reflecting the operation of a testator's mind, it is the proponent's duty to provide a basis for the alleged delusion." It cannot be concluded as a matter of law that the jury erred in finding the proponents failed to establish adequately a reasonable basis for T's belief. Also, the existence of other reasons for T's disposition, such as W's independent wealth, is insufficient to support the validity of the will. A will is invalid when its "dispository provisions were or might have been caused or affected by the delusion." *In re Honigman*, 8 N.Y.2d 244, 168 N.E.2d 676, 203 N.Y.S.2d 859 (1960).
>
> **Note:** The dissent argued that although the evidence established that T's suspicions were groundless, it does not follow that T suffered from an insane delusion or lacked testamentary capacity. Thus, while the provisions of his will may be unreasonable and unjust, T's testamentary wishes should be given effect. Moreover, other and sound reasons, apart from the belief in W's infidelity, existed for T's disposition.

1. **Belief subject to disproof:** There can be no insane delusion unless the delusion is subject to disproof by ***demonstrative evidence***. Thus, a religious belief in the hereafter, the truth of which can neither be proved nor disproved, cannot be an insane delusion.

2. **Eccentricities:** Mere ***eccentricities*** or ***prejudices*** or ***unusual religious beliefs*** do not by themselves constitute insane delusions.

G. **Lucid intervals:** A person who suffers from mental derangement may have **lucid intervals** during which he may execute a valid will.

H. **Other factors:** Moral depravity, illiteracy, extreme old age, great weakness, being deaf and dumb, blindness and severe illness do not disqualify a testator although they may be elements in determining mental capacity.

IV. FRAUD AND UNDUE INFLUENCE

A. **Effect on validity:** A will executed through either undue influence or fraud is ***invalid***.

B. **Undue influence:** The test of undue influence is the ***substitution of another's*** will for that of the testator.

1. **Elements:** The ***elements*** of undue influence are:

    a. a ***susceptible*** testator;

    b. another's ***opportunity to influence*** the testator;

    c. ***improper influence*** in fact; *and*

    d. ***the result showing the effect*** of such influence.

2. **Existence of factors not determinative:** Mere advice, persuasion, affection, or kindness do not ***alone*** constitute undue influence.

3. **Presumption raised:** The existence of a confidential relationship between a testator and a beneficiary may raise a ***presumption*** of undue influence, especially if combined with some other factor such as an unnatural disposition.

    Example: T's will is contested by her two daughters on the ground that it was the product of undue influence exerted on T by B, the will's sole beneficiary. At the time of the will's execution T was recently widowed, physically sick, unable to walk without help, dependent on drugs and an abuser of alcohol. Within ten months before such time, T had executed two other wills, one leaving her estate in equal parts to her two daughters, the other leaving the bulk of her estate to only one daughter. B, who had known T for only two months when the will was executed, bore a confidential relationship to T; she bathed her, gave her drugs, shopped for her, wrote her checks and transported her. Upon learning of T's desire to disinherit her daughters, B urged T to make a new will and took T to a newly admitted-lawyer who knew nothing of T's situation, rather than to the two lawyers who had drawn up T's previous wills. The trial court found for the contestants.

    Held, the trial court's decision that B exerted undue influence on T is affirmed. The seven factors to be considered in determining whether undue influence was exercised are as follows: 1) participation of the beneficiary in the preparation of the will; 2) failure of such a beneficiary to ensure that the testator receives independent, disinterested advice; 3) presence of secrecy and haste; 4) change in the testator's attitude toward others, such as her natural beneficiaries; 5) change in the testator's plan of disposing of her property; 6) existence of an unnatural or unjust disposition, such as one that effectuates the disinheritance of heirs; and 7) susceptibility to influence. *Matter of Estate of Swenson*, 617 P.2d 305 (Or. 1980).

a. **Attorney:** A gift to the testator's ***attorney*** is particularly susceptible to a claim of undue influence because of the confidential and fiduciary nature of the attorney-client relationship. Many courts create a presumption of undue influence in these circumstances.

Example: After M's husband dies, H, her attorney becomes her lover. This relationship continues for a number of years until her death. Three years before her death, M has another attorney, who is completely independent of H, prepare M's will. This will leaves almost all of M's property to H. At M's death, her sister contests the will on the ground of undue influence. H contends that M acted on the independent advice and counsel of one entirely devoted to M's interest.

Held, the will is invalid. The attorney who drafted the will ascertained only that M had no husband and no children. There was no discussion of her relationship with H or the fact that preference was given to a nonrelative to the exclusion of blood relatives. The attorney who wrote the will was little more than a scrivener, and did not offer meaningful advice relating to the testamentary disposition of M's property. Under these circumstances, and in view of the intimate relationship between M and H, the presumption of undue influence was not overcome. *In re Will of Moses*, 227 So.2d 829 (Miss. 1969).

b. **Sexual relationships outside marriage:** Older cases hold that the fact that the testator and the beneficiary had a non-marital ***sexual relationship*** with each other is a strong factor to be considered in determining whether undue influence was exercised. See, e.g., *Reed v. Shipp*, 308 So.2d 705 (Ala. 1975). Modern decisions are less judgmental and do not find that a non-marital relationship is sufficient to raise the presumption of undue influence. See, e.g., *Matter of Launius*, 507 So.2d 27 (Miss. 1987).

C. Fraud: Fraud is distinguishable from undue influence in that fraud involves an element of ***deceit***.

1. **Types of fraud:** Fraud consists of either:

   a. fraud in the ***execution***, (i.e., the testator is deceived as to the character or contents of the document he is signing); or

   b. fraud in the ***inducement***, (i.e., the testator makes the will or provision relying upon a false representation of a material fact made to him by one who knows it to be false).

2. **Innocent misrepresentations:** Innocent misrepresentations will not invalidate a will.

D. Remedies: The general rule is that persons deprived of benefit under a will because of fraud or duress can obtain relief only by ***invalidation*** of the will.

1. **Partial invalidation:** When only a part of a will is affected by undue influence or fraud only the affected part will be invalidated.

2. **Constructive trust:** When a testator has been prevented from executing or revoking a will by fraud, duress or undue influence there is a trend to impose a ***constructive trust*** against the wrongdoer, or anyone else who profited from the wrongdoing even if innocent, in favor of the person who otherwise would have benefitted. McGovern, p. 227.

   Example: Two of T's three heirs, either by physical force or by creating a disturbance, prevent T from executing a will that leaves all of T's property to B, who is not a family member. The two issues presented are: 1) whether a trust should be impressed in favor of B upon the property described in the will and 2) if so, whether the trust should be impressed on the interests inherited by the heir who did not participate in the violent act.

   Held, a constructive trust should be impressed in favor of B on all of T's estate. The constructive trust is a creature of equity that does not interfere with laws of descent and distribution. Legal title still passes to T's heirs; equity, however, demands that the enjoyment of such interests be vested in the party who is in good conscience entitled to the property. Moreover, as the innocent heir would not have inherited but for the wrongful act, equity should act to afford B complete justice and prevent unjust enrichment. *Pope v. Garrett*, 211 S.W.2d 559 (Tex. 1948). See also *Latham v. Father Divine*, 85 N.E.2d 168 (N.Y. 1949).

   Note: The court in *Pope* acknowledged that the constructive trust remedy should be used with caution, especially when, as in the instant case, proof of the wrongful act rests in parol evidence. Influential in the court's decision to resort to the equitable remedy was the fact that the evidence in B's case included the testimony of four disinterested witnesses and T's unexecuted will.

V. MISTAKES

A. Wrong document: If a testator signs the ***wrong document*** in the mistaken belief that it is his will, most courts hold that there is ***no will***.

> **Example:** H and W have their wills prepared at the same time. By mistake H signs W's will and W signs H's will. Neither signed document is admissible to probate. *In re Pavlinko's Estate*, 394 Pa. 564, 148 A.2d 528 (1959). But see *In re Snide*, 418 N.E.2d 656 (N.Y. 1981), holding that the wills are valid in this situation.

B. Omission of provision: If a testator ***omits*** to include some provision in his will there can be ***no relief*** because a will cannot be reformed and the deceased testator cannot comply with the statute of wills.

C. Mistake as to legal effect: If the testator is mistaken as to the ***legal effect*** of the language he uses in his will there cannot be any relief — to grant relief would be to make a will for a decedent.

D. Inclusion by mistake: A provision ***included*** in a will by mistake may be ***omitted*** by the probate court when the will is admitted to probate. This will usually depend upon whether or not the inclusion is ***separable***. This rests upon two considerations:

1. Will the deletion substantially alter other provisions in the instrument?
2. If a substantial alteration will occur, will the intention of the testator be effectuated best by probating the will as written or by deleting the materials mistakenly included and the provision affected by the deletion?

E. Mistake in the inducement: A will generally is not invalid when testator makes it on the basis of a mistake in a material fact, i.e., ***mistake in the inducement***. Thus, e.g., when testator makes no provision for his niece believing her to have married a wealthy man though her husband is in fact a pauper, the will is valid.

F. Pretermitted heir statutes: Some statutes give relief when a testator has made a will mistakenly believing that an absent child is dead. Such statutes usually give the child the share he would have taken had testator died intestate. See protection of children, *supra*, p. 31.

G. Effectuating intent: If both the mistake and the testator's desires but for the mistake, appear on the face of the will, a court may give some remedy to effectuate the intent of the testator. Such cases are extremely rare. Relief in such cases is consistent with cases of dependent relative revocation. See *infra*, p. 66.

H. Malpractice: An attorney who drafts a will has been held ***liable*** to intended beneficiaries if the ***negligent drafting*** of the will prevents them from inheriting as the testator intended. McGovern, p. 243.

> **Example:** In their wills H and W both provide that the other will receive the testator's estate if the other survives by 30 days. The wills also provide that if H and W die in a common disaster, their estates are to be divided between two nephews, A and B. H dies from a stroke and W dies from cancer fifteen days later. Since neither will contains any other dispositive provisions, both estates pass by intestacy to persons other than A and B. A and B sue the attorney who drafted the wills. They allege that H and W did not intend their estates to devolve by intestate succession, and that the intended heirs were A and B.
>
> *Held*, for A and B. The attorney is liable to the intended beneficiaries who are damaged by the negligent drafting of the wills. The attorney owed a duty to H and W to ascertain their intentions in all foreseeable events and draft their wills accordingly. A and B may base their suit either on tort ***negligence*** or in contract as ***third party beneficiaries***. *Ogle v. Fuiten*, 466 N.E.2d 224 (Ill. 1984).

VI. EXECUTION

A. Classification of wills: Depending on the manner in which they are executed, wills may be classified as follows: (1) ***written and witnessed***; (2) ***holographic*** (olographic); or (3) ***nuncupative*** (oral).

1. **Authentication of written and witnessed wills:** The authenticity of a written and witnessed will is vouched for by the ***witnesses***.

2. **Authentication of holographic wills:** The authenticity of a holographic will is vouched for by the genuineness of the testator's ***handwriting***.

3. **Authentication of nuncupative wills:** The authenticity of a nuncupative will is vouched for by the ***circumstances*** in which it is made. See discussion *infra* p. 45.

4. **State regulated:** The formalities required for each type of will are regulated by state statute and vary from state to state. Written and witnessed wills are permissible in every jurisdiction. Holographic and nuncupative wills are valid only in some states.

B. Written and witnessed wills: Every state has a statute prescribing the ***formalities*** requisite to testamentary disposition. These requirements relate to: (1) writing; (2) signing; (3) publication; (4) witnessing or attestation; and (5) presence. An attempt to make a will coupled with an intent to do so will not make a valid will unless the terms of the statute are fulfilled.

1. **Statute of Frauds:** State statutes are usually based on a provision in the English Statute of Frauds which provided: All devises and bequests of any land or tenement shall be in ***writing signed*** by the party so devising the same or by some other person in his presence and by his express direction and shall be ***attested and subscribed*** in the presence of the said deviser by three or four ***credible witnesses*** or else they shall be utterly void and of no effect. 29 Car. 2, c. 3, §3 (1676).

2. **Writing:** To constitute a writing there must be a ***readable inscription*** in any language on a substance which makes the recording thereof relatively permanent. Thus, a writing on the sand would not suffice. A legible inscription on slate, typewritten material, or a writing on paper with lead pencil or ink would satisfy the requirement.

3. **Signing:** ***Any mark*** such as an x, a zero, check mark or a name, intended by a competent testator to constitute his signature as authenticating his will, is a valid signing. This is similarly true of the signature of a witness.

   a. **Who may affix testator's signature:** The signature of the testator may be affixed by himself personally or by some other person in the presence of the testator and at his direction. By the better view the same rule applies in case of a witness.

   b. **Placement of signature:** The ***signature*** of the testator may appear any place on the will, but if the statute requires it to be ***"subscribed"*** or ***"at the end thereof"***, it must be preceded by the contents of the will. This principle also applies to the signatures of witnesses.

   c. **Order of signing:** As between testator and witnesses the order of signing is unimportant if all sign as part of a ***single transaction***. Some cases hold that it is sufficient if the testator signs after the witnesses in their absence, if he later acknowledges his signature to them.

   d. **Uniform Probate Code:** UPC §2-502 requires that a will be written, signed by the testator and witnessed by two persons who sign. However, where a will does not comply with all formal requirements, the document may be treated as a will if there is ***"clear and convincing evidence"*** that the decedent intended the document to be her will. UPC §2-503.

4. **Presence:** Some states require that the testator sign in the presence of witnesses.

   a. **Acknowledgment:** The majority, however, require only an ***acknowledgment*** of the signature to the witnesses. In some states this must be to all witnesses at the same time; in others acknowledgment to each witness separately is sufficient. Thus, if a testator takes his will, which he has already signed, to a witness and shows him the signature stating that it is his signature, it is thus acknowledged. An acknowledgment that "this is my will" is usually sufficient as an acknowledgment of signature. See UPC §2-502.

   b. **"Presence" defined:** The words ***"in the presence of the testator"*** or ***"in the presence of the witnesses"*** usually mean in the ***line of vision*** of the testator or witnesses. They do not mean that one must actually see the signing, but that he could have seen it. Some more liberal cases have held that it is only necessary that the event be close at hand and within general cognizance. Thus, a blind person may make a will with witnesses subscribing in a place that the testator could see if he had sight.

5. **Publication:** A few jurisdictions require the testator to ***publish*** his will. This means that he must declare to the witnesses that the ***instrument is his will***. No jurisdiction requires the witnesses to know the contents of the will.

6. **Witnessing or attestation:** All state statutes require two or three witnesses to the will. These witnesses are usually required both to ***sign*** and to ***attest*** (which are separate functions). Attestation is the state of mind by which the witness intends to bear witness to the performance of the acts required by the statute to validate the will. Signing or subscribing is the physical act of the witness in putting his hand to paper.

   Example: H executes a will prepared by a friend, S. H leaves his entire estate to W and then to his stepson, J, if W predeceases him. H is in the hospital when he signs his will and S notarizes it, but the two witnesses before whom H acknowledges his signature never sign the will. H inherits W's estate when she predeceases him. H dies fifteen months after signing his will, and J claims the estate. The state contends that the will is invalid because it was not signed by two witnesses, and argues that since H had no heirs, the estate escheats to the state.

Held, the will is invalid and the estate escheats to the state. Witnessing requirements consist of the dual acts of ***observation*** and ***signature***. Execution formalities are substantive requirements to prevent fraud, so witnesses must sign a will within a reasonable time after the testator signs or acknowledges his signature. S's signature as a notary can be counted as one witness, but two witnesses are required. This requirement serves an evidentary purpose. If witnesses could testify to their presence at the execution of a will no matter how much time had elapsed, the signing requirement would be useless. *Estate of Peters*, 526 A.2d 1005 (N.J. 1987).

a. **Requesting attestation:** A ***minority*** of states require the testator to ***request*** the witnesses to attest and subscribe. This may be implied by the testator's permitting them to sign.

b. **Competency to testify required:** Witnesses are required to be ***competent*** to testify. The better view is that competency is determined at the time of the execution of the will.

c. **Pecuniary interest:** At common law any witness having a ***pecuniary interest*** in a matter was incompetent to testify; a beneficiary under a will, therefore, could not be an attesting witness. By the more ***modern view*** competent means ***competent under the rules of evidence*** at the time the will is executed. Rules of evidence in about 20 states ***do not disqualify*** a witness for interest; such interest goes only to the witness's ***credibility***. Therefore, in these states a beneficiary may be a witness. UPC §2-505; Waggoner, p. 194.

   i. **Interests of creditors and others:** The interests of creditors, attorneys and executors are usually not sufficient to disqualify them as witnesses.

d. **Purging statutes:** In order to uphold wills, many jurisdictions passed ***"purging"*** statutes eliminating the interest of witness-beneficiaries in order that they might testify.

   Example: T leaves $1,000 to W in her will. W serves as a witness to the will. Under a purging statute W's gift would be struck from the will, leaving W no interest under the will. Having no interest, it would not be to her benefit to testify falsely to make sure the will is admitted to probate and it is assumed that she will testify objectively.

   Note: Even though modern rules of evidence do not in general disqualify a witness for interest, purging statutes may nevertheless eliminate the interest of a witness beneficiary.

i. **Benefit must be direct and financial:** If a purging statute is to prevent a witness from taking under a will, the ***benefit*** must be ***direct*** and ***financial***. If the witness is also an ***intestate successor***, generally only the interest in ***excess*** of the amount he would receive under the will is purged.

ii. **Indirect interests:** A purging statute does not affect ***indirect interests***. Thus, if the testator leaves $100,000 to St. Paul's Church and the witness to the will is a member of the church, the gift to the church will not be invalidated.

iii. **Spouse of beneficiary:** When the spouse of a witness is a beneficiary, some states allow the witness to testify and the spouse to take the interest; others purge the spouse's interest.

e. **Intent to validate:** A witness must sign with ***intent to validate*** the testator's act.

f. **Attestation clause:** An ***attestation clause*** is a certificate signed by witnesses to a will reciting performance of formalities of execution which the witnesses observed.

i. **Prima facie evidence:** An ***attestation clause*** is not required for validity of the will but in some states is prima facie evidence that the statements made therein are true.

g. **Self-proved wills:** The Uniform Probate Code provides for a will to be ***"self-proved"*** by the acknowledgment of the testator and the affidavits of the witnesses reciting the facts of execution, before an officer authorized to administer oaths at the time of execution or subsequent to it. On the testator's death the will may be admitted to probate without the testimony of any subscribing witnesses. UPC §2-504.

C. **Holographic and nuncupative wills:** Many jurisdictions have statutes that recognize certain types of wills which do not meet the usual requirements of either a writing or witnesses. The policy behind such recognition is that such wills are made under ***circumstances that militate against fraud***. These statutes are strictly construed.

1. **Holographic wills:** ***Holographic*** wills are wills completely written and signed in the ***handwriting*** of the testator and usually ***unwitnessed***. Some jurisdictions also require that such wills be dated by the testator's hand. Over thirty jurisdictions recognize these wills. Waggoner, p. 198.

a. **When holographic wills contain material not in testator's handwriting:** There are a ***number of approaches*** concerning the validity of holographic wills containing material not in the testator's hand.

i. **Invalid if part of the will:** Some jurisdictions hold that validity depends on whether the testator ***intended the material to be part of the will***.

Example: T's will is completely handwritten with the exception of a typewritten introductory clause. Even though the typewritten material contains no dispositive provisions, T's will is denied probate when the court finds that the clause was intended by T to be part of her will.

ii. **Severability:** Some jurisdictions hold that the portion not in the testator's handwriting may be ***disregarded***, but only if the testator's intent will still be clear after severing the non-handwritten part.

Example: T buys a printed will form, fills in the blanks by hand, signs it, and has it notarized. Since two witnesses are required, the document is offered as a holographic will. *Held*, probate must be denied, because the handwritten portions are insufficient evidence of a testamentary intent after the printed protions are eliminated. *Estate of Johnson*, 630 P.2d 1044 (Ariz. 1981).

iii. **Modern view:** Some modern statutes on holographic wills require only that the ***signature and material provisions*** be in the handwriting of the testator. See UPC §2-503.

2. **Nuncupative wills:** A ***nuncupative*** will is an ***oral*** will. These wills are recognized in more than twenty states. Waggoner, p. 199.

   a. **Typical statutory requirements:** A typical statute on ***nuncupative*** wills requires:

      i. that the testator be ***dying*** and ***know it***;

      ii. that the will dispose of ***personalty*** only, (as opposed to realty);

      iii. that the testator indicate to the witnesses that he ***wishes them to witness*** his oral will;

      iv. that there be three (or some other specified number) ***witnesses*** over the age of 14 years (or other age); and

      v. that probate of the will be made within ***six months*** from the time the words are spoken unless they are reduced to writing within six (or other number) days after being spoken.

   b. **No special form:** ***No special form of words*** is required to make the will or to call the witnesses to attest.

c. **Soldiers and sailors:** Several states have statutes relaxing statutory requirements for wills of ***soldiers*** and ***sailors***. They usually require that the will be made by soldiers in actual military service or sailors while at sea. These wills are usually limited to dispositions of personalty.

d. **Attempt to dispose of both realty and personalty:** When an oral will attempts to dispose of both realty and personalty the personalty will go according to the will and the realty according to the statutes of descent and distribution as if the testator had died intestate.

VII. TESTAMENTARY INTENT

A. **Animus testandi:** Animus testandi, or ***intention to make a will***, must be present for an instrument to be sustained as a will.

B. **No prescribed form for a will:** The general rule is that ***any writing***, however informal, executed in accordance with statutory requirements, constitutes a valid testamentary disposition if made with the ***expressed intent of the maker to dispose of his property upon his death.*** *Noble v. Fickes*, 82 N.E. 950 (Ill. 1907).

C. **Parol evidence of testamentary intent:** Parol evidence is not ordinarily admissible to establish ***animus testandi*** when there is nothing on the face of an instrument to indicate the presence of testamentary intent. (It may be admissible to interpret ambiguous language on the issue.)

> **Example:** T executes an instrument in the form of a statutory deed that purports to convey certain land to his son Thomas. The deed, which is attested by two credible witnesses, is delivered to a friend with instructions to deliver the instrument to Thomas upon T's death. There is no indication on the face of the instrument that the transfer is intended to take effect only after T's death. At issue is whether parol evidence may be admitted to prove the existence of ***animus testandi***.
>
> *Held*, while the deed was executed in conformance with the Statute of Wills, it does not constitute a valid will. As wills are required to be in writing, an unambiguous deed lacking ***animus testandi*** may not be converted into a will through parol evidence of testamentary intent. *Noble v. Fickes, supra*.

VIII. CONTRACTS TO MAKE WILLS

A. **Law of contracts:** A contract to make a will is to be interpreted and tested by the ***law of contracts***.

B. Writing requirement: Many states have statutes which require an agreement to make a will to be in ***writing***.

1. **Where no statutory writing requirement:** If the state does not have a statute requiring a writing, an oral agreement to leave personal property by will is valid and enforceable. An agreement to devise real property, however, is within the ***Statute of Frauds***.

C. Will must be probated: The last will of a testator must be probated whether or not it conforms to a previously made contract or constitutes a breach thereof.

D. Remedy: The remedy for breach of a contract to devise or bequeath property is through the medium of a trust in a court of equity, rather than by an injunction to enjoin the probate of the last will which constitutes the breach. See *Oursler v. Armstrong, infra*, p. 48.

E. Mutual and joint wills: When mutual and/or joint wills are executed, contractual issues often arise.

1. **Joint will :** A ***joint will*** is a single document executed by two (or more) testators as their will. When one dies it is probated as his will, and when the survivor dies it is probated as her will.

   a. **Contract:** A joint will may constitute a ***contract*** between the two testators, if they so intend.

      Example: H and W execute a joint will providing that the estate of the first to die should go to the survivor. On the survivor's death the estate is to go to a named beneficiary (B). W dies and H inherits. Subsequently, H marries M and executes a new will naming M as sole beneficiary. When H dies, B and M claim the estate. *Held*, for B. H and W intended to make their joint will irrevocable. Thus H received only a power to use the assets during his life and had no devisable property interests for M to inherit. The nature of H's interest was such that M had no right of election as a widow. *Rubenstein v. Mueller*, 225 N.E.2d 540 (N.Y. 1967).

      Note: In reaching its decision the court in *Rubenstein* considered the wording of the will: "Upon the death of the second . . . the estate of the second . . . is hereby bequeathed, ..." This modified the survivor's right to full ownership of the collective property. It "imports the joint disposition of the collective property of both, not the independent disposition by each of his own." Furthermore, this will expressly revoked a prior joint will which gave the survivor the right to alter the disposition made of H and W's property. This omission persuaded the court that H and W intended to make the will irrevocable.

2. **Mutual will: *"Mutual wills"*** are physically separate wills of two (or more) persons which contain similar or reciprocal provisions.

   Example: H and W execute their wills in separate documents. Each person gives the other all of his or her property. These are mutual wills. If H dies first his will be probated, and his property will be distributed to W.

   a. **Not necessarily a contract not to revoke:** Mutual wills (or reciprocal provisions) standing alone without more do ***not*** constitute a ***contract*** between the testators not to revoke; either testator may revoke his will at any time. See UPC §2-514.

      Example: H has four children, two by his first wife and two by his second wife, T. H and T execute wills at the same time. Each will provides: (1) that the residuary estate is to go to the spouse; and (2) that if the spouse fails to survive, the property is to go to H's four children. H dies and T makes a new will that leaves all of her property to her own two children only. H's children from his first marriage seek to impress a constructive trust on the property received by T under H's will.

      Held, as the proof failed to establish the existence of an actual promise by T, express or implied, that she would not afterward change her will, the court will not impress a trust on the property. The existence of a confidential relationship or moral obligation is not enough to justify depriving T of her right to dispose of her property as she wishes. "To attribute to a will the quality of irrevocability demands the most indisputable evidence of the agreement which is relied upon to change its ambulatory nature, and . . . presumptions will not, and should not, take the place of proof." *Oursler v. Armstrong*, 179 N.E.2d 489 (N.Y. 1961).

   b. **Remedy for breach of contract:** If A and B draw mutual wills in favor of each other and ***explicitly contract*** not to revoke them, the parties have in effect made both a will and a contract. Such contractually-linked wills are sometimes called ***"joint and mutual"*** wills. If one will is thereafter revoked, in a majority of jurisdictions the remedy is with respect to the contract and not the will. *Oursler v. Armstrong, supra.*

      Example: After making a joint and mutual will with B, A revokes his will and gives his property to C. On A's death A's later will is probated and the property distributed to C. In most jurisdictions, B now has a choice of remedies, each contractual rather than on the will: (1) B can compel C to hold in constructive trust for B according to the terms of the contract or (2) B can make a claim against A's estate for damages for breach of contract.

i. **Basis for probate:** But in a minority of jurisdictions the courts hold that the breach of contract is enough to allow the older (joint and mutual) will to be admitted to probate.

3. **Uniform Probate Code:** Under the UPC, a contract to make a will may be established ***only*** by the testator's: (1) stating the essential contract provisions in the will, (2) incorporating the contract by reference in the will, or (3) signing a writing evidencing the contract. UPC §2-514.

4. **Quantum meruit:** Where a contract to make a certain disposition of property is unenforceable, there may be a claim against the estate in quantum meruit for the ***value of services*** rendered or in quantum valebant for the value of goods furnished.

   Example: In a non-marital relationship, the surviving partner may have a claim in quantum meruit against the estate for the value of services if they were rendered in reasonable expectation of compensation even without an express promise to devise. *Estate of Zent*, 459 N.W.2d 795 (N.D. 1990); *Suggs v. Norris*, 364 S.E.2d 159 (N.C. 1988).

IX. COMPONENTS OF WILLS

A. **Integration:** ***Integration*** means the determination of what papers constitute the testator's will.

   Example: T makes a first will giving Blackacre to A, a second will giving Whiteacre to B, a third will giving Brownacre to C and a fourth will giving Greenacre and all of the residue of his property to D. T dies. All four of the above wills together constitute the last will and testament of T, since they are wholly consistent with each other and none contains a revocatory clause.

B. **Incorporation by reference:** ***Incorporation by reference*** means that the testator by provision in his will has legally reached out and caused ***extraneous material***, such as a book, record or memorandum, to become part of the will.

1. **Requirements:** For the doctrine of incorporation by reference to apply the following must be established:

   a. that the extraneous material was ***in existence*** at the time of making the will;

   b. that the ***will on its face*** refers to such material as being in existence at the time of the making of the will and ***shows intention to incorporate it***; and

c. that the extraneous material offered as part of the will is the ***identical material*** referred to or described in the will.

Example: T executes a will, dated May 22, 1900, that bequeaths, in clause 12, $50,000 to his wife to be held in trust "for the purposes set forth in a sealed letter which will be found with this will." After T's death, the will is found in T's safe deposit vault along with a sealed envelope containing a letter dated May 12, 1900. The letter is in T's handwriting and signed by him. Referring to "my will just executed" and reciting clause 12, the letter directs T's wife to pay the $50,000 to William Jennings Bryan for his financial aid. At issue is whether the letter may become incorporated by reference into the will.

Held, the reference to the letter fails to incorporate it into the will. To incorporate a paper by reference into a will, the paper must be in existence at the time of the execution of the will and must be described by the will in clear, definite, and unambiguous terms. Here, any sealed letter "setting forth the purposes of the trust, made by anybody at any time after the will was executed, and 'found with the will,' would . . . fully and accurately answer the reference." "The vice is that no particular paper is referred to." *Bryan's Appeal*, 77 Conn. 240, 58 A.748 (1904).

2. **Uniform Probate Code view:** The general rule is that documents not in existence at the time a will is executed cannot be incorporated by reference. But the ***Uniform Probate Code*** provides that a will may refer to a written statement or list to dispose of items of tangible personal property (e.g., jewelry and household goods) if the ***list*** is ***signed*** by the testator and is in existence at the time of the testator's death. See UPC §§2-510 and 2-513.

Note: The ***signature requirement*** is included in the UPC because the lack of a signature may indicate the lack of testamentary intent. However, if the document to be incorporated is unsigned, but there is "clear and convincing evidence" that the testator intended the unsigned writing to dispose of personal property, it may be admissible under UPC §2-503.

3. **Republication:** Even if an informal document is not in existence when the will referring to it is executed, a ***later republication*** of the will by a ***codicil*** will ***satisfy the "existing document" rule*** and will incorporate the document by reference if the document is properly identified in the will.

Example: T executes a will dated March 25, 1932 in which he states that certain property should be distributed as provided in a letter dated March 25, 1932 addressed to his executors. T also executes a codicil dated Nov. 25, 1933 which contains no reference to the letter but does republish the will. A letter addressed to T's executors and dated July 3, 1933 is found with the will. No letter dated March 25 is found among T's effects.

Held, the letter dated July 3 was incorporated into the will when the codicil was executed. Since the letter was written after the will, it was not incorporated by reference when it was written. But the codicil republished the will. Although there is a discrepancy in dates, the evidence of identity is overcome: the letter was in T's safe deposit box with the will; it was addressed to the executors; and no other letter was found. Moreover, the letter was handwritten by T and its terms conform to those described in the will. *Simon v. Grayson*, 102 P.2d 1081 (Cal. 1940).

C. **Doctrine of Independent Significance:** A will may dispose of property by ***reference to certain*** acts and events which have ***significance apart from their effect*** upon the dispositions ***made by will*** whether they occur before or after either the execution of the will or the testator's death. As the acts affecting the will are not done solely for testamentary purposes, they are not treated as invalid amendments to the will and are not subject to statutory will requirements, such as attestation. *Second Bank-State Street Trust Co. v. Pinon, infra*, p. 52. See also Clark, p. 323.

1. **Acts of beneficiaries:** The doctrine may include an ***act of a beneficiary.***

   Example: T leaves property "to the girl my son John marries." The girl's non-testamentory act of marrying John (an act of independent significance) makes her a beneficiary under the will.

2. **Future acts of testator:** The doctrine may apply to *future acts of the testator*. Thus, effect would be given to a testamentary disposition "to such persons as shall be in my employ at the time of my death." The act of employing persons is an act of independent significance not subject to the requirements of wills statutes.

3. **Execution or revocation of another's will:** The execution or revocation of the will of another person is an act of independent significance under the doctrine. See UPC §2-512.

D. **Testamentary gifts to a trust:** When a will makes a gift of property to an inter vivos trust, and the assets are handled and distributed as part of that trust, this is known as a ***pour-over trust***. There are several different approaches, any one of which may suffice to validate a pour-over testamentary gift to a trust in existence at the time of the testator's death, even if the trust itself is not created with testamentary formalities.

1. **Incorporation by reference:** If the trust instrument is in existence at the time of the execution of the will and is referred to therein, it will be ***incorporated by reference*** and a testamentary trust will be created on the terms and conditions contained in the trust document.

2. **Act of independent significance:** In many states, the creation of the trust is deemed to be an ***act of independent significance***, so the gift to the trust is valid even though the trust was created (or amended) without complying with testamentary formalities.

   Example: The wills of T1 and T2, husband and wife, give the residue of their estates to a revocable and amendable inter vivos trust created before the execution of their wills. Subsequent to the execution of the wills, the trust is amended. The question is whether the residue passes: (1) to the trustees under the trust as amended; (2) to the trustees under the terms of the original trust; or (3) otherwise.

   Held, the property should be distributed according to the terms of the amended trust. The amendment to the trust is effective because of the applicability of the doctrine that acts of independent significance are valid even though not executed with the formalities required by the statute of wills. There is no question that the creation and amendment of an amendable, revocable inter vivos trust are acts of independent significance. *Second Bank-State Street Trust Co. v. Pinion*, 170 N.E.2d 350 (Mass. 1960).

   a. **Unfunded pour-over trust:** In the *Pinion* case, *supra*, the court ruled on a trust which had been funded, (*i.e.*, some money had been put into it) before the testators died. When the trust is created at the time of the will, but it is not funded until the testator dies, it is also valid. This modern rule changed the common law where a "res" or corpus was required for a trust.

      Example: T executes a will in which all of her assets are to "pour-over" into revocable inter vivos trusts which T creates the same day. Trust A is a marital deduction trust, i.e., the amount put in it covers the marital deduction for federal estate tax purposes, thereby reducing estate taxes. Trust B contains all other assets. The trusts are never funded during T's life. The principal beneficiary of both trusts is H. The contingent beneficiaries of both trusts are T's nephews and nieces (related to T only by her marriage to H). Subsequently T and H are divorced, but the trusts are not amended to exclude H. T's administrator petitions the court to determine the distribution of trust assets.

Held, (1) T created valid inter vivos trusts even though they were unfunded. (2) H's interest in Trust A was terminated by the divorce, since the purpose of the trust — to qualify for a marital tax deduction — was impossible after the divorce. (3) H's interest in Trust B was also terminated by the divorce. (A statute provides that divorce automatically revokes provisions in a will benefiting a former spouse. The will and trust are an intimately connected testamentary plan. Therefore, the statute should apply to this trust just as it does to a will). (4) The nephews and nieces may take their shares immediately as though H had predeceased T. The statute creates a presumption that gifts to a divorced spouse are revoked, but it is silent about other beneficiaries. Therefore, the divorce did not revoke those gifts. *Clymer v. Mayo*, 473 N.E.2d 1084 (Mass. 1985).

3. **Uniform Testamentary Additions to Trusts Act:** All jurisdictions now have ***statutes*** validating gifts to trusts executed before or concurrently with the execution of the testator's will. These provide that the gift will not be invalided merely because the trust is amendable or revocable or is in fact amended after the execution of the will. See the Uniform Testamentary Additions to Trusts Act and UPC §2-511; also Waggoner, p. 436.

   a. **Gift to a trust under the Act:** Under the Uniform Testamentary Additions to Trusts Act, a gift to a trust which qualifies is deemed to be and is administered as a part of the trust to which it is given. The revocation of the trust prior to the death of the testator causes the devise to lapse.

CONSTRUCTION OF WILLS

I. ADMISSIBILITY OF EXTRINSIC EVIDENCE

A. **Extrinsic evidence defined:** ***Extrinsic evidence*** is evidence found ***outside the body of the will*** (or other instrument or agreement) itself.

B. **General rule:** Extrinsic evidence is ***not ordinarily admissible*** to construe ***clear and accurate descriptions*** in wills of the testator's property or beneficiaries.

C. **Latent ambiguities:** Extrinsic evidence is generally ***admissible to clarify latent ambiguities*** in a will. A latent ambiguity exists when the language of a will, though clear on its face, is susceptible to ***more than one meaning when applied to the extrinsic facts*** to which it refers.

> **Example 1:** T devises the residue of her estate "to Chester Quinn [Q] & Roxy Russell." Roxy is T's dog, who predeceases T. T's natural heir, P, claims one-half of the residue of the estate. P contends that the gift to the dog is void, so the property passes to P by intestate succession.
>
> *Held*, the gift to the dog is void, so half of the residuary estate passes to P. T intended equal shares to go to Q and Roxy. Extrinsic evidence is admissible to establish that Roxy is a dog, because there is a latent ambiguity in the will. The will does not give the entire residuum to Q, and the gift to the dog cannot be expanded to mean a gift of everything to Q to care for the dog. *Estate of Russell*, 444 P.2d 353 (Cal. 1968).

> **Example 2:** T leaves "$1,000 to my nephew John." T has two nephews of that name. Extrinsic evidence, including that of T's expressed intent, is admissible to explain which nephew John was the intended beneficiary.

D. **Patent ambiguities:** In limited circumstances, extrinsic evidence may be admissible to clarify ***patent ambiguities***. A patent ambiguity is one that is ***apparent from the face*** of the will.

> **Example:** A will contains (1) a devise to "George Gord, the son of George Gord"; (2) a devise to "George Gord, the son of Gord"; and (3) a bequest to "George Gord, the son of John Gord." Evidence of the testator's declarations is admitted to show that "George Gord, the son of Gord," was intended to mean "George Gord, the son of George Gord." Ritchie, p. 409 referring to the case of *Doe d. George Gord v. Needs*, 2 M .& W. 129, 150 Eng. Rep. 698 (1836).

II. CONDITIONAL WILLS

A. **Defined:** A conditional will is one which, by its terms, ***operates only upon the occurrence of a stated event.***

B. **Problem of construction:** It is not always clear whether the reference to an occurrence is a ***condition precedent*** to the operation of the will or merely a ***recitation of the motive*** for making the will. Under the latter construction the will is effective regardless of whether the condition is fulfilled. Such an interpretation is considered preferable, but the wording and surrounding circumstances may not support it. Dukeminier, p. 215.

> **Example:** T is an illiterate, uneducated woman. On the eve of embarking on a journey T, on her own, prepares and signs a will that states in part: "I am going on a Journey and may not ever return. And if I do not, this is my last request. . . ." The will leaves T's property to a church and a person she calls her adopted son. T does return from her trip and dies shortly thereafter.
>
> *Held*, the will is not rendered invalid by T's return from her trip. "Courts do not incline to regard a will as conditional where it can be reasonably held that the testator was merely expressing his inducement to make it, however inaccurate his use of language might be, if strictly construed." While the quoted language from T's will may have, in a literal sense, created a condition precedent, it is clear from an examination of the instrument as a whole and surrounding circumstances that such was not T's intention. T, an uneducated person, was apparently stating in concrete form that the contingency of death, on her mind because of her impending journey, was her reason for writing a will. Such an interpretation is supported by the fact that gifts to a church and an adopted son are not of the kind generally subjected to such a condition. *Eaton v. Brown*, 193 U.S. 411, 24 S.Ct. 487 L.Ed. 730 (1904).

III. ADEMPTION AND ABATEMENT

A. **Classification of dispositions under wills:** Dispositions under wills are classified as: (1) ***specific***; (2) ***demonstrative***; (3) ***general***; or (4) ***residuary***. Dispositions are classified for purposes of ***ademption, abatement and lapse***.

1. **Specific:** A ***specific*** devise or bequest is a gift of a particular, identifiable item of property.

> **Example:** I hereby give my Wedgewood tea set to my cousin Jean.

2. **Demonstrative:** A ***demonstrative*** bequest is a gift of a certain amount of property out of a certain fund or identifiable source of property.

   Example: I hereby give $1,000 out of my bank account at Second National Bank to my cousin Margaret.

3. **General:** A ***general*** bequest is a gift of property payable from the general assets of testator's estate.

   Example: I hereby give $5,000 to my cousin Emma.

4. **Residuary:** A ***residuary*** gift is a gift of the ***remaining portion of the estate*** after the satisfaction of other dispositions.

B. **Ademption: *"Ademption"*** is a doctrine by which a gift in a will is ***invalidated***. Ademption operates in two ways: (1) by ***extinction*** and (2) by ***satisfaction***.

1. **Ademption by extinction:** Ademption by ***extinction*** applies to specific devises and bequests of property which (1) are no longer in the estate at all or (2) have been substantially changed in character.

   Example 1: T's will bequeaths $20,000 to H. The next clause bequeaths certain stock and all bank deposits in T's name to T's grandchildren. Shortly before T's death, a son withdraws all T's bank deposits to buy bonds for T as her agent. As a result there is no longer money on deposit to discharge both the gift to H and the gift to T's grandchildren. H argues that there has been an ademption of the bank deposits, and that H should be paid her legacy from the sale of the bonds. The grandchildren argue that the bank deposits merely changed form, and they should be preferred over H.

   Held, there was an ademption, and H receives her bequest. "A substantial change in the nature or character of the subject matter of a bequest will operate as an ademption; but a merely nominal or formal change will not." T's money on deposit no longer exists because of a substantial change. T's bequest to her grandchildren was specific, and it cannot be construed as a gift of investments in bonds. Further, only the fact of the change or extinction is relevant, not the reason for it. *McGee v. McGee*, 413 A.2d 72 (R.I. 1980).

   Example 2: A, by will, makes a gift of "my topaz ring" to B. The topaz ring is later stolen, but proceeds of insurance are available. Under the usual rule the gift is adeemed, and the beneficiary is not entitled to the insurance proceeds.

   a. **Gift of securities:** Under modern statutes, when the testator makes a gift of certain ***securities***, the specific devisee is entitled to so much of such securities as is a part of the estate at the time of death, plus additional securities: (1) of the ***same entity*** owned by testator by reason of increase either through action initiated by the entity (such as a stock split) or as a result of a plan of reinvestent in a regular investment company and (2) of another entity owned by testator as a result of a ***merger***, consolidation, or reorganization of the original securities. *Goode, Executor v. Reynolds, Executor*, 271 S.W. 600 (Ky. 1925).

b. **Unpaid funds related to property:** Under some recent cases and statutes the specific devisee may be allowed to take any part of the specific devise remaining in the estate as well as any ***amounts owing relative to such property*** which were not paid to the testator prior to his death, such as the balance of the purchase price paid for the sale of the property, condemnation awards, and proceeds from fire or casualty insurance.

2. **Ademption by satisfaction:** Ademption by ***satisfaction*** takes place when the testator in his lifetime gives to his legatee all or a part of the gift he had intended to give by his will. It depends on the testator's ***intention*** and applies to general as well as specific legacies.

   a. **Testacy only:** Ademption by satisfaction is applicable only in the case of ***testacy***.

      i. **Distinguished from advancement:** Ademption by satisfaction must be distinguished from the ***doctrine of advancements***. Advancement takes place only when the decedent dies ***intestate*** (*supra*, p. 20).

   b. **Effect of inter vivos gift:** If the subject matter of an ***inter vivos gift*** is the same as the subject matter of a testamentary provision, it is presumed that the inter vivos gift is in lieu of the testamentary gift when there is a ***parent- child*** or ***grand parent-grand child relationship***. In other instances, the presumption is against ademption by satisfaction.

      Example: T makes a will leaving $25,000 to her son, S. Afterward T gives S $15,000 to complete medical school. When T dies, S gets only $10,000, unless there is proof that T had a contrary intention.

   c. **UPC requirements:** Ademption by satisfaction is recognized in UPC §2-609 where the testator, during his life, gives a person a gift, if any of the following is true:

      i. ***the will provides*** for deduction of the gift; or

ii. ***there is a contemporaneous writing of the testator*** stating that the gift is in satisfaction of the devise; or

iii. ***there is a written acknowledgment by the donee*** that the gift is in satisfaction of the devise.

C. **Abatement:** ***Abatement*** is the process of determining the ***order*** in which property in the estate will be applied to the payment of debts, taxes, expenses and dispositions under the will when there is an insufficient amount to pay all claims and dispositions.

1. **Intention of the testator:** If expressed in the will the ***intention*** of the testator governs the order in which property will abate.

2. **General rules of abatement:** In the absence of an expression of the testator's intention in the will the following order of abatement will be applied:

   a. ***intestate*** property (i.e., property not disposed of by the will);

   b. ***residuary*** gifts;

   c. ***general*** bequests;

   d. ***demonstrative bequests*** (if the fund is in existence at the time of death; otherwise they will be treated as general bequests);

   e. ***devises***; and

   f. ***specific bequests***.

   See generally, UPC §§3-902 to 3-916.

3. **Election by the spouse:** In many jurisdictions, statutory provisions have been enacted that provide that the burden to an estate caused by a surviving spouse's election against the will is to be borne ***pro rata by all beneficiaries***. *Supra*, pp. 28. Even where no such statutes exist, such ***pro rata*** abatement is often used in election cases on the grounds that it more closely conforms to the ***presumed intention*** of the testator.

   Example: T executes a will that leaves her husband H a life interest in her entire estate. Upon his death, ten legatees are to receive certain personal effects and cash legacies totalling $53,000; the balance of the estate to be divided among the children of T's deceased brother. After T's death, H renounces the provisions of the will and elects to take his statutory elective share, which is one-half of the estate outright. Such an election serves to reduce the residue designated for next of kin from approximately $50,000 to approximately $4,000. The primary issue is whether the general abatement rules are to control to make up for the depletion caused by the election.

Held, in contravention of the traditional abatement pattern, the elective share in this case should be charged pro rata against all beneficiaries. "This is the sound and equitable approach, and one which more nearly conforms to the presumed intention of the testator" when the diminution in the estate: (1) results from an election by the surviving spouse; (2) in circumstances which produce a substantial distortion of the testamentary scheme; (3) applies to persons who have a natural claim on the bounty of the testator; (4) there is no evidence that the election was foreseeable; and (5) there is no contrary intent manifested in the will as to the order of abatement. *Kilcoyne v. Reilly*, 249 F.2d 472 (D.C. App. 1957).

Note: Section 2-207 of the Uniform Probate Code provides for the priority used to determine the source of the elective share amount. The basic idea is that where the assets left directly to the surviving spouse are not enough to make up the elective share, the shortfall will be ***"equitably apportioned"*** among the other beneficiaries. Usually, this will mean that the other beneficiaries share the burden in proportion to the size of their bequests. See also UPC §3-902.

4. **Same class:** Within the same class, gifts abate ***pro rata***.

Example: D, by will, leaves: $1,000 to each of his nephews A, B and C; his 1939 Ford to H; $1,000 on deposit at First National Bank to E; $1,000 on deposit at Second National Bank to F; and his residuary estate to G. His residuary estate is insufficient by $3,500 to pay all debts and expenses of his estate. A, B, C and G will receive nothing; E and F will each receive $750; and H will receive the 1939 Ford. By virtue of abatement the residuary is first used to satisfy the creditors, to be followed by a pro rata abatement of the general legacies to A, B and C and then the demonstrative bequests to E and F. H receives his special bequest in full.

IV. LAPSE AND ANTILAPSE STATUTES

A. **Lapse:** A gift in a will is said to ***lapse*** when the ***beneficiary dies*** after the execution of the will but before the death of the testator and the will fails to provide an alternative for the disposition of the property.

1. **Beneficiary dead when will executed:** A gift by will to a person ***already deceased*** at the time the will is executed is ***void***; no question of lapse arises in such a case.

2. **Class gifts:** If a gift in a will is to a class and a member of the class dies before the death of the testator, his interest goes to the

surviving members of the class unless the will provides otherwise. *Drafts v. Drafts*, 114 So.2d 473 (1959). *infra*, p. 61.

3. **Passes under residuary clause:** Both void and lapsed gifts pass under a general residuary clause.

4. **Devises versus legacies:** At common law, a lapsed devise of land passed as intestate property while a lapsed legacy passed through the residuary clause. Under the ***modern law*** there is ***no distinction*** between lapsed devises and lapsed legacies.

5. **When residuary legacy lapses:** When a ***residuary*** legacy or devise ***lapses*** it passes as ***intestate*** property. The lapse of specific or general bequests may throw them into the residue.

   Example: T dies testate leaving a will giving Blackacre to A, $1,000 to B and the residuary to C. Both A and B predecease T leaving no lineal descendants. As between C and T's heirs at law, C takes all of the property.

B. **Antilapse statutes:** Many jurisdictions have enacted ***"antilapse" statutes***. These generally prevent lapse by the death of a devisee or legatee before the testator if the devisee or legatee is a ***relative*** and leaves ***issue*** who survive the testator. In such cases the statutes usually provide that ***the surviving issue of the deceased beneficiary take the gift in place of the deceased beneficiary***.

   Example: T devises $5,000 to my sister M "provided she be living at the time of my death." M predeceases T. H, M's daughter, claims the amount devised to M. *Held*, the antilapse statute applies unless the testator specifically provides that the devise be given to another or provides that it lapse (which T did not do). Thus H receives the money. *Detzel v. Nieberding*, 219 N.E.2d 327 (Ohio 1966). In accord, *Estate of Ulrikson*, 290 N.W.2d 757 (Minn. 1980); UPC §2-603(b)(3). Contra, *Estate of Stroble*, 636 P.2d 236 (Kan. App. 1981).

1. **Variations in applicability of statutes:** Jurisdictions vary as to whether or not antilapse statutes apply to the following:

   a. gifts when the devisee is dead at the time of execution of the will;

   b. gifts to a class (as opposed to gifts to a named beneficiary); and

   c. the interest in a class gift of a class member who is dead at the time the will is executed.

   Example: T devises and bequeaths all the residue of her property "to my brothers and sisters, share and share alike." T has seven brothers and sisters, three of whom died leaving lineal descendants before the execution of her will and two of whom died leaving lineal descendants after the execution but before T's death. An antilapse statue in T's state provides in relevant part that when any property is devised or bequeathed to a blood relative of the testator and such beneficiary dies before the testator or before the will is executed, leaving lineal descendants, such gift does not lapse but passes to such descendants. At issue is whether the statute applies to prevent the lapse of the gift to: (1) the class members alive when the will was executed but dead before the death of the testator and/or (2) the class members who died before the execution of the will.

Held, the statute applies to the first group but not to the second. The key to the first question is whether the statute applies to beneficiaries who, rather than being named in the will, are designated as a class. It is clear from the statute's use of the words "blood relative" that the provision was intended to apply to that class of persons who are blood relatives. With respect to the second issue, it is logical to conclude that when a testator provides for his brothers and sisters, he normally intends to include only those brothers and sisters alive at the time, unless his will states otherwise. *Drafts v. Drafts*, 114 So.2d 473 (1959). *Supra*, p. 60.

2. **Uniform Probate Code:** The UPC's antilapse provisions apply to the testator's grandparents, the grandparents' descendants, and the testator's stepchildren. UPC §2-603.

V. MISCELLANEOUS RULES OF CONSTRUCTION

A. **Introduction:** In the absence of a clear intent expressed in the document, courts have developed a ***series of rules to supply presumed intent***. Rules of construction in statutes apply only when it is not made clear in the will that a contrary result was intended.

B. **General rule:** The ***general rule*** is that a will should be interpreted by the language of the instrument in the light of the general circumstances surrounding the testator at the time of its execution.

C. **Intention not found in language:** It is only when the testator's intention cannot be ascertained from the language of the will and surrounding circumstances that statutory and court-made rules of construction apply.

D. **All property passes:** A will is construed to ***pass all property*** which the testator owns at his death, including property acquired after the execution of the will.

Example: T's only property at the time he executes his will is Blackacre. He provides in his will "I give and devise all of my property to Lucy." Thereafter he acquires Whiteacre. On his death he owns both Blackacre and Whiteacre. Lucy takes both properties.

E. **Residue:** If a devise or bequest fails for any reason it becomes ***part of the residue***.

F. **Failure of part of residuary gift:** If the residuary is devised to two or more persons and the residuary gift to one of them fails for any reason his share ***passes to the other residuary devisees*** in proportion to their interests in the residue.

G. **Failure of entire residuary gift:** If a gift of the residuary fails in its entirety, the ***residuary passes by intestacy***.

H. **Deemed to have predeceased the testator:** Many states have statutes which provide that a devisee who does not survive the testator for a ***stated period of time*** (e.g. 120 hours) is treated as if he had predeceased the testator. UPC §2-104.

REVOCATION AND REPUBLICATION OF WILLS

I. REVOCATION

A. **Generally:** A will is ***ambulatory***, which means that it is always subject to ***alteration or revocation*** by a competent testator until the time of his death.

1. **Ways in which to effect revocation:** Revocation may be effected in three ways:

   a. by subsequent ***instrument***;

   b. by ***physical acts*** of burning, tearing, canceling, obliterating or destroying;

   c. by ***operation of law*** (i.e. by certain changes in the testator's circumstances, such as marriage, divorce or the birth of a child).

2. **Requirements:** A revocation is not effective unless there is:

   a. the ***intent to revoke***, which may be express or implied, and

   b. an ***act of revocation***, concurrent with the intent to revoke. *Thompson v. Royal, infra*, p. 64.

3. **Admissibility of evidence of intent:** Declarations made by the testator at or near the time of a physical act of revocation of the will are generally admissible to show his intent.

B. **Revocation by subsequent instrument:** Revocation by ***subsequent*** instrument may be by:

1. **a later will**

   a. which expressly ***revokes the earlier will***, or

   b. which is ***inconsistent with the earlier will***;

2. **codicil; or**

3. **revocatory instrument** executed with the formalities of a will, but which disposes of no property. See *Thompson v. Royal, infra*.

C. **Revocation by physical act:** Statutes usually designate certain physical acts as acts of revocation. These frequently include: burning, tearing, cutting, destroying, mutilating, cancelling and obliterating.

> **Example 1:** After duly executing a will and codicil, T directs her attorney to destroy the instruments. Upon the advice of

her attorney, she instead signs a notation written by her attorney on the back of the cover of the will that states: "This will null and void and to be only held by [my attorney] instead of being destroyed as a memorandum for another will if I desire to make same." A similar signed notation is placed on the back of the codicil. The applicable statute provides that revocation may be effected by: (1) physical act, such as cutting, tearing, obliteration etc.; (2) a subsequent will; or (3) a writing declaring the intention to revoke executed in the manner in which a will must be executed.

Held, T's will was not effectively revoked. Revocation requires (1) the intent to revoke and (2) the doing of one of the acts specified by statute. While the former was established, the latter was not. T's writings did not comply with statutory will formalities, as they were neither attested by subscribing witnesses nor wholly handwritten by T. Furthermore, as the writings were placed on blank parts of the instruments and did not physically affect the written words of the will or codicil there was no mutilation, obliteration or defacement. *Thompson v. Royal*, 175 S.E.2d 748 (Va. 1934).

Example 2: T writes in the margin of her will: "This will is void." The writing does not touch any of the writing on the will. *Held*, the revocation is ineffective. *Kronauge v. Stoecklein*, 293 N.E.2d 320 (Ohio App. 1972).

1. **Uniform Probate Code:** Under the UPC, a will may be revoked by "burning, tearing, canceling, obliterating, or destroying the will or any part of it" with ***intent*** to revoke, "whether or not the burn, tear, or cancellation touched any of the words on the will." This position is a ***minority rule*** and is contrary to the *Thompson* and *Kronauge* cases, *supra*.

2. **Who may do physical acts:** Most statutes permit the physical act of revocation to be done ***by the testator*** or by someone else ***at the testator's direction*** and ***in his presence***.

3. **Partial revocation:** Many statutes have been construed to permit the revocation of a ***part*** of a will by physical act or by the use of language such as ***"nor any clause thereof"*** or ***"or any part thereof."***

   a. **Absence of statutory language permitting partial revocation:** Jurisdictions vary as to whether or not partial revocation by physical act is effective in the absence of such statutory language. UPC §2-507 allows any part of a will to be revoked.

   Example: After executing his will, T draws lines through clauses six and thirteen. His intention is to revoke the two clauses but to leave the rest of the will in effect. The applicable statute provides in pertinent part that revocation may be effectuated by canceling or obliterating the will. Such a provision is derived from a former statute that permitted the revocation of a devise of land "or any clause thereof." The questions presented are: (1) whether the act permitted the partial revocation and (2) if so, what is the effect of the revocation upon the property covered by the clauses.

Held, T's act revoked the two clauses. There is nothing to indicate that the legislature intended to change the former law and limit the power of revocation to a revocation of the whole will. "The power to revoke a will includes the power to revoke any part of it." Additionally, the property covered by the revoked clauses goes to the residuary devisees. The general rule is that all property not otherwise disposed of passes under the residuary clause, unless the will manifests a contrary intention. Moreover, such a ruling does not controvert statutory will requirements. It is not T's unwitnessed act of revocation that disposed of the property covered by the two revoked clauses, but the residuary clause, which was duly executed. *Bigelow v. Gillott*, 123 Mass. 100, 25 Am.Rep. 32 (1877).

b. **Effect of second will:** If a ***second*** will is executed without expressly revoking the first will, the first will is revoked if it is ***inconsistent*** with the second will. UPC §2-507(a)(1). The first will continues to be valid if it is not inconsistent with the second will.

Example: T executes an eight-page will prepared by his attorney. Two years later T writes on a piece of paper that $50,000 in his safe is to be distributed in a certain way. *Held*, the writing is a valid holographic will. But since it did not expressly revoke the first will, and only disposed of property that would pass under the residuary clause of the first will, T did not intend to revoke the first will. Therefore, both instruments are admitted to probate. *Gilbert v. Gilbert*, 652 S.W.2d 663, (Ky.Ct.App. 1983); in accord, UPC §2-507(d).

D. **Revocation by operation of law: *Revocation by operation of law*** occurs when there is a change in either the family situation or the property holdings of the testator, such as the birth of a child or the sale of property devised in the will.

1. **Common law rule:** At common law, ***marriage*** always revoked the will of the ***wife***; ***marriage*** and ***birth of issue*** revoked the will of the ***husband***.

2. **Change in family situation:** Statutes in a number of jurisdictions provide that a will is revoked in its entirety when the make-up of a testator's family changes as a result of events such as ***marriage, divorce, or the birth of a child***.

   a. **Modern trend:** The ***trend is to limit such statutes to the case of divorce,*** which revokes any disposition to the former spouse when accompanied by a property settlement. Omissions of children or a spouse from a will are usually treated now by provisions giving them their intestate shares unless the omissions are intentional. See UPC §§2-301; 2-302; 2-508; 2-802 and 2-804. See also *supra*, pp. 28-31.

3. **Disposition of property:** At common law, if a testator, after the execution of his will disposed of property which was the subject of a devise or bequest, the disposition of the property was said to revoke such devise or bequest. This is more appropriately considered from the standpoint of ***ademption by extinction***. See *supra*, p. 56.

E. **Doctrine of dependent relative revocation:** A ***dependent relative revocation*** is a ***conditional revocation***. There are ***two kinds*** of dependent relative revocation cases.

1. **Expressly conditional revocation:** On occasion a ***revocation clause*** is, by its terms, ***dependent on a condition***. The intent is that the will be revoked only upon the fulfillment of some condition. Such cases are straightforward but relatively rare.

2. **Mistaken revocation:** The most common type of dependent relative revocation involves a ***revocation induced by a mistake*** in law or fact. Revocation under such circumstances is said to be "dependent on the existence of the situation as believed by the testator" and thus ineffective to revoke the will.

   a. **Fiction of conditional revocation:** The doctrine in cases of mistake is thus based on the circumstance that revocation was dependent or conditioned upon a ***fictional*** event. See Haskell, p. 62.

   b. **Purpose:** The purpose of the doctrine under such circumstances is to permit a mistaken revocation to be ***undone***. *Ibid.*

   c. **Mistaken revocation by physical act:** The doctrine of dependent relative revocation applies to mistaken or partial revocations by ***physical act***.

   Examples of mistaken revocation:

   Example 1: T duly executes a will. She subsequently executes another instrument without the requisite formalities and draws lines through her first will believing she no longer needs the instrument. As her revocation of the first will was based on the mistaken assumption that the second will was valid, the doctrine of dependent relative revocation may be applied to nullify the revocation. Haskell, p. 62.

Example 2: T's will leaves A $25,000. T later decides to increase the legacy by crossing out "$25,000" and inserting above it "$30,000." T dies. The substitution of the figure "$30,000" is invalid as it was not properly executed. The revocation was thus made on the mistaken assumption that the substitution of the higher figure had testamentary validity. The partial revocation should therefore be held invalid, since T would clearly have preferred that A receive $25,000 rather than nothing. Haskell, p. 63.

Example 3: T executes a will in 1955, then another will in 1959 which expressly revokes the first will. Subsequently T revokes the 1959 will in the mistaken belief that she is thereby reviving the 1955 will. Applying the doctrine of dependent relative revocation, the 1959 will is entitled to probate. *Estate of Alburn*, 118 N.W.2d 919 (Wisc. 1963).

i. **Parol evidence:** Parol evidence is ***admissible*** to establish the testator's ***mistaken state of mind*** when the mistaken revocation is by physical act.

d. **Mistaken revocation by subsequent written instrument:** The majority of courts hold that the doctrine also applies to cases in which revocation is by ***subsequent written instrument***. Thus, when a codicil revokes a legacy to certain relatives upon the ***stated reason*** that the beneficiaries have died though they have ***not*** in fact died, the revocation may be nullified.

i. **Face of the instrument:** In cases involving revocation by subsequent instrument, the ***mistake must appear on the face*** of the subsequent instrument.

F. **Lost wills:** If a will cannot be found at the testator's death and it was last known to be in his possession, it is presumed that he revoked it. If, however, it cannot be found and was last known to be in the possession of a third person there is no such presumption.

1. **Parol evidence:** The contents of a lost and unrevoked will may be provided by parol evidence.

II. REPUBLICATION

A. Definition: ***Republication*** is a term used to describe the following:

1. the revival by subsequent will, instrument or codicil of a ***valid will that has been revoked*** but not physically destroyed;
2. the reaffirmance by codicil of a valid will for the purpose of ***making the will speak as of the date of the codicil***;
3. the restoration of a will by ***revocation of a subsequent will that had revoked the first will***; and
4. the validation of a ***prior invalid will***.

B. Divergence of views: Jurisdictions vary with respect to ***revival of a prior will by revocation of a revoking will***.

1. **Common law rule:** Some courts follow the common law rule that revocation of a revoking will automatically revive the first will, regardless of the testator's intention.
2. **Ecclesiastical Court rule:** Some have adopted the ecclesiastical court rule which makes revival dependent on the ***testator's intent***. Under this approach, ***parol evidence*** is admissible to establish intent.
3. **Modifications:** Some jurisdictions apply ***modified versions*** of the above two rules. Some, for example, basically follow the common law rule but allow for an exception in cases in which an ***unreasonable result*** would be effected.
4. **Statutory rules:** Other jurisdictions have enacted statutes to address the issue. One such statute provides that there can be no revival by mere revocation of the revoking will, regardless of the testator's intention. Some states allow revival only if the first will is ***reexecuted*** or if a ***codicil*** is executed showing an ***intent to revive***.
5. **Uniform Probate Code:** Under the UPC, a revoked will may be revived "if it is evident from the circumstances of the revocation of the subsequent will [or codicil] or from the testator's contemporary or subsequent declarations that the testator intended the previous will to take effect as executed." UPC §2-509.

C. Variations on validating invalid will: Strictly speaking, a subsequent instrument cannot revive a will that was never valid. Some jurisdictions justify such revivals on the basis of the ***incorporation by reference*** of the first will into the subsequent instrument. In such jurisdictions, courts often find the revival of a will ineffective due to incapacity, undue influence or lack of due execution.

1. **Jurisdictions that do not recognize the doctrine of incorporation by reference:** In jurisdictions that do not allow

incorporation by reference, such as New York, courts generally permit revival only when the will's invalidity was based on incapacity or undue influence (as opposed to lack of proper execution).

III. CODICILS

A. **Defined:** The word codicil means ***little will***.

B. **Function:** A codicil is usually executed to bring about a ***change in the will*** without the necessity of re-executing the will in its entirety. Codicils usually undertake to revoke, modify, alter or republish a will.

C. **Requirements:** A codicil must be executed with the same ***formalities*** as any other will.

D. **Contents:** A codicil makes specific reference to the will, identifies it by its date of execution and states the ***changes*** to be effected by it. Except as to modifications made by the codicil the will is affirmed in all other particulars.

NATURE OF TRUSTS

I. INTRODUCTION TO TRUST TERMS AND CONCEPTS

A. Definition of trust: A trust is a fiduciary relationship in which one or more persons hold property subject to equitable duties to deal with the property for the benefit of other persons. See Bogert, pp. 1-5; Rest. of Trusts, 2d §2.

B. Split title: The concept of a trust is that of ***split title:*** one person, the trustee, holds ***legal title*** to particular property for the benefit of another person, the beneficiary, who is said to hold ***equitable title***.

C. Legal/equitable interests: The ***interest*** of the ***trustee***, or title-holder, is said to be ***legal***, while that of the ***beneficiary*** is ***equitable***.

D. Uses for trusts: The trust form is adaptable to numerous situations:

1. It is a means of ***holding*** and ***disposing of property***.

   > **Example:** S desires to transfer Blackacre to her children who are minors, but does not want them to control legal title until they are ***sui juris***. She therefore transfers title to a trustee to hold and manage the property until her youngest child reaches age 21, at which time the property is to be conveyed to her children.

2. It is also a ***mode of relief*** against persons who are holding title to property in circumstances in which it is ***unjust*** for them to keep it.

   > **Example:** A fraudulently induces B to convey Blackacre to him. Although A then holds legal title, the property justly belongs to B. A court will declare A a constructive trustee for B.

E. Definitions of trust elements:

1. **Settlor:** The ***settlor*** is the person who ***creates a trust***.

2. **Trust property:** The property interest held by the trustee is the ***trust property***. It may also be called the ***corpus, res*** or ***subject matter of the trust***.

3. **Trustee:** The ***trustee*** is the person who holds title to the trust property.

4. **Beneficiary:** The ***beneficiary*** (or ***cestui que trust***) is the person for whose benefit the trustee holds the trust property.

5. **Terms of the trust:** ***Terms of the trust*** are those duties and powers of the trustees and rights of the beneficiary intended by the settlor at the time of creating the trust.

   Example: A transfers property to B with the instruction that B is to pay the income to C during C's life. B has the duty to pay the income to C and C has an enforceable right to such income. See Rest. of Trusts, 2d §4.

F. Trust classifications: A trust is classified on the basis of:

1. the ***intent*** manifested by its creator;
2. the ***duties*** imposed upon the trustee; (i.e., whether it is active or passive); and
3. the ***method*** by which it is ***created***. See *infra*, pp. 80-88.

G. Classification as to intent: Trusts are classified as to ***intent*** as follows:

1. ***express trusts,*** which fall into two categories:
   a. ***private trusts***, and
   b. ***charitable trusts***;
2. ***resulting (implied) trusts***; and
3. ***constructive trusts***.
4. **Trusts compared:** An express trust requires an overt manifestation of an intention by the settler (trustor) to create a trust. By contrast, a resulting trust is similar to an express trust except that the intention to create it is inferred from the circumstances. See *infra*, p. 118.

   a. **Constructive trust:** A constructive trust is a ***remedy*** imposed when property is obtained by fraud, duress or undue influence. It is used to divest title from a person who is not legally entitled to it and convey title to the person who should have it.

      Example 1: X induces T to devise property to X through undue influence exerted on T by X. When undue influence is established, the court will declare a constructive trust over the property for the benefit of T's rightful heirs.

      Example 2: If a person murders his testator and through that act receives title to property, the murderer holds the property in constructive trust for those who would otherwise take the property.

   b. **Terminology used:** The term ***express trust*** is used when it is necessary to contrast a formal trust with a resulting trust or a constructive trust. The term ***private trust*** is used when it is necessary to contrast an express trust for private purposes with an express charitable trust.

H. Active and passive trusts: An ***active trust*** is one in which the trustee has some affirmative duty to perform, (e.g. to collect rents and distribute the income to the beneficiaries). A ***passive trust*** is one in which the trustee is the mere title-holder and has no duties with respect to the trust res.

1. **Legislation abolishing passive trusts:** In many jurisdictions either the ***Statute of Uses***, see *infra,* p. 74 or similar legislation is in force that abolishes passive trusts. As a result of such legislation the trustee of a passive trust takes nothing and the beneficiary takes legal title automatically. Most states apply this rule to trusts of personalty as well as realty.

2. **Duty to execute and deliver a deed:** There is a split of authority among jurisdictions as to whether or not a trust in which the only duty of the trustee is to execute and deliver a deed to the beneficiaries, is passive.

3. **When purpose of trust ceases:** Some states have statutes which provide that when the purposes for which an express trust is created cease, and the trust becomes passive, the trust automatically ceases.

II. ANALYSIS OF TRUST PROBLEMS

A. Essential determinations: The essential determinations to be made in any trust fact situation are:

1. the ***existence*** of a valid trust:

2. the ***terms*** of the trust with respect to the intent of the settlor; and

3. the ***enforcement*** thereof.

B. Existence of valid trusts: The first step in analyzing whether or not a trust exists is to ***determine if all elements of a trust are present***.

1. **Classification as to trust intent:** To ascertain the presence of necessary trust elements, the trust should first be ***classified as to trust intent***, express or implied. See *supra*, p. 71.

2. **Does any rule of law render trust invalid?** Once it is determined that all trust elements are present, it is then necessary to determine if any rule of law will operate to make the trust (or any trust interest) invalid or unenforceable. In the event that a trust or any interest in a trust is invalid, it is then important to determine the effect of such invalidity on the trust property.

C. Terms of trust: If a valid trust is established, the intent of the creator of the trust as to the ***rights and duties of each party*** should be identified.

1. The ***powers, duties, and liabilities*** of the ***trustee*** vis-a-vis the trust property and the various parties related to the trust must be determined with reference to the intent of the creator and applicable provisions of law (*infra*, pp. 92-94, 185-205).

2. **Relationships of the parties:** In this regard, it is important to examine the ***relationships of the various parties***:

   a. to each other and

   b. to the trust property.

3. **Distinctions between and among parties:** In analyzing relationships in the trust, careful distinctions must be made between and among settlors, trustees, beneficiaries, creditors and other third parties. See *infra*, pp. 76, 94.

   Note: The same person may relate to the trust in more than one capacity. In answering a question in the area of trusts, reference to an individual must include specific reference to the particular capacity he fills and the rights and liabilities related to each.

D. Enforcement issues: Whenever a breach of trust occurs or an interest in a trust is rendered invalid, it is important to consider: (1) who has standing to raise the issue, and (2) the ability of the court or the parties to change or modify the intent of the creator.

1. **Constructive trust is not intent-enforcing:** It is important to keep in mind that the ***constructive trust is not intent-enforcing***. It is a ***remedial device*** and as such it will often be subject to special rules that have little application in the general law of trusts.

III. HISTORICAL DEVELOPMENT

A. Original and definition of "uses": The trust developed out of the ***common law system of uses***, in which one person held land ***"for the use of another."*** The system of uses originally involved a transfer from A to B for certain purposes and B's agreement to carry out such purposes by a gentlemen's agreement.

B. Purposes of uses: Uses were usually created to achieve the effect of a will for real property (wills not then being allowed), to escape taxes on death and to give the benefit of the land to persons who could not hold title.

C. Enforced in courts of equity: The common law courts would not enforce agreements with respect to uses, but the ***courts of equity*** became increasingly liberal in affording ***remedies***.

D. Statute of Uses: The ***Statute of Uses***, passed by the English Parliament in 1535, attempted to eliminate uses by "executing" uses; i.e., turning equitable estates into legal estates.

> **Example:** If A transferred land to B to the use of C, the use would be executed and B's legal estate would thereby be vested in C, who thus became the fee simple owner.

1. **Exemptions:** The Statute of Uses did not apply to certain transactions involving uses. ***Exemptions*** were:

   a. ***a use of personal property***;

   b. ***an active use*** (i.e., one in which the trustee had active duties to perform other than holding and conveying legal title); and

   c. ***a use on a use*** (i.e., A to B to the use of C to the use of D).

   These exemptions allowed the development of the ***modern law of trusts***.

2. **Adoption by states of Statute of Uses:** Some states have either adopted the Statute of Uses by legislative enactment or consider it adopted as part of the common law.

   a. **States in which Statute not in effect:** In other states the Statute of Uses is not in force. Much the same result, however, is achieved by legislation and court rulings providing that when the purposes for which an express trust is created cease, the estate of the trustee also ceases. For further discussion, see *supra*, p. 72.

IV. DISTINCTIONS BETWEEN TRUSTS AND OTHER RELATIONSHIPS

A. Introduction: Trusts must be distinguished from ***other relationships which resemble trusts*** in that one person may be acting with respect to or holding property for another, but ***are not true trusts***. Among such relationships are bailment, guardianship, executorship and administratorship, agency, debt, mortgages, pledges, liens, third party beneficiary contracts, and corporate directorships.

B. Importance of correct classification: It is important to classify such relationships correctly. As the distinctions involved frequently have their origins in the historical difference between several kinds of courts (common law, canon law and equity), the remedies will vary depending upon the classification.

C. **Bailment:** A ***bailment*** exists when one person, the ***bailee***, has rightful possession of personal property, title to which is in another, the ***bailor***.

1. It is ***similar*** to a trust in that:

   a. the bailee has possession of the subject property and

   b. the bailment may be created for the benefit of a third party.

2. It is ***different from*** a trust in that:

   a. the bailee has ***no title*** to the subject of the bailment and ***cannot transfer title*** to a bona fide purchaser, except in estoppel situations and under certain provisions of the Uniform Commercial Code (see UCC §2-403);

   b. ***real property*** or ***intangible property not embodied in a document*** cannot be the subject matter of a bailment;

   c. there is no ***fiduciary duty*** between the bailee and the bailor or a third party for whose benefit the bailment was created; and

   d. it is enforced by ***legal***, rather than equitable remedies.

      Example: A delivers furniture to B to be stored in B's warehouse for six months while A is in Europe and to be returned to A upon demand. A bailment is created. Only possession has passed to B, not title.

D. **Executorships and administratorships:** ***Executorships*** and ***administratorships*** are limited in purpose to the ***winding up of the estate of a decedent***. They derive their authority by court appointment.

1. Executorships are ***similar to*** trusts in that (the same similarities and differences apply to administrators):

   a. the executor has a fiduciary duty to the beneficiaries of the estate and

   b. the executor ***holds title*** to the personal property in the estate.

2. Executorships are ***different from*** trusts in that:

   a. the executor ***does not hold title to real property*** in the estate;

   b. the ***duties*** of the executor are ***limited*** in scope to those necessary to collect the property of the decedent, pay decedent's debts and expenses and distribute the remaining property;

   c. executors ***do not*** ordinarily ***have a duty to make investments***; and

d. executors are always ***subject to court supervision of their administration*** while certain trustees are not.

E. **Guardianship:** ***Guardianship*** involves a court's appointment of an official, the ***guardian*** or ***conservator***, to deal with the property of a third person, the ***ward***, who lacks legal capacity.

1. It is ***similar to*** a trust in that:

a. the guardian has a ***fiduciary relationship to the ward*** and

b. the guardian must ***take possession of and manage*** the ward's property.

2. It is ***different from*** a trust in that:

a. the guardian ***does not have title*** to the ward's property — only certain powers to deal with it;

b. the guardians' powers and duties are ***fixed by statute*** and he is ***subject to court supervision*** of his guardianship; and

c. the guardianship exists only as long as the ward ***lacks capacity***.

F. **Agency:** An ***agency*** is a relationship in which one person, the ***agent***, acts for another, the ***principal***, and is in his control.

1. It is ***similar to*** a trust in that the agent has a ***fiduciary duty*** to the principal.

2. It is ***different from*** a trust in that:

a. the agent is ***subject to the control of the principal*** (whereas a trustee is under a duty to act for the benefit of the beneficiary but subject to the terms of the trust rather than the control of the beneficiary);

b. an agent ***does not have title*** to the property of the principal, except in certain circumstances in which it is necessary to have title to carry out the agency;

c. an agent may ***subject his principal to personal liability*** (whereas a trustee cannot so subject the beneficiary or the trust); and

d. an agency is ***terminated by revocation, death or incapacity of the principal***.

Example 1: A authorizes B to find a buyer for his house. A dies prior to B's finding such a buyer. B's agency terminates on the death of A and he is no longer authorized to find a buyer.

> **Example 2:** A deeds his house to B with directions to sell it and pay the proceeds to C. A dies. B is a trustee and may proceed to sell the house and carry out the terms of the trust.

See *Agency & Partnership*, Smith's Review, pp. 13-19, 56-80, 91-97.

G. Debt: A ***debt*** is a ***contractual relationship*** involving a personal obligation on the part of one person, the ***debtor***, to pay money to another, the ***creditor***. It is ***different from*** a trust in that:

1. the debtor has ***no fiduciary duty*** to the creditor;
2. a creditor has only a ***personal claim*** against the debtor — he has no interest in the debtor's property;
3. the creditor's remedies against the debtor are at law in the first instance; and
4. the creation of a debt ***requires consideration***.

H. Liens and pledges: ***Liens*** and ***pledges*** are ***security interests*** which are ***contractual*** in nature.

1. They are ***similar to*** trusts in that:
   - **a.** the lienholder or pledgee must have ***possession*** of the subject property and
   - **b.** the lienholder or pledgee has certain rights with respect to the subject property.
2. They are ***different from*** trusts in that:
   - **a.** there is ***no fiduciary duty*** between the parties;
   - **b.** the lienholder or pledgee acquires ***no property right*** in the subject of the lien or pledge; and
   - **c.** they are dependent upon the ***existence*** of a debt and ***terminate*** when it has been paid.

I. Mortgages: ***Mortgages*** are ***security interests*** in real property in which one person, the ***mortgagor***, grants an interest in property to another, the ***mortgagee***, who holds it for his own benefit as security for the repayment of a debt.

1. A mortgage is ***similar to*** a trust in that:
   - **a.** the mortgagee, in some jurisdictions, may have legal title to the property and
   - **b.** both legal and equitable duties and remedies are involved in the relationship.

2. A mortgage is ***different from*** a trust in that:

   a. there is no fiduciary relationship between the mortgagee and mortgagor and

   b. in most jurisdictions ***legal title remains in the mortgagor*** with the mortgagee having only a security interest.

J. Third party beneficiary contract: A ***third party beneficiary contract*** is a mere personal undertaking to a second party to make payment to a third party.

1. It is ***similar to*** a trust in that the beneficiary has the ***right to enforce the contract***.

2. It is ***different from*** a trust in that:

   a. the obligor has ***no fiduciary duty*** to the beneficiary;

   b. the obligee as well as the beneficiary may enforce the contract;

   c. the beneficiary has ***no equitable interest*** in the property; and

   d. the ***remedies*** of the beneficiary are at law in the first instance.

K. Equitable charge: An ***equitable charge*** is created when a person gives, by will or inter vivos transfer, property to another person for the benefit of the other person but ***subject to a payment to a third party***.

1. It is ***similar to*** a trust in that:

   a. the transferee of the property holds it ***subject to an equitable interest in a third party***; and

   b. the transferee of the property can transfer it to a bona fide purchaser ***free*** of the equitable interest.

2. It is ***different from*** a trust in that:

   a. ***no fiduciary relationship*** is created;

   b. the transferee has ***both*** the legal title and beneficial interest in the property; and

   c. once the equitable charge is paid the transferee holds it ***clear of any interest in others***.

      Example 1: A devises Blackacre to B "subject to the payment of $100 per month to Mary during her life." B holds Blackacre subject to an equitable charge in the absence of evidence of a different intention. B holds Blackacre beneficially, having both legal and equitable title.

      Example 2: A devises Blackacre to B "in trust" to pay Mary during her life $100 a month from the income, and to B on Mary's death. A trust is created. B holds only legal title to

Blackacre during Mary's life.

L. Directors of corporations: ***Directors of corporations*** are in a special relationship to the corporation.

1. The relationship of directors to a corporation is ***similar to*** that of trustees in that they ***owe fiduciary duties*** to the corporation.
2. It is ***different from*** that of a trustee in that they ***do not hold title*** to the property of the corporation.

M. Fiduciary relationship: A ***fiduciary relationship*** is the relationship in which one person is under a duty to act ***solely for the benefit of another*** within the scope of the relationship. See *infra*, pp. 185-205.

PRIVATE EXPRESS TRUSTS

I. GENERALLY

A. Elements: Every private express trust consists of four distinct elements: (1) an ***intention*** of the settlor to create a trust; (2) a ***res*** or subject matter; (3) a ***trustee***; and (4) a ***beneficiary*** or ***cestui que trust***. For definitions of trust elements see *supra*, pp. 70-71.

II. INTENTION TO CREATE A TRUST

A. Overt manifestation of intent: It is essential to the creation of an express trust that the settlor ***overtly manifest*** an intention to create a trust. The settlor must intend to impose enforceable duties on a trustee to deal with property for the benefit of another.

1. **Words or conduct:** Intent may be made manifest by ***words, conduct*** or both; no particular words or form of conduct are necessary.

   a. **"In trust" or "trustee":** The words ***"in trust"*** or ***"trustee"*** are not necessary to create a trust. Conversely, the presence of such words does not make it certain that a court will find the intent to create a trust.

   Example: X and Y make gifts to D for P's education, but there is no written agreement. D is P's father. P sues D for an accounting. D claims no trust exists, and that the money was all spent on P's education anyway.

   Held, a valid trust was created and D must account for the funds. Although the donors did not expressly tell D to hold the money in trust, this was not essential to create a trust relationship — It was enough that the transfer was made to D with intent to vest beneficial ownership in P. When D spent money for P, D may have intended to discharge his duty to P as a parent, or may have intended to follow the directions of the trust. That is a question of fact, and all doubts must be resolved against the trustee who fails to maintain accurate records. *Jimenez v. Lee*, 547 P.2d 126 (Ore. 1976).

   b. **Evidence of words or conduct may be inadmissible:** It is important to remember that although the settlor's intention may be made manifest by his words and conduct, such evidence may, in appropriate cases, be excluded by the ***parol evidence rule***, the ***statute of frauds***, the ***statute of wills*** or other rules of law. Also, statutes in some instances require that the intention be shown in a particular form, such as the requirement of a writing in the case of trusts of interests in land or testamentary trusts.

2. **Precatory words:** Precatory words are words of ***hope, wish, desire*** or ***recommendation***.

   a. **Early view:** The early view was that if the transferor ***expressed a desire*** that a certain use be made of the property, the expression of desire in itself was ***sufficient*** to form a trust.

   b. **Modern view:** Under the more modern view, ***precatory words alone do not create a trust***. Such words may create a trust only if it is found that the transferor ***intended to create enforceable obligations***. The entire language of the instrument is considered in the light of the situation of the transferor, his family and the alleged beneficiaries at the effective date of the document.

      Example: T gives $208 to her sister-in-law, B, each month. T then devises her property to her children, but states: "I request [that] my two children . . . pay to B $208 per month as long as she shall live." *Held*, the "request" created a trust in B's favor. This intent to create a trust is shown by the fact that T paid that amount to B for many years, T expressed herself clearly, stated the exact amount and the duration of payments. Further, since the request was made to her children, T would believe the words had the force of a command. *Spencer v. Childs*, 134 N.E.2d 60 (N.Y. 1956).

3. **Failure to describe elements clearly:** The failure of the transferor to describe clearly any of the ***elements*** required for a trust is evidence that he did not intend a trust.

4. **Moral claim:** Courts tend to find a trust created by precatory words when the beneficiary has a ***moral claim*** on the transferor.

   Example: If a testator, having for many years supported his retarded, institutionalized child, Mary, leaves his entire estate to his other child, "with the hope that he will provide for the comfort and maintenance of Mary," the court, recognizing testator's obligation to his helpless child, may hold a trust to have been created.

5. **Precatory language separated from dispository language:** If the transferor makes an absolute gift of property in one sentence and inserts precatory language in a separate sentence or article, courts usually find no trust intent.

   Example: "I give, devise and bequeath all the rest, residue and remainder of my property to my wife to be her absolute estate forever. It is my request that upon her death my wife shall devise Blackacre to my brother, John." No trust in favor of John is created. To do so would cut down the prior gift of the fee. See *Comford v. Cantrell*, 151 S.W.2d 1076 (Tenn. 1941).

B. Lack of intention to create a present trust: A trust requires a ***present legal transaction*** rather than a future one. The manifestation of the settlor's intention to create a trust in the future does not create a trust.

> **Example 1:** S, the owner of bonds, tells T that he intends on the following day to transfer the bonds to T in trust for B. No trust arises until the transfer is made to T.

> **Example 2:** S tells B that he intends to purchase 1,000 shares of ABC stock and, when he does, to hold them in trust for B. Even if S purchases the shares no trust arises until he declares himself trustee for B. The previous declaration of intent will not suffice.

1. **Trust will not immediately arise:** A trust will not arise immediately if the settlor manifests the intention that it shall not arise immediately or does not immediately designate the beneficiary, the trustee or the trust property.

> **Example:** A delivers to T bonds to be held in trust for such person as A may designate by letter to T. A dies prior to such designation. No trust has arisen.

2. **Distinguished from other situations:** A promise to create a trust in the future is to be ***distinguished from*** a present trust of an enforceable promise to be performed in the future and a present trust in which the interest of the beneficiary will not take effect in enjoyment until a future date.

   i. **Future interest:** If there is a manifestation of present intention to create a trust, a trust will arise although by the terms of the trust the interest of the beneficiary is a ***future interest***.

> **Example:** A declares himself trustee of 1,000 shares of stock to pay income to A for ten years and then to B for the remainder of B's life. Although B's interest is a future interest a trust is created ***in presenti***. Rest. of Trusts, 2d §26, Comment g.

3. **Enforceable promise:** If one party makes an ***enforceable promise*** to pay money or transfer property to another person as trustee, and if the promisee manifests the intention that his rights under the promise shall be held in trust, a present trust is created at the time of the promise. In the absence of evidence of a different intention the inference is that the promisee intended an immediate trust

and he becomes trustee of his rights under the promise.

Example: In consideration of a payment of $100,000 made by S to X, X promises in writing to convey property to S in trust for B. There is no other evidence. S holds his rights against X in trust for B. See Rest. of Trusts, 2d §26, Comment n.

C. **Savings bank trusts:** If a person makes a deposit in a bank in his own name "in trust" for another, he may have intended any of the following: (1) to create a ***revocable trust***; (2) to create an ***irrevocable trust***; or (3) ***not to create*** a trust. The courts resolve these questions by examining the situation of the depositor and his relationship to the beneficiary and other facts and circumstances.

1. **Totten or tentative trust:** When there is no evidence of the testator's intention other than the form of deposit, most states hold that a ***revocable trust is created***. The depositor may withdraw all or any part of the funds during his lifetime and on his death the beneficiary may enforce the trust as to any part remaining on deposit at his death. This is called a ***tentative*** or ***Totten*** trust. The word "Totten" refers to the famous case establishing this principle. *Matter of Totten*, 71 N.E. 748 (N.Y. 1904).

   a. **Control by depositor:** In spite of the fact that the depositor has had ***complete control*** over the deposits during his life, the trust is not held invalid as a testamentary transfer. The trust is considered to arise at the time of the deposit.

   Example 1: S makes a deposit in a savings account in her name as trustee for B. S gives no notice to B of the deposit, retains the passbook in her own possession and makes withdrawals from and additions to the deposit. At issue is: (1) whether the fact that the deposit was made was sufficient to show an intention to create a trust and, if so, (2) whether the other circumstances had the effect of disproving such intention.

   Held, a deposit in a savings account in the settlor's name in trust for another is presumptively a tentative or Totten trust. Neither the retention of the passbook, the absence of notice to B, nor the withdrawals from and additions to the deposit, is effective to rebut the presumption. Moreover, the requirement that an express trust be in writing is satisfied by the fact that a written entry of deposit was made on the bank records, a passbook evidencing the deposit was issued and S signed an identification card as trustee for B. Furthermore, the deposit was not testamentary in character merely because B's enjoyment of the interest was postponed until S's death and S retained the power to revoke or modify the trust. The deposit constituted an executed trust as of the time of its execution; it arose during S's lifetime (rather than upon S's death) and was therefore nontestamentary. *Wilder v. Howard*, 4 S.E.2d 199 (Ga. 1939).

Example 2: H buys stock through a stock purchase plan where he works. He has the shares issued to H and W as joint tenants to avoid probate and legal expenses when he dies. H never indicates that he intends to transfer any present interest to W. W does not claim half ownership or ask for half of the dividends. The parties are then divorced, at which time W asks for a half interest in the stock

Held, H is the sole owner of the stock. The same principles apply to joint stock certificates as apply to joint bank accounts. H merely made a present gift to W of a future interest, reserving a life interest to himself and the power to revoke W's interest. *Blanchette v. Blanchette*, 287 N.E.2d 459 (Mas. 1972).

b. **Statutes validating tentative trusts:** Many states have enacted statutes ***validating the tentative trust***. These statutes generally establish a ***"conclusive presumption"*** that the depositor intended to create a trust for the beneficiary, if the beneficiary survives.

c. **Revocation:** A tentative trust may be ***revoked*** at any time prior to the depositor's death by: (1) ***withdrawal*** of any part of the deposit, which operates as a revocation to the extent of the withdrawal; (2) the ***death*** of the beneficiary prior to the death of the depositor; or (3) any other ***manifestation of intention*** to revoke.

   i. **Revocation by will:** If the depositor's ***will*** purports to revoke the trust, there is a conflict of authority. Some courts allow revocation of savings accounts and money market certificates by will. See *Estate of Bol*, 429 N.W.2d 467 (S.D. 1988). Other courts hold that a testator cannot exercise the power to revoke a lifetime trust in a will. See *Estate of Kovalyshyn*, 343 A.2d 852 (N.J. Super. 1975).

   ii. **Uniform Probate Code:** The UPC provides that "A right of survivorship arising from the express terms of the account . . . may not be altered by will." UPC §6-213.

d. **Depositor's creditors:** Tentative trusts are subject to the rights of the depositor's creditors.

e. **Subject to statutory rights of surviving spouse:** Whether tentative trusts are subject to statutory rights of a surviving spouse in the depositor's estate varies from jurisdiction to jurisdiction. By the better view they are. See *Montgomery v.*

Michaels, *supra*, p. 29.

D. **Illusory trusts:** If a settlor ***in form*** either declares himself trustee of, or transfers to a third party, property in trust but by the terms of the trust, or by his dealings with the trust property ***in substance*** exercises so much control over the trust property that it is clear that he ***did not intend to relinquish any of his rights in the trust property***, the trust is invalid as illusory. See *Newman v. Dore*, *infra*, pp. 86-87.

1. **Present interest:** The ***test*** whether or not the creation of an inter vivos trust is illusory is whether the beneficiary receives a ***present interest*** in the trust property or instead is to receive an interest only at or by reason of the death of the settlor. In the latter case the trust is testamentary and must comply with the statute of wills. See *Farkas v. Williams*, *infra*, pp. 86, 136.

2. **Reservation of income:** The mere ***reservation*** by the settlor of income for life will not render a trust illusory.

3. **Reservation of income plus right to revoke:** By the more modern view, the settlor's reservation of income for life plus a retained right to revoke will not render a trust illusory.

   Example: S transfers Blackacre to T in trust to pay all rents and income to S for life and on S's death to convey Blackacre to B. S retains the right to revoke the trust.

   Held, the trust is valid. A present interest passes to B with possession and enjoyment postponed. The interest may be defeated by a subsequent revocation, but until such revocation takes place the beneficiary's interest is a validly existing interest.

4. **Reservation of income, right to revoke and additional rights of control:** A reservation of income for life combined with both the right to revoke and additional retained rights of control (such as the right to determine investment) ***may*** render the trust illusory. The fact that the settlor has made himself the trustee in addition to retaining the right to revoke and the reservation of income does not necessarily render the trust illusory. The results in any given case may depend upon the ***degree of control*** actually retained and exercised by the settlor.

   Example 1: Prior to dying intestate, D purchases securities from S and executes a written application requesting S to issue the securities in D's name as trustee for B. He also signs declarations of trust that reserve to D as settlor the right: (1) to change the beneficiary or revoke the trust at any time upon written notice to S; (2) to receive during his lifetime all cash dividends; and (3) to retain for his own use the proceeds from the sale or redemption of any portion of the trust property.

The declarations also give D the right to act as sole trustee with the attendant power to vote, sell, redeem, exchange or otherwise deal in the securities. The questions arising in determining whether the instruments create valid inter vivos trusts are: (1) whether upon the execution of the instruments B acquired an interest in the subject matter of the trusts and (2) whether D, as settlor-trustee, retained such control over the subject matter as to render the instruments attempted testamentary dispositions (which would be invalid for failure to comply with required will formalities).

Held, the instruments created valid inter vivos trusts. With respect to the first issue, B acquired a present interest in the trust property as a direct result of D's relinquishment, upon executing the instruments, of some of the incidents of absolute ownership. D assumed a fiduciary duty to B with respect to the trust res and obligated himself to give written notice to S in order to change the beneficiary or revoke the trust. Concerning the second question, it is well established that the retention by the settlor of the power to revoke and a life interest in the property does not render the trust invalid. Moreover, the fact that D also made himself the sole trustee does not alter the character of the transaction. By assuming the duties of trustee, D actually placed limitations on his control of the property as he thereby obligated himself to act in accordance with the standards imposed on fiduciaries. *Farkas v. Williams*, 5 Ill.2d 417, 125 N.E.2d 600 (1955).

Note: The court in *Farkas*, in finding the trust valid, also considered the formality of the transaction creating the trust. D had executed four separate applications expressing his intent to place the stock in his name as trustee for B, as well as four declarations of trust in which he declared that he was holding the property in trust for B. D's intent was thus manifested in a "solemn and formal manner."

Example 2: Three days before his death T executes a trust agreement transferring all of his property to trustees in trust for a named beneficiary. By the terms of the trust, D retains: (1) the power to revoke the trust; (2) the income of the trust for life; and (3) the right to control trustees as to the administration of the trust. Under state law, T's surviving spouse W may elect to take a one-third share in the property owned by T at death. T's trust is created for the purpose of defeating W's rights to his property upon his death. At issue is whether the transfer of T's property to the trust was effective.

Held, for W. The transfer was an unlawful invasion of W's expectant interest. The fact that T's motive in creating the trust was to defeat W's interest is not controlling. The test is whether the transfer was real or illusory. T's retention of the power to revoke, the right to income for life, and the right to control trustees makes it clear that he never intended to divest himself of his property, even when death was near. The creation of the trust was "intended only as a mask for the effective retention by [T] of the property which in form he had conveyed." *Newman v. Dore*, 275 N.Y. 371, 9 N.E.2d 966 (1937).

Note: The court's ruling in *Newman* was limited to finding the trust invalid in light of the fact that it deprived W of her expectant interest. It did not reach the issue of whether the trust could be held valid under other circumstances. In some states the fact that a trust was created with intent to defeat the spouse's share will invalidate the trust. See *supra*, p. 29.

5. **Actual exercise of retained power:** The ***actual exercise*** of retained power used by the settlor will be influential in a court's determination of whether a transfer is real or illusory.

   Example: S transfers all of his property in trust including his home and club memberships. He retains the income for life plus the right to revoke and full power to control investments. S then uses this right to revoke in order to pay bills and in his general business. He makes revocations for as little as $12 to pay personal expenses. The trust is clearly illusory. The trustee is no more than a depositary and an agent for the settlor. See *Osborn v. Osborn*, 10 Ohio Misc. 171, 226 N.E.2d 814 (1966).

6. **Type of attack made on trust:** The central issue in cases involving illusory trusts is the emphasis placed by the court on the ***degree of control*** retained by the settlor. This varies from court to court, and depends upon the facts of the particular case and, to some extent, the ***type of attack*** made upon the trust. See *Newman v. Dore, supra.*

7. **Creditors of settlor:** During the lifetime of the settlor, the settlor's ***creditors*** can reach the ***maximum amount*** which the trustee can pay or apply to the settlor's benefit under the terms of the trust.

   a. **Power to revoke:** Where the settlor has retained the power to ***revoke*** the trust, court decisions are in conflict about whether his creditors can reach the trust res after his death. The trend of modern decisions is to ***allow*** creditors to reach the trust res.

Example: S creates an inter vivos trust, retaining the power to revoke or amend and to direct the disposition of principal and income during his life. S transfers shares of stock to the trust, and provides in his will that his residuary estate goes to the trust. Subsequently S obtains an unsecured loan of $75,000 from a bank. About four months later S dies in an accident, and S's estate has insufficient assets to repay the loan. The bank seeks to reach the trust assets. The trust beneficiaries argue that when S died, his power over the trust died with him, and the interest of the beneficiaries became vested.

Held, creditors may reach trust assets over which S had control at his death to the same extent that S could use the trust assets for his own benefit during his life. A revocable inter vivos trust is a common estate planning vehicle. S retained all substantial incidents of ownership and thought of the property as "his." "It is excessive obeisance to the form in which property is held to prevent creditors from reaching property placed in trust under such terms." *State Street Bank & Trust Co. v. Reiser*, 389 N.E.2d 768 (Mass. App. 1979).

III. THE SUBJECT MATTER OF THE TRUST

A. Generally: An essential element of every trust is the ***trust property*** or ***res***.

1. **Requirements:** The trust property, both at the time of creation and throughout the existence of the trust, must normally be in ***existence***, and must be definite or definitely ascertainable.

2. **Voluntarily transferable:** At the time of the creation of the trust the trust property must be ***voluntarily transferable*** by the owner.

   a. **Intangibles:** An interest in an ***intangible*** such as a chose in action, patent, trademark or copyright, if transferable, may be held in trust.

   b. **Equitable interests:** ***Equitable interests***, such as a beneficiary's interest in another trust, if transferable, may be held in trust.

   c. **Contingent interests:** ***Contingent interests***, such as contingent remainders, if transferable, may be held in trust.

      i. **Jurisdiction:** The transferability of contingent remainders depends upon the ***jurisdiction***.

3. **Expectancy:** A ***mere expectancy***, such as the interest of a person who expects to receive property as a devisee under a will, cannot be held in trust.

4. **Contract to make a trust:** As noted, the general rule is that the trust corpus must exist at the time the trust is created. An important ***exception*** to this general rule is that if the settlor receives ***consideration*** for declaring a trust of property expected to come into existence in the future, then a trust will be found to exist once the property in fact comes into existence. In other words, ***a contract to make a trust will be specifically enforced,*** but all requirements for contracts (including consideration) must be satisfied.

    Example: In December 1927 T declares a trust of his profits from stock speculation for the following year. T states that the profits will be distributed equally to his mother, wife and two minor children, after deducting a reasonable compensation for his services, and that he will personally assume any losses. The profits for the year 1928 are divided among the beneficiaries and they pay taxes on them. T pays taxes only on his compensation. The federal government claims that all profits are taxable to T.

    Held, T did not create a valid trust. T voluntarily agreed to hold profits in trust if T made a profit in the stock market. There was no trust in December 1927 because there were no profits at that time — no corpus to the trust. Further, there was no enforceable contract to hold future profits in trust because there was no consideration. T's profits are his own property until he sets them aside for the beneficiaries. Since the profits are T's when earned, and do not become trust property automatically, T must pay taxes on all profits. *Brainard v. Commissioner*, 91 F.2d 880 (7th Cir. 1937).

    Note: But as the court indicated in *Brainard*, if T had been given consideration for declaring a trust of future profits, then a trust would have attached to the profits when they were realized. This is so because there would have been an enforceable contract. See, e.g., *Clark v. Rutherford*, 298 S.W.2d 327 (Ark. 1957); Bogert, p. 74.

5. **Destruction of trust property:** A ***trust ends*** with the ***destruction of trust property***. Thus, if the trust property consists solely of lumber which is destroyed by fire and there is no insurance, the trust comes to an end. The beneficiary may have a claim against the trustee for breach of trust if the trustee was negligent in failing to insure.

6. **Duration or extent of trustee's interest in trust property:** The duration or extent of the trustee's interest in the trust estate in the absence of the manifestation of a different intention by the settlor, will be:

a. in the case of ***real property***, whatever estate in land the trustee must have to accomplish the trust purpose;

b. in the case of ***personal property***, an interest of unlimited duration.

Example: A transfers land and 100 shares of ABC stock to T in trust to pay the income to C for life. T has a life estate for the life of C in the land and a fee simple in the ABC stock.

B. Insurance trusts: If a person takes out a ***policy of insurance*** on his life, he may create a trust of the policy and its proceeds by: (1) making the policy payable to a ***designated person as trustee***; (2) making the policy payable ***absolutely*** to a designated beneficiary who in turn agrees with the insured to ***hold the proceeds in trust***; (3) assigning the policy to a ***third party as trustee***; or (4) ***declaring himself*** trustee of the policy.

1. **Present inter vivos trust created:** In each of the cases set forth above a ***present inter vivos trust is created***. The beneficiary named in the policy holds his rights as beneficiary in trust for such persons and on such terms as specified by the insured. The one who purchases the policy is the settlor. The beneficiary or assignee is trustee and the ***rights to the policy are the trust res***.

2. **Nontestamentary:** An insurance trust is ***not testamentary*** and therefore need not comply with the ***Statute of Wills*** even though the insured reserves the power to change the beneficiary or to revoke or modify the trust. For a discussion of trusts and the Statute of Wills, see *infra*, pp. 136-38.

3. **Trust arises immediately:** The fact that the beneficiary's rights can be terminated at any time by the insured or may be enjoyed by the trust beneficiaries only after death does not prevent a trust from arising immediately.

Example: D makes his life insurance policies payable to Trust Co., as trustee. At the same time he and Trust Co. execute a trust agreement that: (1) provides for the administration and disposition of the policy proceeds; (2) obligates Trust Co., for compensation, to administer and dispose of the proceeds in accordance with the terms of the agreement upon D's death; (3) binds Trust Co. to hold the policies unless and until D requests otherwise; (4) reserves to D the right to terminate or amend the trust, change the beneficiaries, and receive dividends or interest from the policies; and (5) provides that D shall pay the insurance premiums to keep the policies in force. Upon D's death, his estate is insufficient to pay the claims of creditors. Creditors seek to have the insurance trust declared invalid and the proceeds held under a resulting trust in favor of the estate. In support of their action, creditors argue that: (1) there was no disposition by D of any interests in the policies during his lifetime; (2) there was no actual corpus of the trust while D was alive; (3) D failed to assign the policies to Trust Co.; and (4) D failed to relinquish the power to change the beneficiaries of the policy.

Held, the trust agreement created a valid trust. The insurance policies constituted the corpus of the trust. D's designation of the Trust Co. as beneficiary of the policy proceeds was as effective as an assignment to manifest his intention with respect to the payment of the policy. Furthermore, the nomination of Trust Co. as beneficiary transferred to Trust Co. during D's lifetime an interest in the policies which, if no revocation occurred, would vest in Trust Co. upon D's death. The interest, which consisted of the right to receive the proceeds of the policies, was not impaired by D's unexercised right to change the beneficiary. Moreover, the mere fact that D retained the right to change the beneficiary did not make the policies or their proceeds a part of D's estate. To be an asset of an estate, a life insurance policy must be made payable to the insured or his executors or administrators. *Gurnett v. Mutual Life Insurance Co.*, 191 N.E. 250 (Ill. 1934).

a. **Rights may be held in trust even though they may be defeated:** The rights of the beneficiary of an insurance policy may be held in trust even though such beneficiary's rights may be subsequently defeated by the insured's changing the beneficiary of the policy.

   Example: H purchases a policy of life insurance on H's life and names W as beneficiary but reserves the power to change the beneficiary. W declares herself trustee of her interest for her daughter D. A valid trust is created in which W is trustee for D even though H may later change the beneficiary and defeat W's interest, at which time the trust will terminate.

4. **When insurance policy payable only to members of a particular class:** If an interest in an insurance policy can be transferred only to members of a particular class, a trust of such interest cannot be created for persons outside the class.

   Example: The National Service Life Insurance Act of 1940 originally provided that the insurance issued to members of the Armed Forces under the Act should be payable only to certain classes of relatives of the insured. Soldier A takes out a policy payable to B, a member of the class. B agrees to hold the proceeds in trust for C, a non-member of the class. The trust for C is invalid.

IV. THE TRUSTEE

A. Who may serve as trustee: Any person who has the ***capacity*** to take, hold and administer property for his own use may take, hold and administer property in trust.

1. **Infants and insane persons:** ***Infants and insane persons*** can take and hold property in trust, but since their contracts are voidable they cannot properly administer a trust and will usually be removed as trustee.

2. **Non-residents:** ***Non-residents*** of the state in which the trust is to be administered may be trustees. In some states, however, courts have discretion pursuant to statute, to ***refuse to confirm*** the appointment of a non-resident as testamentary trustee.

   a. **Resident agent:** When a non-resident is named as trustee, the court may require the appointment of a ***resident agent*** for service of process.

   b. **Aliens:** At common law the extent to which an alien could take and hold real property was severely restricted and today whether or not aliens may act as trustees is regulated by statute in many states.

3. **Corporations:** The extent to which a ***corporation*** may act as trustee will depend upon the statutes of the jurisdiction of its incorporation and the purposes for which it is incorporated. Non-domiciliary corporations are often disqualified.

4. **Governmental body:** The ***United States*** or a ***state*** may take and hold property as trustee. But because of the ***doctrine of Sovereign Immunity***, under which a government cannot be sued without its consent, the trust is unenforceable against the government in the absence of a statute or special act of the legislature and/or unless special courts (e.g., U.S. Court of Federal Claims) have been established to handle claims against the government. Bogert, p. 93.

   Example: Land may be devised to a government to hold in trust for a special purpose such as a home for insane persons or for the benefit of soldiers.

5. **Partnership:** A ***partnership*** may serve as a trustee to the extent it is recognized as an ***entity*** by the applicable law of the jurisdiction.

B. When no trustee named: A trust will not be permitted to fail for want of a trustee.

Example: M by will leaves certain land in trust for C. Suppose that no trustee is named, or the named trustee has died.

The court will appoint a trustee to administer the trust, and will order the person having legal title to the property to convey it to the appointed trustee. (Before the court's order, the title would be either in M's heir or in M's residuary devisee). See, e.g., *Perfect Union Lodge No. 10 v. Interfirst Bank*, 748 S.W.2d 218 (Tex. 1988).

C. **Succession:** If a sole trustee dies intestate the title to the trust real property descends to his heir and the title to the trust personal property passes to his personal representative, but such heir or personal representative will ***not be permitted to administer the trust***. The court will appoint a successor trustee.

Example: T holds land and bonds in trust for C. T dies intestate leaving H his sole heir and A is appointed his administrator. The title to the land passes to H and the title to the bonds passes to A. The equity court will appoint a new trustee and order H and A to transfer the land and the bonds respectively to such newly appointed trustee.

Note: This same principle of succession holds true if T dies testate and devises the land to H and the bonds pass to T's executor, A.

D. **Survivorship:** Two or more trustees always hold the title to the trust property in joint tenancy. The ***doctrine of survivorship*** applies even in a jurisdiction where tenancy in common is preferred by statute over joint tenancy.

Example: A, B and C hold land and a herd of sheep in trust for X. A dies (testate or intestate). B and C by survivorship hold title to the land and the sheep. B then dies. C by the doctrine of survivorship holds the title to the land and the sheep.

E. **Resignation:** A trustee cannot ***resign*** without permission of the equity court unless the trust instrument so provides or all of the beneficiaries are ***sui juris*** and consent to the resignation. The court will usually permit the trustee to resign if continuing to serve will be unreasonably burdensome to him and will not cause great detriment to the trust. Rest. of Trusts, 2d, §106.

F. **Removal:** Whether or not to ***remove a trustee*** is within the sound ***judicial discretion*** of the equity court. A trustee may be removed for habitual drunkenness, dishonesty, incompetency in handling of trust property, or dissipation of the trust estate. Mere ***friction*** or ***incompatibility between the trustee and beneficiary*** is not enough to justify removal unless it endangers the trust property or makes impossible the accomplishment of the purpose of the trust. *Blumenstiel v. Morris*, 180 S.W.2d 107 (Ark. 1944).

G. **When creation of trust dependent upon acceptance of particular trustee:** If the settlor conditions the ***creation of a trust*** on the acceptance of a particular person as trustee, the trust fails upon the failure or refusal of the designated person to act.

H. **Beneficiary as trustee:** The extent to which a beneficiary of a trust may also be a trustee of the trust is governed by the following rules:

1. The ***sole beneficiary cannot be the sole trustee***. This would vest the same person with identical legal and equitable interests and a merger would take place, giving the trustee- beneficiary an absolute interest.

2. One of ***several beneficiaries*** may be one of several trustees.

3. One of two or more beneficiaries can be the ***sole trustee***. The trustee's interest as trustee is different from his interest as beneficiary. No merger results because the same person is not vested with the absolute legal and equitable interests.

4. The sole beneficiary can be one of two or more trustees. Absolute title does not vest in the beneficiary upon the death of the other trustees, and a substitute trustee will be appointed based on the implied intent of the settlor.

5. If there is more than one beneficiary all the beneficiaries may be all the trustees.

> **Example:** A conveyance to B and C in trust for B and C creates a valid trust. As trustees B and C hold as tenants in common, so their interests do not merge.

I. **Settlor as trustee:** The ***settlor*** of the trust may be the trustee. This is always the case in a declaration of trust. See *Farkas v. Williams, supra*, p. 85-86.

> **Note:** For further discussion of the role of the trustee, see *infra*, pp. 185-205.

V. THE BENEFICIARY

A. **Ascertainable identity:** In every private trust there must be a specifically named beneficiary or a beneficiary so described that his identity can be ascertained when the trust is created or within the period of the Rule Against Perpetuities.

B. **Who may be a beneficiary:** A beneficiary may be:

1. **Natural person:** A ***natural person*** who has capacity to take and hold legal title to property has capacity to be the beneficiary of a trust.

2. **Aliens:** ***Aliens*** may be beneficiaries of a trust unless restricted by special rules of the jurisdiction. In some states it is held that although an alien may take ***title to land*** the state may bring a proceeding to forfeit the land to the state. In such states the equitable interest of an alien trust beneficiary could also be forfeited. See Rest. of Trusts, 2d §117, Comment b. The question of the constitutionality of state statutes restricting the rights of aliens to inherit has been frequently raised in other contexts.

3. **Corporations:** ***Corporations*** may be beneficiaries of a trust ***to the extent they are empowered to take and hold legal title to property***. A corporation not yet organized may be the beneficiary of a trust to the extent it could be if in existence and if it is certain to come into existence within the period of the Rule Against Perpetuities.

4. **Trustee as beneficiary:** The beneficiary may also be a ***trustee*** of a trust except that the sole beneficiary may not be the sole trustee. See *supra*, p. 94.

5. **Settlor as beneficiary:** The person who creates an ***inter vivos trust*** may be a beneficiary or the sole beneficiary of the trust. The settlor has been held to be the sole beneficiary in the following instances:

   a. Settlor creates an inter vivos trust to pay income to herself for a period of years and then reconvey the property to her.

   b. Settlor creates an inter vivos trust to pay income to herself for life and on her death to convey the property to her personal representative or to whomever she shall appoint by deed or will.

   c. Settlor creates an inter vivos trust to pay the income to himself for life and on his death to pay the principal to his next of kin or heirs.

6. **Class as beneficiary:** The beneficiary may be a ***class of persons*** as long as the class is ***definite or definitely ascertainable***.

   Example 1: If A leaves property in trust for "my children," the class is definite and the trust would be valid.

   Example 2: If a trust is designated "for my family," the validity of the trust will depend upon whether the court construes the term to mean immediate family, in which case the class is sufficiently definite, or all relations, in which case the trust would fail since the class is indefinite.

   Example 3: If a trust is designated "for my relatives" and this is interpreted to mean "next-of-kin" the class is sufficiently definite and the trust is valid.

a. **Power of trustee to select from ascertainable class:** If the beneficiary is a definite or definitely ascertainable class, the fact that the trustee is given ***power to select from the class*** does not affect the validity of the trust.

b. **Vague or indefinite designation of class:** If the settlor's designation of a class of beneficiaries is so ***vague or indefinite*** that the class of beneficiaries cannot be determined with reasonable certainty, the trust must fail.

Example: The ninth clause of T's will in essence gives "to my trustees my property [of a described type] in trust to make disposal of to such of my friends as they shall select." The question presented is whether the clause provides for definite and ascertainable beneficiaries so that the bequest can be sustained as a private trust.

Held, the trust must fail. In order to ensure that someone has standing to compel performance by the trustee, it is required that the beneficiary of a private trust be a definite person or class of persons. Unlike terms such as "relations" or "issue," the word "friends" is incapable of precise application. There are no accepted statutory or other limitations to such a concept. Moreover, the will clause itself fails to provide criteria to govern the selection of individuals from the class. To allow the trustees to simply "select" friends without restriction is in effect to substitute the will and discretion of the trustees for that of T. As such the clause contravenes the policies of the Statute of Wills which requires such dispositions to be made in accordance with formal will requirements. *Clark v. Campbell*, 82 N.H. 281, 133 A. 166 (1926).

Note: Upon failure of the trust, the trustees in *Clark* were to hold title to the property described in clause nine of the will and to dispose of it as part of the will's residue.

c. **Unrestricted power of disposition:** A ***trust created for the benefit of any person or persons whom the trustee may select is not a trust***. Unless an intent is expressed to the contrary, in such instances the trustee is considered to have an ***unrestricted power of disposition*** and takes an ***absolute gift free of trust***.

i. **Resulting trust in favor of settlor's heirs:** This situation is to be distinguished from that in which the settlor manifests an intention that the transferee not dispose of property for his own benefit, but fails to name a beneficiary. In this latter case the trust fails and the trustee, rather than holding for his own benefit, holds on a resulting trust in favor of the settlor's heirs. For a further discussion of resulting trusts, see *infra*, pp. 118-23.

d. **Disposition for benefit of family:** If property is transferred to a person for the benefit of that person and his family, it is a question of interpretation whether the transferor intended to create a trust or intended to make a beneficial gift to the person named with an expression of the motive for making the gift. See Rest. of Trusts, 2d §25, comment d.

e. **Partnerships and unincorporated associations:** Even though at common law a partnership or an unincorporated association cannot as such hold legal title to real property or be a trustee, either may be a beneficiary of a trust and hold the equitable title to the trust property.

   i. **Individual members who are determinable:** Individuals who are members of any such association at a given instant and therefore determinable, may be beneficiaries.

   ii. **Individual members of association with indefinite succession:** The individual members of an association with indefinite succession may be beneficiaries, provided either the trustee or such members or a committee thereof has power to terminate the trust.

   Example: S leaves securities to T in trust "for the members of the Sioux County Bar Association who pay their annual dues, but at any time T may, in his discretion, terminate the trust and distribute the corpus of the trust property to the members." The trust would be invalid under the Rule Against Perpetuities if T did not have power to terminate it. Many members might in the indefinite future pay their annual dues and the equitable title to the trust res would vest in them long after the time allowed by the Rule. The fact that T may at any instant terminate the trust prevents a violation of the policy of the Rule. There is always someone who has power to dispose of the property both legally and equitably.

f. **Tenants in common:** The beneficiaries of a trust hold their equitable interest as ***tenants in common*** unless the trust instrument provides that they shall hold as joint tenants.

   Example: S transfers property to T in trust for A, B, and C. Each of these beneficiaries owns an undivided one-third of the equitable title in the trust property.

C. **Trusts for unborn beneficiaries:** Trusts for unborn children are ***valid if there is another beneficiary*** in existence at the time of creating the trust who can enforce the trust from its inception.

> **Example:** A transfers property to T in trust for A's children then living or born thereafter. A trust is created. The living children can enforce the trust from its inception.

1. **No beneficiary in existence:** If there is no beneficiary in existence at the time of the creation of the trust but a beneficiary may be born thereafter, it is important to ***determine whether the trust is created by a transfer in trust or by a declaration of trust***.

   a. **Transfer in trust:** In the case of a ***transfer in trust***, the trust is ***valid***. The trustee is considered a ***resulting trustee*** for the benefit of the settlor who may enforce the trust until a child is born.

   Example: A transfers property to T in trust for A's children. Even though A has no children at the time of transfer, a trust is created.

   b. **Declaration of trust:** In the case of a ***declaration of trust*** (for example, A declares himself trustee for his children, but no children are in existence at the time), there is disagreement as to whether or not a trust is created.

      i. **No trust view:** One view is that since there is no beneficiary in existence who can enforce the trust against A, ***no trust is created***.

      ii. **Rule Against Perpetuities view:** Another view is that as long as the interest must vest in a child within the period of the ***Rule Againt Perpetuities***, a valid trust is created.

2. **Doctrine of worthier title:** There is a split of authority as to the result when ***settlor transfers property in trust to hold for the benefit of settlor for life and then to the "settlor's heirs":***

   a. **Disposition creates reversion:** Some jurisdictions hold that under ***the doctrine of worthier title*** the disposition in favor of the settlor's heirs creates a reversion in the settlor and no interest in the heirs.

   b. **Intention of settlor:** Other jurisdictions hold that the doctrine of worthier title is not an absolute rule of law and the rule is ***only a matter of construction***. The question here is whether the ***settlor*** in the particular case ***intended*** to create an interest in the heirs.

   c. **Remainder to heirs:** Still other jurisdictions hold that the heirs have a ***remainder***.

3. **Disposition to third person for life and then to his heirs:** When a disposition is made to a third person for life and then to his heirs, that third person is the sole beneficiary of the trust in the following instances:

   a. in jurisdictions where the Rule in Shelley's Case is in force and the res is realty (for the Rule in Shelley's Case, see Restatement of Property, §§312, 313; see also Emanuel on *Property*.) and

   b. when it is found that the settlor intended the entire equitable interest to go to the designated third person.

D. **Honorary trusts:** When there is ***no definite ascertainable beneficiary***, a trust for specific ***non-charitable*** purposes is ordinarily ***not*** an ***enforceable*** trust. Such distributions are known as ***honorary trusts***. Common examples of such dispositions are trusts for the erection of monuments, the care of graves, the saying of masses, and the care of ***specific*** animals.

1. **Trustee may carry out intent of settlor if he wishes:** The general rule is that the ***purported trustee of an honorary trust may carry out the intent of the settlor if he chooses to do so***. Since there is no beneficiary who can enforce the trust, the carrying out of the trust depends upon on the ***honor*** of the trustee.

   Example: T's will bequeaths his dog to F. T directs his executor to deposit $1,000 in a bank and pay 75 cents per day to F for the keep and care of the dog. When the dog dies any balance is to be divided among F and others. A question is raised whether this honorary trust is valid, and whether it violates the Rule against Perpetuities (*infra*, p. 144.)

   Held, this honorary trust is valid, since F has volunteered to carry it out. T's purpose for the trust is not capricious or illegal, and F accepted the dog. *In re Searight's Estate*, 95 N.E.2d 779 (Ohio App. 1950).

   a. **Resulting trust:** If the trustee chooses ***not*** to carry out the trust duties, he will be deemed to hold the property for the ***settlor*** or the ***settlor's heirs***, under a ***"resulting trust"***.

2. **Variations among jurisdictions:** Jurisdictions vary as to the extent to which honorary trusts will be recognized, if at all.

   a. **UPC allows:** UPC §2-907 recognizes honorary trusts. But it authorizes the court to reduce excessive amounts of such a trust, and to limit the trust's duration to 21 years.

   b. **Special statutes:** In many jurisdictions special legislation exists validating provisions for the upkeep of graves and monuments. In many jurisdictions, trusts for saying mass are upheld as charitable trusts, *infra*, p. 112.

3. **Limitations due to public policy:** Honorary trusts are limited by considerations of public policy.

   a. **Rule Against Perpetuities:** Honorary trusts must satisfy the ***Rule Against Perpetuities***. But the Rule will often be construed in a way that is favorable to the upholding of the trust.

      Example: Consider *Searight's Estate*, *supra*, where T willed his dog to F and left $1,000 in trust to be paid to F for the dog's care and feeding, at the rate of 75 cents per day. The court held that the Rule was not violated by the trust. The court noted that the Rule limits contingencies to a *human* life plus 21 years. The life of an *animal* with great longevity such as an elephant or sea turtle cannot be used, the court said. At 75 cents per day the trust fund would be depleted in about four years. Therefore, the period of the trust would not violate the Rule.

   b. **Amount may not be unduly large:** The ***amount*** of the honorary trust must not be ***unreasonably larger*** than needed for the purposes to be accomplished.

   c. **Not capricious purposes:** The ***purposes*** of the trust must be those of a reasonably normal settlor, and may not be ***capricious***.

      Example: "I leave $1,000,000 to T in trust to burn $1,000 on each anniversary of my death." This would be a capricious purpose, and the trustee would not be allowed to carry it out.

4. **Specific animals:** Honorary trusts for the benefit of specific animals, sustained in only some jurisdictions, are to be ***distinguished from charitable trusts*** for the benefit of ***animals in general***, which are sustained everywhere. For a discussion of the distinction between honorary trusts and charitable trusts see *infra*, p. 112.

E. **Protecting the beneficiary's interest from claims of creditors and others:** A beneficiary's interest in a trust is freely transferable to the same extent that a similar legal interest is transferable unless there are express or implied restraints on transfer. The interest can be reached by creditors of the beneficiary in the absence of such restraint. Neither consideration nor notice to and consent of the trustee is necessary for the transfer of the beneficiary's interest.

1. **Devices to protect interest from alienation:** Various devices have been developed to protect the beneficiary's interest from alienation. The most common are: (1) the ***spendthrift trust***; (2) a ***forfeiture provision***; (3) ***discretionary trusts***; and (4) ***support***

trusts.

a. **Devices merely prevent alienation of funds while in hands of trustee:** Such devices are directed to protecting the trust interest while it is still in the hands of the trustee. Once funds have been paid over to the beneficiary, any attempt at imposing a restraint on alienation is invalid.

2. **Spendthrift trusts:** A spendthrift clause in a trust is an ***express provision against alienation*** (voluntary, involuntary or both) of the beneficiary's right to receive principal, income or both.

Example: A clause in T's will provides: "Each beneficiary hereunder is hereby restrained from alienating, anticipating, encumbering or in any manner assigning his interest hereunder nor shall such interest be subject to his liabilities or obligations nor to judgment or other legal process, bankruptcy proceedings or claims of creditors or others."

a. **Majority rule:** In a majority of jurisdictions spendthrift provisions are held ***valid*** on the theory that the settlor who had the entire interest in property can give away a qualified interest if he chooses.

Example: The eleventh article of T's will states in essence: "I give the sum of $75,000 to Trustee in trust to pay the net income thereof semiannually to my brother B during his natural life, such payments to be made free from the interference or control of his creditors, my intention being that the use of said income shall not be anticipated by assignment." At issue is whether B's creditor C can attach the income of the trust fund created for B's benefit before it is paid to B.

Held, against C. A person having the entire right to dispose of his property may place it in trust in favor of a beneficiary and "provide that it shall not be alienated by him by anticipation." Creditors may reach all nonexempt property of a debtor but cannot enlarge the gift of the settlor and take more than the settlor has given. "The rule of public policy [that] subjects a debtor's property to the payment of his debts does not subject the property of a donor to the debts of his beneficiary, and does not give the creditor a right to complain that, in the exercise of his absolute right of disposition, the donor has not seen fit to give the property to the creditor, but has left it out of his reach." *Broadway National Bank v. Adams*, 133 Mass. 170, 4 Am.Rep. 504 (1882).

b. **Minority rule:** Some jurisdictions hold spendthrift provisions ***invalid*** on the theory that a person should not be able to live according to the standards which he claims for himself and at the same time repudiate any obligation to pay for anything that he purchases on credit.

c. **Any language that manifests intent: *Any form of words*** which shows the settlor's intention to impose a direct restraint on alienation of the beneficiary's interest may be used to create a spendthrift trust.

d. **Involuntarily and voluntary alienation:** Courts often will hold that the settlor intended to ***restrain both involuntary and voluntary alienation*** even if the settlor expresses only one or the other. It is thought contrary to public policy to permit a settlor to restrain involuntary alienation without restraining voluntary alienation.

e. **No spendthrift trust for settlor:** A settlor may ***not*** create a spendthrift trust for himself.

f. **Exceptions to rule that income cannot be reached:** In jurisdictions where spendthrift trusts are valid, exceptions are often made to the rule that creditors and other claimants may not reach the income of the trust. Some jurisdictions hold that only restraints on income are valid and invalidate restraints on the corpus. Some jurisdictions hold restraints valid only to the extent of income necessary for the support of the beneficiary and hold additional income subject to creditors.

g. **Specific statutes may govern:** In a number of states spendthrift provisions are governed by specific statutes.

Example: A New York statute allows creditors of the beneficiary to reach that part of a spendthrift trust income in excess of the amount needed for the support and education of the beneficiary. N.Y. Est., Powers and Trusts law §7-3.4.

h. **Special classes of claimants may reach interest:** The ***modern trend*** is to allow certain special classes of claimants to ***reach the beneficiary's interest*** in a spendthrift trust on the ground of public policy. These include:

i. persons the beneficiary is bound to ***support*** (i.e., claims for alimony and child support).

Example: B, the beneficiary of a spendthrift trust, has two children by his first marriage to whom he is obligated to pay child support. B is also obligated to pay alimony to his second wife and support for two children of his second marriage. B disappears and his whereabouts are unknown. Suit is brought against the trustee bank to obtain the alimony and support money as provided in the divorce decrees. The bank defends the action on the grounds that it is the testator's privilege to dispose of his property as he pleases and the trust should be free of alienation.

Held, interest from the spendthrift trust is subject to claims for alimony and child support. B should not be allowed to enjoy the benefits of a trust and at the same time refuse to pay obligations arising out of marriage. Public policy requires this result. Therefore, income from the trust is payable for child support and alimony where the alimony has been ordered by a court.

As to the trust's corpus, the trust provides that B has no right to the principal unless the trustee determines that he is entitled to it. However, the trust provides for payment of the principal in case of emergency by B or his children. The failure to support children is such an emergency, so the principal (corpus) may be used for child support. It may not be used for alimony because the trust makes no provision for B's wife. *Shelley v. Shelley*, 354 P.2d 282 (Ore. 1960).

ii. persons who render necessary ***personal services*** to the beneficiary (e.g., the physician who gives the beneficiary medical treatment);

iii. persons whose ***services preserve the beneficiary's interest*** in the trust (e.g., the lawyer who by bringing suit for the trust saves the trust's income);

iv. ***tort claims***; and

v. claims by the ***United States*** or a ***State***.

3. Support trusts: A trust containing a direction that the trustee shall pay or apply only so much of the income and principal as is necessary for the ***education and support*** of the beneficiary is a ***support trust***. The interest of the beneficiary cannot be transferred because of the nature of the beneficiary's interest.

Example: A clause in T's will provides: "I hereby transfer $100,000 to D in trust to pay or apply so much of the income as is necessary for the education and reasonable support of C during C's life."

a. Partial restriction on alienation: In a trust for support, ***restrictions on alienation are implied only to the extent actually necessary to effectuate the settlor's purpose of providing support*** for the beneficiary. If the beneficiary has a right to any additional amount from the trust such additional interest is freely alienable.

b. Distinguished: A support trust must be distinguished from a trust in which the settlor has ***expressed support and***

education as the motive for the trust but which does not limit the beneficiary's interest to an amount necessary to his support. In such cases the interest of the beneficiary can be transferred and is subject to his creditors.

Example: A transfers property to T to pay the annual income to B during his life for his comfort and support. B is entitled to the entire income and can assign it and his creditors can reach it. See Rest. of Trusts, 2d §154.

c. **Exceptions:** Support trusts are subject to the same exceptions for alimony, child support and necessaries as are spendthrift trusts.

d. **Settlor as beneficiary:** If a settlor creates a support trust for his own benefit his creditors can reach the maximum amount that the trustee could apply for or pay to him under the trust terms.

4. **Discretionary trusts:** A trust whose trustee is given discretion as to the amount of income or principal to give to the beneficiaries is called a ***"discretionary trust."*** In a discretionary trust, the trust instrument might set a general standard such as "comfort," "happiness" or "support," but no specific standard is set forth by which the trustee is to base his discretion.

a. **Beneficiary has no vested interest:** In a discretionary trust the beneficiary has ***no vested interest*** in the trust that can be alienated or reached by creditors until the trustee has elected to make a payment to the beneficiary. An assignee of the beneficiary, however, may hold the trustee liable for any future payment to the beneficiary by giving the trustee notice of his assignment, such assignment being considered an assignment of a future payment.

Example 1: S delivers $5,000 to T in trust for C. The trust instrument provides that all payments to C from corpus or income shall be in T's sole discretion, and that T may choose to make no payment at all to C. Before T has elected to make any payment to C as beneficiary, C assigns to X a right to $25 of any payment T elects to make to C. X notifies T of such assignment and demands that if T elects to pay C any amount up to $25, T shall make the payment to X and not to C. T need make no election to pay C and if he does not do so, X has no right to receive anything from the trust; however, if T does elect to pay C $25 T is liable to X for that amount.

Example 2: The state seeks payment from the corpus of a discretionary trust for care furnished to a beneficiary who is in a mental institution. The trustees decline to make payment to the state. *Held*, payments from the corpus cannot be compelled unless the trustees act ***dishonestly***, ***arbitrarily*** or with an ***improper motive***. There is no such showing in this case, since the trustees considered B's future needs and other purposes of the trust in reaching their decision. *First National Bank of Maryland v. Dept. of Health & Mental Hygiene*, 399 A.2d 821 (Md. 1979).

Note: The court in *Bank of Maryland* noted that the supplier of necessaries has a claim against the corpus of a *support* trust. However, the court held that the trust involved in that case was *not* a support trust.

b. Settlor as beneficiary: If a settlor creates a discretionary trust for ***his own benefit*** his creditors can reach the maximum amount that the trustee could apply for or pay to him under the trust terms.

c. Judicial Review: A court will not interfere with the reasonable exercise of discretion by a trustee. On review a court will look to the standard, if any, in the trust instrument. Very little review is possible if distributions are to be made "as the trustee deems best". However, where income or principal is to be paid "as may be necessary . . . for the comfortable support" of the beneficiary, a court will order a trustee to adhere to the terms of the trust if payments are inadequate for "comfortable support." *Old Colony Trust Co. v. Rodd*, 254 N.E.2d 886 (Mass. 1970).

d. Forfeiture provision: A ***forfeiture provision*** in a trust may provide that the interest of the beneficiary immediately cease or that the ***trust automatically change to a discretionary trust,*** if the beneficiary attempts to assign or his creditors try to reach his interest. A gift to another is provided for in such case.

Example: P transfers property to T in trust to pay the income to B during B's life and then the principal to C. The trust instrument provides that if at any time B should attempt to assign his interest or be adjudicated a bankrupt or if a creditor should attempt to subject the interest to creditors' claims, B's interest under the trust will cease and the property shall be paid to C. If a creditor brings an action to reach B's interest, the interest automatically terminates and is vested in C and B has no further interest in the trust. See Rest. of Trusts, 2d §150.

CHARITABLE TRUSTS

I. HISTORY OF CHARITABLE TRUSTS

A. Origins: Charitable trusts developed in England out of the desire of individuals to make gifts ***for religious purposes***. Previously, direct gifts to charity had been either:

1. ***forbidden*** by restrictions on mortmain, *supra*, pp. 31-32, or

2. ***unacceptable*** because of the vows of poverty of the Franciscan friars.

B. Initially honorary: Initially the duties of the trustee (feoffee to uses) were merely ***honorary*** and unenforceable in the courts.

C. Became enforceable: As early as the ***fifteenth century***, charitable trusts were being ***enforced*** by the Chancellor.

D. Statute of Charitable Uses: The Statute of Charitable Uses was adopted in 1601 to provide for the enforcement of charitable trusts. It authorized the Chancellor to appoint commissioners from time to time to inquire into abuses and to make orders for the redress of abuses involving charitable bequests and donations. This remedy was seldom used in England and never in the United States. Sec. 43 Eliz. I, c. 4 (1601).

E. Enforceablility in the United States: Charitable trusts have been upheld and enforced in the various states of the United States whether or not the Statute of Charitable Uses is in effect.

II. ELEMENTS

A. Six elements: A charitable trust is a public trust and must have ***six distinct elements to be valid***: (1) an intention of the settlor to create a trust; (2) a trustee to administer the trust; (3) a res or subject matter; (4) a charitable purpose expressly designated; (5) a definite class to be benefited; and (6) indefinite beneficiaries (within the defined class) who actually receive the benefit.

B. Comparison to private trusts: The requirement of: (1) the intention, (2) the trustee; and (3) the res, are the same in a charitable trust as in a private trust.

> **Example:** S, by will, leaves the residuary of his estate to "T in trust for the purpose of furnishing food, clothing and shelter for the poor children of City X." A charitable trust is created as (1) S is the settlor and his intention to create a charitable trust is expressed in clear language; (2) T is designated as trustee; (3) the property in S's estate constitutes the

res or subject matter of the trust; (4) furnishing food, clothing and shelter for the children is an express charitable purpose that has as its object benefiting, uplifting or developing mankind, mentally, morally, physically or spiritually; (5) "poor children of City X" constitutes a specifically designated class of persons to be benefited; and (6) the specific children who will receive food, clothing and shelter from the trust remain indefinite at the creation of the trust (which takes place when S's will becomes effective upon his death). See Rest. of Trusts, 2d §§348, 351.

1. **Manner of creation:** A charitable trust is created in the same manner as a private express trust. It may be created by a declaration of trust, a transfer inter vivos, a transfer by will, a power of appointment, and a promise in trust. See Rest. of Trusts, 2d §349.

2. **Enforceability:** For a private express trust to be valid, it must have definite beneficiaries who can enforce it. By contrast, a trust having ***indefinite beneficiaries*** will be valid, if it has a ***charitable purpose***. As such, it is ***enforceable by the attorney general***.

Example: T by will leaves her residuary estate "to the Reverend H.J. Lambert, to be used by him at his discretion for religious and educational purposes."

Held, T's gift created a valid, public charitable trust. That the beneficiaries are indefinite does not invalidate the trust since a trust is not charitable when all the beneficiaries are "definitely ascertained." The purposes of T's trust are sufficiently certain for a charitable trust: religious and educational purposes to be selected in the discretion of a named trustee. While the court cannot specify what religious and educational purposes are to be chosen, it can compel the trustee to make a selection and then insure that trust property is applied to such purposes. Moreover, religious and education purposes are the very essence of public charitable trusts. *Yeager v. Johns*, 484 S.W.2d 211 (1972).

III. CHARITABLE PURPOSES

A. **Definition:** A purpose is charitable when it is to benefit, improve or uplift mankind mentally, morally, physically or spiritually. Charitable purposes include relief of poverty, improvement of government, advancement of religion, education or health, and other goals that benefit the community.

Example 1: Trusts "for the benefit of the poor" or "for widows" are construed to be "for poor people" and "poor widows" — for the ***relief of poverty*** — and are therefore charitable.

Example 2: Trusts "to erect and maintain a bridge, a street and a park" are construed to ***improve government*** and are therefore charitable. This benefits taxpayers as a class and within the class, the particular taxpayers who would be taxed for such improvements.

Example 3: Trusts "to prevent cruelty to animals," "to build a monument to Abraham Lincoln," "to beautify Town X" or "to improve the United States Constitution" respectively promote ***kindness to animals, patriotism, community happiness*** and ***better government*** and are therefore charitable.

Example 4: Trusts "to build a statue of St. Paul," "to distribute Bibles," or "to support foreign missionaries" tend to promote ***religion*** and are therefore charitable.

Example 5: Trusts "to provide scholarships," "for educational purposes," "to promote Boy Scouts and Girl Scouts," "to promote birth control," "to encourage vivesection," "to discourage vivisection," or "to set up a fund for low interest loans to needy students" promote ***education*** and are therefore charitable.

Example 6: Trusts "to study cancer," "to provide a sewage disposal plant for Town Y," "to encourage vegetarianism" or "to prevent cruelty to children" promote health and are therefore charitable.

1. **Derivation of definition of charitable purposes:** The definition of charitable purposes is derived from the preamble to the Statute of Charitable Uses adopted in England in 1601 (43 Eliz. I. c. 4) which enumerates charitable purposes. It was early determined that the list was not complete and that other purposes of the same general character are also charitable. See Rest. of Trusts, 2d §368. Comment a.

2. **Trust for "benevolent" purposes:** A trust for ***"benevolent"*** purposes may or may not be a charitable trust. If the word is construed to be the equivalent of "charitable," the trust is valid. On the other hand if it is found to mean "good will toward man" or mere liberality, the trust fails.

Example 1: T by will bequeaths all of her personal property to the Bishop of Durham in trust to dispose of the residue "to such objects of benevolence and liberality as the Bishop of Durham in his own discretion shall most approve of."

Held, the trust is not a charitable trust. The terms "benevolence and liberality" are broad enough to include non-charitable purposes. As the Bishop would thus not be bound to apply the property to strictly charitable purposes, the State cannot enforce the trust. *Morice v. Bishop of Durham*, 10 Ves. 522, 32 Eng. Rep. 947 (1805).

Note 1: Since there was also no beneficiary to enforce the trust in *Morice*, and there was no intention by T to make an outright gift to the Bishop, the Bishop in *Morice* was found to hold the property for T's heirs on a resulting trust.

Note 2: Modern court decisions treat "benevolent" as a synonym of "charitable," so a modern court would probably enforce a charitable trust on the facts of *Morice*. Bogert, p. 207; compare *Wilson v. Flowers, infra*, p. 111.

Example 2: T creates a testamentary trust from which income is to be paid equally to all first, second and third grade school children at a specified school just prior to Christmas and Easter each year. The money is to be used to further their education. An heir of T sues, contending that the will does not create a valid charitable trust and that the funds should go to T's heirs.

Held, the trust must fail. The trustee here has no power to control the use of the money once paid, so the stated purpose of educational advancement cannot be assured. The money is given at a time when the minds of the children are far removed from studies. It appears that T wanted to bestow gifts on the children to bring them happiness during the holidays, but that is not an educational trust. The trust here is a benevolence, a private trust, and may not be upheld as a charitable trust. *Shenandoah Valley National Bank v. Taylor*, 63 S.E.2d 786 (Va. 1951).

Note: The distinction between private and charitable trusts is important because of the Rule Against Perpetuities. A private trust is subject to the Rule; it must end within the perpetuities period or it is invalid. A charitable trust is public and is not subject to the Rule. Therefore, to continue indefinitely into the future the trust must be charitable. Otherwise the trust fails, as it did in the *Shenandoah Valley* case.

3. **Two requirements concerning beneficiary:** The ***class*** to be benefited in a charitable trust must ***be definite***; that is, it must be large enough so that the community in general is affected and interested in the enforcement of the trust, but must not include all of mankind. Furthermore, ***within this class, the specific persons to benefit from the trust must be indefinite***.

Example 1: A trust "for the benefit of orphans of veterans of World War II" is charitable. The class, the orphans of the veterans of World War II, is definite. The indefinite persons within the class are those who are ultimately selected by the trustee to receive the benefits. The class is large enough so that the community is interested in the enforcement of the trust.

Example 2: A trust to "establish an athletic field for the X High School" is charitable. If this is considered a trust for governmental purposes because it furnishes a facility which would otherwise have to paid for at governmental expense, the class to be benefited is all taxpayers of the school district and the indefinite beneficiaries within the class are the particular taxpayers who would otherwise be taxed to pay for the field. If this is considered a charitable trust for educational purposes as part of the physical education program of the high school, the class to be benefited is the entire class of high school students; the indefinite beneficiaries within the class are the students who use the athletic field.

Example 3: A trust "to erect and maintain a monument of George Washington in the yard of the County Courthouse of Z Country" is charitable as promoting patriotism. The class to be benefited is the entire immediate community and within the class the indefinite beneficiaries are the people who actually view the monument.

Example 4: A trust to "charity" is valid, but leaves to the trustee the selection of the particular charitable purpose to which the trust's res will be applied. If no trustee is named in the will, the court appoints a trustee to carry out the trust. *Jordan's Estate*, 197 A. 150 (Pa. 1938).

Note: In the example above the trustee could set up a "hospital for stray dogs and cats." Such a trust would be charitable because it is for all dogs and cats generally, and not for specifically named ones. Such an institution engenders a general feeling of kindliness toward animals. The class of persons which is benefited is made up of the people in the immediate community and the indefinite persons to be benefited within the class are those who come in contact with institution and are affected by it.

4. **Unacceptable purposes:** A trust for ***named persons*** or a trust for ***profit*** cannot be a charitable trust.

IV. TRUSTS FOR BOTH CHARITABLE AND NON-CHARITABLE PURPOSES

A. Inseparability: A trust for both charitable and non-charitable purposes ***will fail if the two are inseparable***.

Example: S bequeaths $100,000 to T "to hold in trust for the benefit of all the schools in City X." P is the residuary legatee. Some schools in City X are public and charitable institutions and some are private and operated for profit. S has not indicated how much of the $100,000 may be used for the public schools and how much may be used for the private schools. The valid part being inseparable from the invalid part, the whole must fail as a charitable trust and T holds in resulting trust for P.

B. When primary purpose is charitable: If the primary purpose of the trust is charitable but the trustee is authorized to apply part of the property to non-charitable purposes, a valid charitable trust is created. Since the power to apply to non-charitable objects is invalid, the trustee ***must apply the entire property to the intended charitable purpose***. Rest. of Trusts, 2d §398, Comment g.

Example: Income from certain trust assets is to be contributed "to such philanthropic causes as my trustees may select." The trust is challenged as invalid. Heirs contend that the gifts should pass by intestate succession. They reason that the testator intended "philanthropic" to have a broader meaning than charitable causes, so that the gift is void either for uncertainty or as a violation of the Rule Against Perpetuities. (Remember that a trust of indefinte duration violates the Rule if it is not a charitable trust.)

Held, the trust is a valid charitable trust. While "philanthropic" may be technically broader than "charitable," in modern usage it has come to mean the same thing. Further, evidence of the testator's intent shows that he equated the word with "charitable". Thus the trust is valid. The trustees are directed to contribute solely to organizations which qualify as charities under federal and state law. *Wilson v. Flowers*, 277 A.2d 199 (N.J. 1971).

C. When maximum amount for non-charitable purposes is known: If a trust has both charitable and non-charitable purposes and it is possible to determine the maximum amount that can be used for non-charitable purposes, the ***trust fails only as to that amount and the remainder is a valid charitable trust***.

D. Division of trust: If a number of purposes are specified for a trust, some non-charitable and some charitable, the court may direct a ***division*** of the trust into as many equal shares as there are trust objects. The shares for charitable objects then create valid charitable trusts; the shares for non-charitable objects fail.

Example: S bequeaths to T $10,000 for the following purposes: (1) to pay the hospital bills of children who become infected with rabies and (2) to spread rabies among the dogs and create a scourge on the people of the Town of X. ***Five thousand dollars is to be used for each purpose***. The trust for purpose one is charitable and will be enforced. The trust for the second purpose, which is vicious and injurious to mankind, will fail; T will hold the $5,000 for the invalid purpose in resulting trust for S's statutory heir or residuary legatee.

V. CHARITABLE TRUSTS DISTINGUISHED FROM HONORARY TRUSTS

A. Erection of monuments to testator or his family: A trust for the ***erection of monuments to the testator or his family*** is usually private and may only be upheld as an honorary trust. If, however, the monument is to recognize an individual who has performed great service to the public, it may be charitable.

B. Care of cemetery plots: Trusts for the ***care of cemetery plots*** are usually not charitable and must be sustained either as honorary trusts or under special statutes. Trusts for the maintenance of a public cemetery, however, may be charitable.

C. Specific animals: Trusts for the benefit of ***special animals*** are private and fail for the lack of a human beneficiary. They may be upheld as honorary trusts.

D. Saying masses: Trusts for saying masses are generally held to be charitable. *In re Hamilton's Estate*, 181 Cal. 758, 186 P. 587 (1919). In a few states (particularly when the trust is for the purpose of having masses said for the soul of the settlor) such trusts are held to be private trusts which fail for want of a living beneficiary. Under such circumstances they may be upheld as honorary trusts. For further discussion of honorary trusts, see *supra*, pp. 99-100; Bogert, p. 221.

VI. ENFORCEMENT AND DURATION OF CHARITABLE TRUSTS

A. Enforcement: In a private trust the beneficiary named or designated is the proper person to enforce the trust. By contrast, in a charitable trust the ***Attorney General*** of the State, representing the public, is generally the proper person to enforce such trust.

1. **Those who may not enforce charitable trust:** A suit for the enforcement of a charitable trust ***cannot*** be maintained by:

   a. the settlor;

   b. the settlor's heirs or personal representative;

c. members of the general public; or

d. possible beneficiaries not identifiable as being entitled to a benefit under the trust.

Example: A leaves property in trust for the poor children of Cleveland. No particular poor child may enforce the trust.

2. **Those who may enforce charitable trusts:** In addition to the ***Attorney General***, those who may have a right to enforce a charitable trust are:

a. particular persons entitled to receive a benefit under the trust.

Example: A leaves his home in trust to be used as a residence for the Dean of the Yale Law School. The Dean of the Law School, in office, may enforce the trust.

b. members of an unincorporated association or a small class for whose benefit the trust is created.

Example: A leaves property in trust for the benefit of the Sunlight Chapter of the Daughters of World War II Veterans. Any member of the chapter may maintain a suit to enforce the trust on behalf of herself and of the other members. See co-trustees, *infra*, pp. 188 and 200.

3. **Modern trend:** The modern trend is to enlarge the group that may enforce the trust. In a few cases, a member of the class of potential beneficiaries has been allowed to bring an action on behalf of the whole class.

4. **Doctrine of deviation:** Under the ***doctrine of deviation*** (which is also applicable to private trusts) a trustee may deviate from a term of a charitable trust if compliance is impossible or, due to circumstances not foreseen by the settlor, would prevent accomplishment of the purposes of the trust.

a. **Distinguished from cy pres:** The doctrine of deviation is to be distiguished from the doctrine of cy pres, *infra*, p. 14. The former has to do with the methods of accomplishing the trust purposes, whereas the latter involves applying the trust property to different purposes.

B. **Duration:** A charitable trust may last for an ***indefinite or unlimited*** period.

1. **Successor:** A charitable trust will generally not fail for want of a trustee. If the person named as trustee is unable or unwilling to serve in that capacity, the court will appoint a successor.

2. **When duties personal to particular trustee:** If the duties of the trustee are personal to a particular trustee and that trustee dies or

refuses to serve, the trust will fail.

> **Example:** D lies leaving $300,000 to T in trust for the benefit of such charity as T and D shall select. If T is dead at the time of D's death the trust will fail since no one is left to make the selection.

3. **Statutes of Mortmain:** Many jurisdictions place limitations on charitable trusts in the form of statutes of mortmain. For further discussion on gifts to charity, see *supra*, pp. 31-32.

VII. DOCTRINE OF CY PRES

A. **Definition:** If a settlor establishes a trust for a charitable purpose and evinces both a general charitable intent and an intent to apply the fund to particular charities and it becomes impossible or impracticable to accomplish the latter, the equity court may order that the trust fund be applied to another charity ***"as near as may be"*** to the particular ones designated by the settlor. This is the doctrine of ***judicial cy pres*** and is applied only in charitable trusts.

B. **Common law "prerogative" cy pres:** Common law recognized ***"prerogative" cy pres*** in addition to ***judicial cy pres***. This doctrine allowed the crown to apply the property of a failed charitable trust to any other charitable purpose it might select regardless of how close it was to the settlor's specific purpose. This doctrine ***is not accepted in the United States***.

   1. **Differences:** In ***"prerogative"*** cy pres it is not necessary that there be a finding of general charitable intent or that the property be applied to a purpose like the particular one designated by the settlor. Both are necessary for judicial cy pres.

C. **Modern trend in judicial cy pres:** The modern trend in judicial cy pres is to ***expand the ability*** of the court to choose among several schemes and ***not be limited*** to the one most like that designated by the settlor.

D. **Mere inefficiency not enough:** It is not enough that attainment of the trust's purposes has now become more ***difficult*** or ***inefficient***, due to changes unforeseen by the settlor — the purposes must be shown to have become ***illegal***, ***impossible***, or highly ***impractical***.

> **Example:** T leaves her estate to a charitable trust to be used for Marin County residents. The estate consists of oil stock worth about $7 million at T's death. Subsequently, the value rises to over $400 million and generates an annual income of $30 million. The trustee seeks to expand the trust purposes based on the cy pres doctrine so that income can be spent in other nearby counties.

Held, the purpose of the trust should not be expanded. The cy pres doctrine should not be applied unless the purpose of a trust become illegal, impossible, or impractical. The residents of Marin County have substantial unmet needs which are within the terms of the trust. Therefore, the terms should not be changed merely because the trustees believe that they can spend the income more wisely elsewhere. The fact that philanthropy is inefficient does not mean it is "impractical." *Estate of Buck,* 21 U.S.F.L.Rev. 691 (Super.Ct.Marin County, Cal. 1986).

E. **Termination provision:** If property is given in trust to be applied to a ***particular charitable purpose*** and it is provided in the trust that it is to ***terminate*** if the purpose fails, cy pres ***will not be applied***. The fact that the settlor specifies that the property is to be used for the specific purpose ***"forever"*** or ***"upon condition"*** that it be applied for such purpose, does not preclude the use of cy pres, although it may be ***evidence of the settlor's specific intention***.

F. **General charitable intent:** When the specific trust purposes have failed and the court finds a ***general charitable intent***, the court usually directs that a plan be presented for application of the trust property within the settlor's general charitable intent. In choosing a plan the court will consider the language of the trust as well as other circumstances to achieve the probable choice of the settlor.

1. **When no general charitable intent:** If the court does not find a general charitable intent, a resulting trust in favor of the settlor or settlor's heirs will be raised. For further discussion of resulting trusts, see *supra* p. 96 and *infra*, pp. 118-123.

Example 1: In 1911, Senator Bacon of Georgia executes a will that conveys property in trust to the City of Macon, Georgia for the creation of a public park for the exclusive use of the white people of that city. In his will Senator Bacon states that while he has the kindest feeling for "Negroes," he is of the opinion that in their social relations the races should be forever separate.

The U.S. Supreme Court rules that the park cannot continue to be operated on a racially segregated basis. The Supreme Court of Georgia subsequently holds that Senator Bacon's intention to provide a park for whites only has become impossible to fulfill, that the trust has thus failed, and that the trust property has reverted by operation of Georgia law to Senator Bacon's heirs. Petitioners, black citizens of Macon, contend that this termination of the trust violates the Fourteenth Amendment rights to due process and equal protection. The question presented is thus whether the Georgia

Supreme Court's failure to apply the cy pres doctrine to save the trust by striking the will's racial restrictions and opening the park to all citizens violated petitioners' constitutional rights.

Held, the Georgia Supreme Court's ruling that the trust failed is affirmed. The Georgia courts, construing the language of the testator's will, concluded that Senator Bacon's intent "was not 'general' but extended only to the establishment of a segregated park for the benefit of white people." It was found that racial separation was an inseparable part of Senator Bacon's intent and, in effect, that Senator Bacon would rather have had the whole trust fail than have the park integrated. Under such circumstances, the Georgia Supreme Court had no choice, under long standing and race neutral state trust laws, but to hold the cy pres doctrine inapplicable and terminate the trust. There is no violation of the Fourteenth Amendment when neutral and non-discriminatory state trust laws operate to deprive everyone, whites as well as blacks, of the benefits of a trust. *Evans v. Abney*, 396 U.S. 435 (1970).

Example 2: Wilson devises his estate to a bank as trustee to apply the income for scholarships to young men from X school (a public school) with the highest grades in certain subjects as certified by the school superintendent. In another trust Johnson makes the Board of Education trustee to award scholarships to young men. The trustees of both trusts allege that participation by the school districts violates federal law prohibiting gender discrimination in federally financed education programs.

Held, in the Wilson trust, the Court, exercising its cy pres power, strikes the clause requiring the district's certification. Candidates may apply directly for the scholarships. In the Johnson trust, the trustee is replaced by a private trustee who will carry out the trust as written. A court cannot invoke its cy pres doctrine unless the testator's specific purpose can no longer be performed. The specific purpose of the trust is the education of male students. So long as the named schools graduate males with the requisite qualifications, the purpose is not "impossible or impracticable." Although there is strong public policy favoring equal treatment of men and women, the gender-based limitation on beneficiaries of a private charitable trust is not illegal. In fact many trusts bestow their benefits exclusively on women. Those trusts would be unlawful if the present trusts were held illegal. Presently the trusts cannot be performed because the school districts will not cooperate. That impediment can be remedied by using the court's general equity power over all trusts to eliminate the necessity for action by the school districts. *Estate of Wilson*, 452 N.E.2d 1228 (N.Y. 1983).

Note: The state would violate the Equal Protection Clause of the Fourteenth Amendment of the U.S. Constitution if it awarded scholarships that are gender restrictive. But *Wilson*, *supra*, involved only ***private discrimination***, which the state has no affirmative obligation to prevent. By enforcing the trust, the state does not discriminate, compel another to discriminate, or allow another to assume a state function and discriminate. The court's decision facilitates the administration of the trusts; it does not enforce their discriminatory provisions.

G. Consent not necessary: Cy pres may be ordered without the consent of either the settlor, if living, or the trustee.

H. Surplus remaining: When the charitable purpose to which trust property is to be applied is accomplished with a ***surplus remaining***, the court will usually direct the surplus to be applied to a charitable purpose which falls within the settlor's general intent.

I. Causes for failure of charitable purpose: Frequent ***causes for failure*** of specific charitable purposes are:

1. amount of property insufficient for the purpose;
2. specific purpose already accomplished;
3. third person whose consent is necessary ***refuses to give it***;

    Example: A gift of a historical house in trust is to be open to the public if the town consents to maintain it. If the town refuses consent, the gift will fail as to the specific charitable purpose.

4. useless purpose;
5. illegality;
6. gift to a corporation that is incapable of becoming a trust beneficiary;
7. impracticality of specific site; or
8. particular purpose impractical due to changed circumstances;

    Example: A gift to establish an orphanage when orphanages are no longer considered a sociologically sound way of caring for parentless children, would be an impractical purpose due to changed circumstances.

RESULTING TRUSTS

I. GENERAL PRINCIPLES

A. Definition: A resulting trust arises when: (1) property is disposed of (2) under circumstances that raise an unrebutted inference (3) that the transferor does not intend the transferee to have the beneficial interest therein and (4) such beneficial interest is not disposed of otherwise. In such cases the person holding the beneficial interest is not entitled to it; the interest therefore ***"results"*** to the transferor. The person having legal title holds it in a ***"resulting trust"*** for such transferor. See *supra*, p. 97.

B. Purpose: The resulting trust attempts to do with the property ***what it is presumed the transferor would have wanted*** had he anticipated the situation.

C. Elements: A resulting trust is similar to an express private trust except that the ***intention is inferred*** from the circumstances instead of being expressed, and has the following four elements: (1) an ***inferred intention*** to create the trust; (2) a ***trustee***; (3) a trust ***res***; and (4) a ***beneficiary***.

D. Distinguished from constructive trust: A resulting trust should be distinguished from a constructive trust. A constructive trust is not based on the settlor's intent, but is rather an attempt by the court to correct fraud. A resulting trust is based on the settlor's ***presumed*** or ***implied intent***. For further discussion of constructive trusts, see *infra*, pp. 96-97.

E. When it arises: A resulting trust arises in three general situations:

1. when an ***express trust fails***;

    Example: S conveys land to T to hold in trust for C. Without S's knowledge C has predeceased the conveyance to T. The express trust fails for want of a beneficiary. T holds the land in resulting trust for the settlor, S. See Rest. of Trusts, 2d §411.

2. when an ***express trust does not use or exhaust*** all of the trust property;

    Example 1: S transfers $100,000 in trust to pay Bonnie $1000 a month from principal during her life and makes no further disposition. Bonnie dies after having received $25,000. The trustee holds the unexpended funds in a resulting trust for S.

Example 2: S conveys land to T in trust for the purpose of selling it and paying S's creditors in full. S owes X, Y and Z each $1,000. T sells the land for $5,000. After the creditors are paid in full, T still has $2,000 from the sale. T holds this $2,000 in a resulting trust for S. See Rest. of Trusts, 2d §430.

3. **Purchase money resulting trust:** when property is purchased and paid for by one person and title is taken in the name of another. Here, a resulting trust arises in favor of the person who pays the money. This is usually referred to as a ***"purchase money resulting trust."***

Example: A, B and C each pays $1,000 to X for certain land. X is instructed to and makes the deed to T as grantee. T holds one-third of the land in resulting trust for A, one-third for B and one-third for C. This is true whether the payment is made in money, goods, credit or anything else of value. See Rest. of Trusts, 2d §440.

F. **Passive trust:** A resulting trust is always a ***dry, naked or passive trust***. The trustee has ***no active duty to perform*** except that he must ***transfer the legal title to the trust property to the person entitled to it*** (*supra*, pp. 72, 76).

G. **Statute of Frauds:** The ***Statute of Frauds*** has ***no application*** to the creation of a resulting trust. A resulting trust's existence can be proved by parol evidence showing: (1) the ***failure of an express trust***; (2) the ***performance*** of an express trust without exhausting the trust property; or (3) that a ***conveyance has been made*** to one person and the consideration therefor has been paid by another.

1. **Transfer of equitable interest in land:** A transfer by the beneficiary of his equitable interest in land held for him in resulting trust must comply with the Statute of Frauds.

Example: T holds land in resulting trust for S. S makes an oral agreement to sell his equitable interest in the land to P. P seeks specific performance and S sets up as a defense the Statute of Frauds. The defense is valid. The equitable title held by S is an interest in land, the transfer of which requires a writing signed by S to be enforceable. See Rest. of Trusts, 2d §407, Comment c.

2. **Purchase money resulting trust:** A purchase money resulting trust may be extinguished by parol, but resulting trusts of land which arise from failure of an express trust, or performance of an express trust without exhausting the trust property, require ***compliance*** with the Statute of Frauds to be extinguished. That is, these two types of trusts can only be extinguished by a writing signed by all beneficiaries.

H. Intention to give away property for specific purpose only: If a gratuitous transfer of property is made to a trustee and the express trust fails or does not exhaust the trust property, the resulting trust is based on the theory that the ***grantor did not intend to give away his property except for the purpose for which the express trust was created***.

> **Example:** S transfers land to T in trust for C. C disclaims any interest in the property. This causes failure of the express trust for lack of a beneficiary. It is inferred that S intended to transfer his property only for C; therefore if C will not or does not take, T holds in resulting trust for S. The express trust is created by a deed in writing. The resulting trust is created by the ***inferred intention*** and need not comply with the Statute of Frauds. See Rest. of Trusts, 2d §411.

II. SPECIAL PROBLEMS

A. Applicability of cy pres doctrine: When a charitable trust fails, a resulting trust will be inferred only if the doctrine of cy pres is found not to apply. See *First Univ. Soc. of Bath v. Swett*, 90 A.2d 812 (Me. 1952). For further discussion of the cy pres doctrine, see *supra*, pp. 114-117, and *infra*, p. 150.

B. Public policy against wrongdoers: If the settlor creates an express trust for an ***illegal purpose*** and it fails for this reason, a resulting trust does not arise if the policy against giving relief to a person who has committed an illegal act outweighs the policy against unjust enrichment. Rest. of Trusts, 2d §422.

> **Example:** Settlor conveys money to a trustee to defraud his creditors or the government. The court will not infer a resulting trust, because this would reward settlor or his heirs for his wrongful act. See Rest. of Trusts, 2d §444; *Stone v. Lobsien*, 247 P.2d 357 (Cal. App. 1952).

1. **Illegality after creation:** A private trust, lawful when created, may become illegal due to a ***change in law***. This terminates the trust, and the settlor or his heirs are entitled to a return of the property.

> **Example:** The beneficiaries of a trust are aliens. During a war, a law is enacted which provides for seizure of property of enemy aliens by the Attorney General. Since the beneficiaries are now enemy aliens, they may not benefit from the trust, so a resulting trust will be inferred for the benefit of the settlor. *In re Solbrig's Will*, 96 N.W.2d 97 (Wisc. 1959).

C. When express trust fails and consideration has been paid: A resulting trust will not be raised in favor of a ***grantor who has been***

paid for the trust property.

> **Example:** T wishes to establish a trust in certain land, which is owned by S, for T's son, C. T pays S $5,000 for the land and has the deed made to "T in trust for C." C rejects the trust entirely, which causes the express trust to fail. T holds the land for his own benefit and not in resulting trust for S, because T has paid for the property so S has no right either to the $5,000 or to the equitable interest in the land.

D. Rebutting inference in purchase money cases: The inference that a resulting trust arises when one person takes title and another pays the purchase price is ***rebutted*** if the person paying the purchase price ***manifests the intention*** that ***no resulting trust shall arise***. Parol evidence is admissible to show such intention even if the property transferred is land and the Statute of Frauds is in force. Rest. of Trusts, 2d §441; Bogert, p. 269.

1. **Ways in which intention may be shown:** A number of situations serve to rebut the inference that a resulting trust was intended. Thus, if A pays the purchase price of Blackacre to V and has title conveyed to B, a resulting trust does ***not*** arise in A if:

   a. A pays as a ***loan*** to B;

   b. A pays in ***discharge of a debt*** to B;

   c. A pays as a ***gift*** to B;

   d. A pays in ***discharge of a debt to a third party***; or

   e. A pays as a ***loan*** to a ***third party***.

E. Family relationship: If the transferee is the wife, child, or other natural object of the payor's bounty, the presumption is that a ***gift was intended***. This presumption can be rebutted by showing that no gift was intended. Parol evidence is admissible to show that no gift was intended, even if the property transferred is land and the Statute of Frauds is in effect. *Watkins v. Watkins*, 142 A.2d 6 (Pa. 1958).

> **Example:** H purchases land from V and has title conveyed to W, his wife. W orally agrees to hold the land in trust for their son, C. Normally, H will be presumed to have intended to make a gift to W. But the presumption of gift to W can be rebutted by evidence of the oral trust. If such rebutting evidence is produced, a resulting trust (or in some circumstances a constructive trust) arises. Rest. of Trusts, 2d §442.

1. **Husbands and parents:** At common law, husbands and parents were not considered natural objects of bounty, and no presumption of gift arose when property was conveyed to them. But modern decisions accept the presumption of a gift. *Peterson v. Massey*, 53

N.W.2d 912 (Neb. 1952).

F. **When only part of purchase price paid by resulting trust claimant:** If a ***part of the purchase price*** is paid by the resulting trust claimant he is presumed to have intended a trust in a proportionate part of the property to the extent of his contribution to the purchase price. See Rest. of Trusts, 2d §454; Bogert, p. 266.

1. **Agreement to the contrary:** The parties may agree that the person paying part of the price is entitled to more or less than his proportionate share. When the agreement is enforceable (i.e., no Statute of Frauds violation exists) there is a ***resulting trust to the extent of the specific interest agreed upon***. Rest. of Trusts, 2d §454.

   a. **Agreement is unenforceable and purports to give payor more than his proportionate share:** If the agreement grants the payor more than his proportionate share but is unenforceable due to a violation of the Statute of Frauds, the payor is entitled ***only to his proportionate share***.

   Example: A pays one-half the purchase price for a conveyance of land to B. A and B orally agree that A is to have a three-quarters undivided interest. B holds one-half the property on a resulting trust for A and one-half free of trust. The oral agreement is unenforceable because of the Statute of Frauds.

   b. **When agreement is unenforceable but manifests payor's intention to take less than his proportionate share:** Even if unenforceable due to the Statute of Frauds, an oral agreement that the payor will take less than his proportionate share serves to ***cut down the payor's share*** to the agreed upon amount. "In such a case, the ***inference*** that he intended to acquire a fractional interest proportionate to his contribution to the purchase price is in part rebutted." Rest. of Trusts, 2d §454, Comments g-i.

   Example: A pays one-half the purchase price for a conveyance to B. A and B orally agree that A is to have a one-quarter interest. B holds one-quarter on a resulting trust and three-quarters free of trust. The oral agreement may be used to rebut the presumption of resulting trust in half.

2. **Aliquot share of purchase price:** A few jurisdictions hold that a resulting trust claimant must either pay the entire purchase price or a part that represents an ***aliquot share*** of the purchase price. "Aliquot share" has been held in different jurisdictions to mean:

a. capable of being divided into the total price without leaving a remainder or

b. "a particular fraction of the whole as distinguished from a general contribution to the purchase money." *Skehill v. Abbott*, 184 Mass. 145, 68 N.E. 37 (1903).

G. Purchase money resulting trusts abolished in some jurisdictions: A number of jurisdictions have ***abolished*** the purchase money resulting trust by statute, because it has the effect of ***rendering land titles uncertain***.

CONSTRUCTIVE TRUSTS

I. GENERALLY

A. Nature of constructive trust as remedy: The constructive trust is a ***remedy created by courts of equity*** to obtain title from a person who ought not to have it, and force him to convey it to the one who should have it.

1. **Not intent-enforcing:** The constructive trust is not ***"intent-enforcing."*** It is ***"fraud rectifying."*** See Bogert, pp. 287-290.

   Note: Compare the theory of a constructive trust with that of a resulting trust which enforces a presumpton of intent. See *supra*, p. 118.

2. **Created by court orders:** A constructive trust is created by the court's decree that a ***wrong-doer holds property as a constructive trustee***.

   Example: T by fraud induces C to convey C's Blackacre to T for no consideration. T holds legal title to Blackacre and C has only a cause of action against T. T can cut off C's equity by selling and conveying Blackacre to a bona fide purchaser. If C sues T in equity prior to any such conveyance the equity court will enter a decree that T is holding title to Blackacre as a constructive trustee for C. The constructive trust comes into existence when the court of equity makes its decree. Because such a "construed" trust is always dry or passive, the court orders legal title transferred to the injured party.

II. COMMON APPLICATIONS

A. Introduction: A constructive trust may be decreed by a court having equitable jurisdiction in any situation in which one person is holding title to property which rightfully belongs to another. Common instances include the following:

1. ***title to property*** is obtained by fraud, duress, mistake or undue influence;

2. a person murders another in order to ***inherit the victim's property***;

3. one ***takes property*** from a trustee with notice of the trust;

4. a grantee obtains property by ***absolute deed on an oral promise to hold in trust*** and the oral trust is ***voidable*** under the Statute of Frauds;

5. a person obtains a gift ***by will or intestacy on an oral promise to hold in trust for another***;

6. one is holding property by reason of a ***breach of fiduciary duty***.

B. **Fraud or mistake:** Fraud or mistake may be the basis for a constructive trust.

> **Example:** S agrees to sell and P agrees to buy Blackacre from S for $5,000. P pays the money and S executes a deed to P but by mistake describes both Whiteacre and Blackacre. Title to Whiteacre is then in P by mistake when it should have remained in S. Note three elements: (1) title to Whiteacre is in P; (2) if permitted to keep it, P will be unjustly enriched; and (3) it is inequitable for P to retain title to Whiteacre. On these facts S may have a decree in equity making P a constructive trustee of Whiteacre and ordering its reconveyance to S.

C. **Murder:** If a person ***murders*** his ancestor or testator and as a result receives title to property, the ***murderer holds the property in constructive trust*** for whomever would otherwise take the property. See also *supra*, p. 23.

> **Example:** T makes his will giving $10,000 in United States government bonds to M and the residue of his property to C. M murders T and the title to the bonds comes to M. But M cannot profit by his own wrong. The legacy in favor of M will be treated as though it were revoked. M holds the bonds in constructive trust for the residuary legatee.

1. **Contrary cases:** There are many cases which hold to the contrary. Thus, it has been held that a murderer is not barred from inheriting from his victim ***except*** where by statute such limitation is imposed. See *Bird v. Plunckett*, 139 Conn. 491, 95 A.2d 71 (1953).

D. **Obtaining property with notice of trust:** When the ***trustee of an express trust wrongfully transfers the trust property to a third person who knows of the trust***, such third person holds the property in constructive trust for the beneficiary of the express trust.

> **Example:** T holds United States government bonds in trust for C. The terms of the trust prohibit T's disposing of such bonds. In breach of trust T transfers the bonds to X who knows about the trust but pays T full value for the bonds. C may in equity compel X to hold the bonds in constructive trust for C. The reason is that having taken with notice, X is not a bona fide purchaser. It is inequitable for X to hold the bonds for himself as against C even though X paid full value for them. For a discussion concerning the tracing of trust funds,

see *infra*, pp. 204-05.

E. Oral promise to hold in trust: When property is conveyed to a person who ***orally promises*** to hold it in trust for a third person but who later refuses to carry out the trust, claiming that the trust is voidable under the Statute of Frauds, a constructive trust for the benefit of such third person may be imposed.

1. **Traditional majority rule:** The majority rule is that a ***constructive trust will not be decreed*** either for the grantor or the intended beneficiary if to do so would circumvent the Statute of Frauds.

   Example: T conveys property to D, his brother, by a deed that is absolute on its face. Parol evidence demonstrates that there was an oral agreement that D would hold the property in trust for the use and benefit of T and his heirs. Acknowledging that the parol evidence is inadmissible under the Statute of Frauds to prove the existence of the trust, T's heirs claim that such evidence is admissible to establish D's fraud in refusing to execute the trust.

   Held, against T's heirs. While parol evidence would be admissible to prove fraud in the procurement of the conveyance (which is not alleged here), it is not admissible for the purposes of this case. For the parol evidence to establish that D committed fraud by refusing to execute the trust, it would first have to establish the existence of the trust. As the latter is clearly prohibited by the Statute of Frauds, to allow the former would constitute an indirect violation of the statute. *Rasdall's Administrators v. Rasdall*, 9 Wis. 379 (1859).

   a. **Exceptions:** Exceptions to this rule have developed. Courts adhering to the traditional majority rule generally decree a constructive trust when any of the following is true:

      i. ***there is actual fraud at the time of the promise*** (i.e., the grantee obtains the property by misrepresentation as to his intended performance of the trust);

      ii. ***the transfer is made in contemplation of death***. Rest. of Trusts, 2d §44; *Harrington v. Harrington*, 448 P.2d 364 (Ore. 1968); or

      iii. the grantee is in a ***confidential relationship with the grantor***; see Bogert, pp. 302-08.

      Example: T deeds lands to her eldest daughter and the latter's husband to be held in trust for the benefit of all of T's children under an oral understanding. T dies and the trustees repudiate the oral agreement, claiming the property for themselves. At issue is whether a constructive trust should be placed on the property in favor of T's children, as beneficiaries.

Held, for T's children. "The underlying principle of a constructive trust is the equitable prevention of unjust enrichment which arises from fraud or the abuse of a confidential relationship." In the instant case the Statute of Frauds prevents the enforcement of the express agreement between the parties because the understanding was not put in writing. Parol evidence, however, is relevant and admissible to show that the grantees have been unjustly enriched by their repudiation of the agreement. As such evidence demonstrates that the grantees were unjustly enriched by abusing a confidential relationship, a constructive trust should be imposed. *Masino v. Sechrest*, 66 N.W.2d 740 (Wisc. 1954). See also *Person v. Pagnotta*, 541 P.2d 483 (Ore. 1975).

2. **Traditional minority view:** Some jurisdictions will enforce a constructive trust in favor of the intended beneficiary when the grantee would otherwise be unjustly enriched. See Bogert, pp. 302-08.

   a. **Modern cases:** Many modern cases adopt the traditional minority view and do not require a ***showing of fraud or confidential relationship but only unjust enrichment***.

3. **Promise implied from facts:** Where there is a confidential relationship between the parties, in all courts an express promise to hold in trust is not necessarily required. A promise may be ***implied*** in order to prevent unjust enrichment.

Example: P, a widower, develops a very close relationship with D. P is a farmer with an eighth grade education and D is a school teacher. D assists P with his wife's estate and performs domestic tasks for him. P executes a deed transferring ownership of his farm to D. D then moves onto the farm with P and orders P to vacate the premises. D does not at any time expressly promise P that D will hold the farm in trust for P. P sues to recover the farm.

Held, a constructive trust is declared for P's benefit. A constructive trust may be placed on property transferred in reliance upon a confidential relationship. A promise may be implied from the transaction itself. P transferred the only land he owned to D. While there was no express promise to hold for P's benefit, such a promise is superfluous in view of the relationship between the parties. P would not have conveyed his farm, which was his home and means of earning a living, without at least the tacit consent of D to permit P to continue to live on and operate the farm. A constructive trust will be imposed if D received a benefit the retention of which would be unjust. *Sharp v. Kosmalski*, 351 N.E.2d 721 (N.Y. 1976).

a. **Promise implied by law:** One ***unmarried cohabitant*** may raise claims based upon unjust enrichment following the termination of the relationship, if the other attempts to retain an unreasonable amount of the property acquired through the efforts of both. In such a situation the court may impose a constructive trust to prevent unjust enrichment. *Watts v. Watts*, 405 N.W.2d 303 (Wisc. 1987).

F. **Inherit by making oral promises:** Whenever a person obtains property by ***will or intestacy*** because the decedent in making a will or remaining intestate relied upon his ***promise to hold the property in trust for another***, he holds it in constructive trust for the intended beneficiary. The essential elements are:

1. **express or implied promise** to hold in trust by the donee; and
2. **reliance by the decedent.**

Example: D asks his brother T if he will hold Blackacre in trust for their parents M and F, and at the death of the survivor, distribute it to all D's nephews and nieces, then living. T agrees to do so. A then executes a will and bequeaths Blackacre to T and dies. T will be compelled to hold the property upon a constructive trust for M and F and D's nephews and nieces. This is sometimes referred to as a secret trust. See Rest. of Trusts, 2d §55.

Note: This cites the position adopted by a majority of the cases and the Restatement of Trusts, 2d. Other courts have held it a violation of the Statute of Wills to raise a constructive trust in such cases.

G. **Breach of fiduciary duty:** If a fiduciary obtains property in a transaction with the person to whom he owes a fiduciary duty ***without full disclosure and utmost good faith*** he may be holding the property as a constructive trustee for such person.

Example: A director of a corporation purchases property from the corporation with the knowledge, which he does not disclose, that it is to be appropriated for a highway. He will hold the property as a constructive trustee for the corporation.

H. **Theft or conversion not a basis for constructive trust:** A constructive trust ***cannot*** be based on a ***theft or a conversion*** as the thief or converter does not acquire title through his wrong.

Example: D steal P's lumber. P cannot sue D in equity to make him a constructive trustee as the theft cannot lodge the legal title to the property in D. Such title is still in P and his remedy is in law in an action in replevin to get back the lumber in specie, or in trover for its value.

CREATION, MODIFICATION AND TERMINATION OF TRUSTS

I. METHODS OF CREATING TRUSTS

A. Introduction: A trust may be created in any of the following ways:

1. declaration of trust;
2. transfer in trust, either
   a. ***inter vivos*** or
   b. ***by will***;
3. exercise of a power of appointment;
4. contractual agreement
5. statute.

The method used for creating the trust will depend upon the ***relationship of the settlor to the property interest*** which is to constitute the trust res.

B. Declaration of trust: A trust is created by a ***declaration of trust*** when the owner of property ***declares*** that he holds it in trust for the benefit of another.

> **Example:** S is the owner of 100 shares of stock. S declares himself trustee of the shares for the benefit of B. S is trustee for B.

1. **No need for a transfer of title:** In the case of a declaration of trust there is no need for a transfer of title since the settlor already has legal title and an oral declaration is usually sufficient to transfer equitable title. But an oral declaration may be ineffective as to land. For a further discussion of the requirement of a writing and the Statute of Frauds, see *infra*, pp. 134-36.

2. **Conveying property to settlor as trustee:** When the owner of property executes an instrument conveying property to himself as trustee the instrument has the ***same effect as if he had declared himself trustee***.

> **Example:** S, the owner of certain land, executes, acknowledges and records a deed in statutory form conveying it to S as trustee for B. S is the trustee of the property for B.

C. Transfer in trust: A trust is created when ***property is transferred in trust to a trustee*** for the benefit of a third person or of the settlor.

Example 1: S is the owner of certain land. He conveys it to T in trust for the benefit of B. Legal title is passed to T as trustee for B, to whom equitable title has passed. There is no interest left in the settlor S.

Example 2: S is the owner of certain land. He conveys it to T in trust for S. Legal title is passed to T as trustee for S, who has retained equitable title.

1. **Types:** A transfer in trust may be either by ***deed***, called an ***inter vivos or living trust***, or by ***will***, called a ***testamentary trust***.

D. **Exercise of a power of appointment:** A person holding a ***general power of appointment*** may appoint to anyone including himself or his estate. He can create a trust by appointment to a person as trustee for himself or for others.

1. **Special power of appointment:** A person holding a ***special power of appointment*** can only appoint among particular persons or classes or persons. He can create a trust by appointment to a trustee for the benefit of such persons, depending upon the intent of the donor of the special power of appointment.

Example 1: D devises real property to S for life with a testamentary power of appointment in S to appoint the remainder among A, B, and C in such shares and interests as S shall determine. S appoints to T in trust for A and B during their joint lives and on the death of the first to convey to the survivor. A trust is created. The exercise of the special power of appointment is within S's power because it is to be inferred that S is to have the same power of disposition in making the appointment as he would have in property he owns outright, so long as the donor has not instructed him to the contrary.

Example 2: D devises real property to S for life with a power to appoint the remainder outright among A, B, and C. S may not appoint to T in trust for A, B, and C. The testator has manifested the intention that the property pass outright.

See Rest. of Trusts, 2d §17, comment f.

E. **Contractual agreement:** Trusts may be created by various kinds of contractual arrangement:

1. The ***insured under an insurance policy*** who has the right to change or designate the beneficiary directs the beneficiary to hold the proceeds in trust for a third person.

2. " . . . a person makes an enforceable promise to pay money or to make a conveyance of property to another person as trustee thereby creating a present trust . . . , the rights of the promisee being held

by him as trustee," provided there is an intention to create a present trust. Rest. of Trusts, 2d §26, Comment n.

> **Example:** For consideration of $10,000, A promises by written agreement to convey certain land to B in trust for C. B thereby holds in trust for C, the right to specific performance of the agreement as well as the right to damages if A breaks his promise. Rest. of Trusts, 2d. §26, Comment n, Illustration.

F. Statutes: Statutes may provide for the creation of trusts in various instances. In the case of ***wrongful death*** the statute often provides that a right of action exists in the widow or executor of the decedent. Any recovery, however, is to be held in trust for designated beneficiaries.

II. CAPACITY TO CREATE A TRUST

A. Same as capacity to transfer outright. The capacity required in the settlor to create a trust is that which would be required for the transfer of the same property outright.

1. **Declaration of trust:** A settlor must have ***capacity to make an inter vivos transfer of legal title*** to the trust property if he declares himself the trustee of property for the benefit of another.

2. **Inter vivos trust:** A settlor must have ***capacity to make an inter vivos transfer of legal title*** to the trust property to the trustee in order to make a tranfer in trust.

3. **Testamentary trust:** A settlor must have ***testamentary capacity*** to create a trust by will.

III. CONSIDERATION IN TRUST CREATION

A. Consideration: ***No consideration is necessary*** to create a valid trust. In fact, most trusts are gratuitous. Thus lack of consideration does not render a trust unenforceable or revocable. Bogert, p. 65.

B. Present declaration of trust as to chattels: Thus a present declaration of trust as to ***personal property*** is valid and enforceable without any consideration.

> **Example:** T is owner of some sheep, a promissory note signed by X, and a one year lease on certain land. T orally declares himself trustee of all of such property ***here and now*** for the benefit of C. C can enforce the trust.

C. Present trust of real property: Similarly, an owner of ***real property*** can create a trust of such property by his declaration or by a conveyance, even though it is unsupported by consideration. However, the declaration or conveyance must comply with the ***Statute of Frauds***.

Example 1: By a writing signed by T, owner of Blackacre, T gratuitously declares, "I hereby make myself trustee of Blackacre for the benefit of C and his heirs." Even though T received nothing of value in exchange for the writing, there is a trust enforceable by C.

Example 2: S, owner of Blackacre, executes a deed and delivers it "to T and his heirs in trust for C." The trust is valid and enforceable by C even though S received no consideration.

D. **Promise to create a trust in the future:** But a promise to create a trust to ***take effect in the future*** is ***unenforceable unless it is supported by consideration*** of the sort required for a contract.

Example: T owns 10 cows. T gratuitously promises C that beginning one week from now he, T, will hold such cows in trust for C. There is no enforceable trust and no enforceable contract, due to lack of consideration of the sort that would be required for a contract. For a trust to exist it must be complete and the trustee must have presently enforceable duties to perform.

1. **Contract to create trust:** If valuable consideration *is* given in exchange for the promise to create a trust, then the promise is enforceable. The consideration is the same as that required for an enforceable contract. "Love and affection," or a duty to support, are not sufficient consideration in most states. Bogert, pp. 67-68.

IV. NOTICE TO AND ACCEPTANCE BY TRUSTEE AND BENEFICIARY

A. **Beneficiary:** It is ***not necessary*** that the ***beneficiary*** have ***notice*** of the creation of a trust, or that he ***accept*** it.

B. **Trustee:** It is ***not necessary*** that the ***trustee*** have notice of the creation of a trust, or that he accept the trust.

C. **Disclaimers:** Either the trustee or the beneficiary may ***disclaim*** his interest if he has not by words or conduct manifested acceptance of the trust. Disclaimers are retroactive to the date of creation of the trust.

V. PAROL EVIDENCE RULE

A. **Generally:** If a written document evidences the transfer of legal title to property a ***question*** may arise as to the ***admissibility of extrinsic evidence to show that the transferor intended (or did not intend) to create a trust***. Under the parol evidence rule, when the writing is adopted by the settlor as a ***complete expression*** of his intention, extrinsic evidence (absent fraud, duress or mistake) is not admissible to contradict or vary the writing. If the meaning of the writing is ***unclear or ambiguous***, extrinsic evidence may be admitted to determine its interpretation (*supra*, p. 54).

B. **Specific applications:** As applied to trusts the parol evidence rule operates as follows:

1. **Writing declares nontrust intent:** If the writing provides that the transferee is to take the property for his ***own benefit***, parol evidence is ***not admissible*** to show that the transferee was intended to hold the property in trust. Such evidence would vary or contradict the writing and circumvent the Statute of Frauds.

   Example: Property is given "to X for her own use and benefit." Parol evidence is not admissible to show that the donor intended that X hold the property in trust for another.

2. **Writing declares trust intent:** If the writing provides that the transferee is to hold the property ***in trust for a particular purpose***, parol evidence is ***not admissible*** to show that the transferee was intended ***not*** to hold the property in trust, or to hold the property for some ***different purpose***.

   Example: Property is given "to T in trust for A." T may not present oral evidence that he is to take as beneficial owner. Similarly, B may not show that he is to be a beneficiary together with A.

3. **Writing silent or ambiguous:** If the writing does not make it clear whether the transferee is to take the property for his own benefit or to hold it in trust, most courts ***allow*** parol evidence to show that the transferee was intended to hold the property in trust either for the transferor or for a third party. This does not contradict the writing, but only supplements the incomplete writing.

4. **Writing by owner:** When the owner of property by a writing has stated that he holds property in trust, parol evidence may not be admitted to show that he intended to hold free of trust or for a different trust.

VI. THE REQUIREMENT OF A WRITING: THE STATUTE OF FRAUDS

A. **Generally:** An enforceable trust can be created without a writing unless otherwise provided by statute.

B. **Oral trusts of personal property:** An oral trust of ***personal property*** is valid and enforceable in most jurisdications.

C. **Trusts of real property:** But almost all jurisdictions have statutory provisions requiring that express trusts of ***real property*** be evidenced by a ***signed writing***.

1. **Basis for statutes:** Statutes requiring a writing for the enforcement of a trust in land are usually based on the English Statute of Frauds of 1677, which required that an express trust of real property be ***"manifested and proved"*** by a writing signed by the party enabled to declare such a trust. If there was no such writing, the alleged trust was ***"utterly void and of none effect."***

   a. **Applicability of other statutes requiring writings:** In states that have not set out Statute of Frauds provisions with respect to trusts, statutes requiring a writing either in the case of a contract as to land or a conveyance of land have been held applicable to the creation of a trust in land.

2. **Applicability of Statute of Frauds:** The Statute of Frauds applies to both:

   a. ***declarations of trust*** and

   b. ***transfers in trust***.

3. **Oral trusts of land merely voidable:** The Statute of Frauds has been construed to make oral trusts of land only ***voidable not void***. Only the trustee has standing to set up the Statute of Frauds. No other person may do so. Therefore, the trustee may perform the oral trust, but may not be forced to do so.

4. **No special form for writing:** To satisfy the Statute of Frauds the memorandum ***does not need to be in any special form***. The only requirements are that it be ***signed*** and that it contain the ***essential terms*** of the trust: a description of the ***trust property***, the ***beneficiaries*** and the ***purpose***. It must be signed:

   a. in the case of a ***declaration of trust***—by the owner of the property prior to, at the time of, or subsequent to the declaration of trust (but prior to any transfer of the interest to a third party);

   b. in the case of a ***transfer in trust***—

      i. by the transferor prior to or at the time of the transfer and

      ii. by the transferee prior to, at the time of or subsequent to the transfer, but prior to any transfer to a third party.

      Note: The requirements of the Statute of Frauds are satisfied by the execution of the writing. If the writing is later lost or destroyed, parol evidence is admissible to establish the contents of the writing. Rest. of Trusts, 2d §49.

5. **Minority rule:** A minority of states has held that the Statute of Frauds requires that the trust be created by a writing, not merely

proved by it. In these jurisdictions a memorandum prepared after the transfer of the property would be insufficient. See Rest. of Trusts, 2d §40.

6. **Part performance of an oral trust of real property:** ***Part performance*** by the trustee of an oral trust concerning real property may take it out of the Statute of Frauds in some jurisdictions. Such part performance may consist of:

   a. **Possession:** the trustee's ***delivering possession*** of the land to the beneficiary. (This is sufficient in some jurisdictions; other jurisdictions require possession plus some other act, such as making repairs or paying taxes.)

   b. **Improvements:** the trustee's permitting the beneficiary to make ***valuable improvements*** on the land; or

   c. **Detrimental change of position:** any act of the beneficiary, done in ***reliance*** on the trust and with the trustee's consent, that irrevocably changes the beneficiary's position.

VII. TRUSTS AND THE STATUTE OF WILLS

A. **Definition of testamentary trusts:** A trust is testamentary when the ***transfer*** in trust becomes ***effective only upon and by reason of the death of the settlor***.

> **Example:** S executes and delivers to T a deed transferring to T in trust for B such shares of stock as S shall own at his death. No trust is created either at the time of the deed or at S's death.

1. **Not testamentary when interest in beneficiary created during settlor's lifetime:** An inter vivos trust in which the settlor reserves a life interest with the power to revoke, alter, modify or control the administration of the trust during his life, does not become testamentary if an interest is created in a beneficiary during the settlor's lifetime. The mere fact that the beneficiary's enjoyment is postponed does not make the trust testamentary. See *Farkas v. Williams*, *supra*, pp. 85-86.

B. **Requirements for creation of testamentary trusts:** Only a ***valid*** will (one that complies with the Statute of Wills) can create a ***testamentary trust*** of either real or personal property. It is ***not*** necessary that the will ***name a trustee***; a trustee will be appointed by the court if necessary.

1. **Ascertainability of trust elements:** To comply with the Statute of Wills all of the elements of the testamentary trust (intention to create a trust, purposes of trust, identification of beneficiaries and trust res) must be ascertainable either:

a. from the face of the will; or

b. from the face of the will and from an existing document properly incorporated by reference; and/or

c. from facts which have independent significance apart from the intended testamentary disposition. See *supra*, p. 51.

C. **Secret trusts:** The term ***"secret trust"*** describes the situation where property is devised to a person without any indication on the instrument of transfer that the property is to be held in trust for another. Courts usually admit extrinsic evidence of the promise to hold in trust. If the court is convinced that the decedent has ***relied*** on the legatee's or devisee's promise to hold the property in trust for another, the court will impose a constructive trust to ***prevent unjust enrichment.***

> **Example:** Testator leaves Blackacre to Dave, Testator's lawyer, in Testator's will. Steve, Testator's son, offers evidence in court that before Testator wrote his will, he said to Dave, "If I leave Blackacre to you, will you promise to hold it in trust for the use of my son Steve?" and that Dave responded, "Yes". The court will hear this extrinsic evidence. If the court believes the evidence, the court will impose a constructive trust, by which Dave will be ordered to hold the property for Steve's benefit. (The court cannot find an ***express*** trust to exist, because the Statute of Wills does not allow oral modification of the clear terms of a will.)

1. **Semi-secret trust:** In another scenario, the will indicates that the property is to be held in trust, but the benficiary of the trust is not named. Such a ***"semi-secret"*** trust is ***not recognized*** in most jurisdictions, and the assets go into a resulting trust for the benefit of the testator's heirs.

> **Example:** T devises the residue of her estate to X, to distribute in his discretion so as "to carry out wishes which I have expressed to him or may express to him." X states that T said the money was to be used for poor, aged, infirm and needy persons at St. Stephen's Mission, which X operates. T's heirs contend that the trust is too indefinite to be carried out.
>
> *Held,* the trust is not valid. The beneficiaries of the trust are not named in the will and may not be established by extrinsic (parol) evidence. If T wanted property to go to persons other than her heirs she should have named them in her will. X was named trustee and T's heirs were neither specifically excluded nor were others named as beneficiaries. Therefore, the heirs should have the benefit of the intestate succession laws. *Olliffe v. Wells*, 130 Mass. 221 (1881).

Note: But some states, and Rest. of Trusts, 2d §55, have adopted the English view, by which semi-secret trusts are ***enforced***. See, e.g., *Linney v. Cleveland Trust Co.*, 165 N.E. 101 (Ohio App. 1928); *In re Hartman's Estate (No. 2)*, 182 A. 232 (Pa. 1936).

VIII. PROHIBITED TRUST PURPOSES

A. Trusts for illegal purposes prohibited: A trust may not be created for an ***illegal purpose***.

B. Types of purposes that are illegal: Trusts for illegal purposes include:

1. trusts that involve the commission of a crime or tort by the trustee;
2. trusts the enforcement of which would be against public policy such as:
   a. provisions encouraging divorce, preventing marriage, restraining religious freedom, or discouraging performance of public duties or
   b. provisions for holding property in trust for a period longer than the Rule against Perpetuities or for capricious purposes, or providing for unreasonable periods of income accumulation or for unreasonable restraints on alienation;
3. trusts created for the purpose of defrauding creditors or other third parties; or
4. trusts for which the consideration is illegal.

C. May result in failure of trust: If the illegal provision goes to the ***whole trust***, the trust fails in its entirety.

1. **Partial invalidity:** If the illegal provision does not affect the whole trust, only the illegal provision is stricken and the balance of the trust is given effect without it.

IX. POWER TO REVOKE OR MODIFY

A. Generally: In general, if the settlor has not expressly ***reserved the power*** to ***revoke or modify*** a trust, the power to do so does ***not exist***.

B. Parol evidence: If the trust is written and ***unambiguous***, the parol evidence rule will apply to exclude evidence that the settlor intended a power to revoke. See *supra*, pp. 133-34, for further discussion of the parol evidence rule; see also Emanuel on *Contracts*.

1. **Ambiguous or oral terms:** If the ***terms*** of the trust instrument are ***ambiguous or the trust is oral***, extrinsic factors that may show that the settlor reserved the power of revocation include:

a. improvidence of setting up the trust without such a power;

b. relationship between the settlor and beneficiary;

c. purposes for creating trust;

d. nature of the trust property; and

e. impact of federal taxes on provision as drafted.

C. **Omission of power to revoke through fraud or mistake:** General rules with respect to rescission and reformation will be applied if it is claimed that the provision for revocation was omitted through fraud or mistake.

D. **Extent of reserved power:** If no method is specified, the power may be exercised in any way sufficient to manifest the intention to revoke or modify.

1. **Power expressly limited:** If the settlor reserves the power to revoke or modify only in a ***particular manner*** he may only revoke or modify in such manner.

    Example: A power to revoke with the consent of a third party.

2. **Power to revoke:** The power to revoke also includes the power to revoke in part and to modify.

3. **Power to modify reserved:** Whether the power to modify includes the power to revoke depends on all the ***circumstances***.

E. **Statutory presumptions:** In many states statutes have been enacted which provide that in the absence of an express provision to the contrary, the trust is ***presumed to be irrevocable***. Others ***presume*** it to be ***revocable*** in such circumstances.

F. **Unanticipated circumstances:** When a trust is in effect, there may arise circumstances which were ***unknown*** or ***unanticipated*** by the settlor. A court may exercise its discretionary power to act in certain limited situations.

1. **Changes in distribution to beneficiaries:** A court may allow a trustee to depart from the terms of a trust if there are unanticipated circumstances which would ***substantially impair*** the ***purposes*** of the trust. Rest. of Trusts §167.

    Example: By will, H leaves his estate in trust. The income is to be paid to W for life, and at her death the principal is to be divided among H and W's children. W becomes ill and the income is not sufficient to support her. The trustees, joined by the children of H and W, petition the court to modify the trust so that the principal may be used to provide support for W.

Held, petition granted. The use of the principal to benefit W is neither authorized nor forbidden in the will. Further, the primary purpose of the will is to provide for W, and a strict reading of the trust would impair that purpose. The court is empowered to act in this situation, so the trustees are authorized to use the principal for W. *Petition of Wolcott*, 56 A.2d 641 (N.H. 1948).

2. **Administrative deviations:** A court has power, ***in emergencies***, to protect beneficiaries from serious loss or a total destruction of trust assets by allowing changes in the ***administrative provisions*** of a trust.

    Example: The principal assets of T's estate include stock in a newspaper publishing company. The stock is left in trust, but the trustees are denied power to sell the stock. While profitable at T's death, the newspaper begins to run large deficits. The only way to prevent further substantial losses is to sell the newspaper. *Held*, the court may imply a power of sale of this asset in a case of *necessity*, as exists here. *Estate of Pulitzer*, 139 Misc. 575, 249 N.Y.S. 87 (Sur.Ct.1931), *aff'd mem.*, 237 App.Div. 808, 260 N.Y.S. 975 (1932).

X. TERMINATION OF TRUSTS

A. **Termination regardless of consent:** The trust will be terminated in the following instances whether or not the settlor, trustee or beneficiaries consent:

1. upon the expiration of the period for which the trust was created;
2. upon the fulfillment of the condition upon which the trust is to terminate;
3. when the purposes for which the trust was created become impossible or illegal; and
4. when the continuance of the trust would defeat the purpose for which the trust was created.

B. **Termination by settlor who is sole beneficiary:** If the settlor is the sole beneficiary of the trust, he can ***compel termination of the trust*** even if there has been no reservation of a power to revoke and the trust purposes have not been accomplished.

C. **Merger of titles of trustee and beneficiaries:** A ***trustee*** and ***beneficiary*** generally have ***no power to terminate*** a trust unless the power to terminate is given to one of them by the terms of the trust. If, however, the trustee transfers his interest to the beneficiary, a ***merger of legal and equitable title*** occurs and the trust is ended even if material purposes of the trust have not been accomplished and a judicial termination could not have been obtained. See Ritchie, p. 661.

1. **Beneficiary of legal age:** A beneficiary who is of legal age and capacity when he consents to termination may not hold the trustee liable for breach.

2. **Beneficiary lacking legal capacity:** A beneficiary lacking legal capacity to enter into an agreement of termination is not ***estopped from suing for breach***.

   Example: T creates a testamentary trust that provides that the income from B's share of the trust principal is to be paid to B in monthly installments until he reaches age 31, at which time the principal is to be delivered to him. After turning 21, B induces the trustee to terminate the trust and transfer the principal to him. B squanders all the property, then brings an action against the trustee for an order: (1) setting aside as void the transaction that terminated the trust; and (2) directing the trustee to reconstitute the trust estate.

   Held, for the trustee. The general rule is that a beneficiary "may authorize the trustee to perform an act which would otherwise be a breach of trust and thereby estop himself from holding the trustee liable therefor. . . ." Similarly, a beneficiary cannot have a settlement with the trustee (who has acted honorably) set aside without returning the consideration paid to him by the trustee. Here, B was of full age and capacity when he demanded that the trustee terminate the trust. The trustee acted honorably and only upon the insistence of B. Moreover, B, who has lost all the trust property, is incapable of returning it to the trust. Thus, the trust may not be reinstated and the trustee is not liable to B for breach. *Hagerty v. Clement*, 195 La. 230, 196 So.330 (1940).

D. **Consent of settlor and all beneficiaries:** If ***all of the beneficiaries and the settlor*** consent to termination even though the trust purposes have not been accomplished, the ***trust will be terminated***.

E. **Consent of beneficiaries alone:** If all of the beneficiaries of a trust (but not the settlor) consent to its termination:

1. **Majority rule:** Under the ***majority rule***, the trust will ***not*** be terminated if the trust is an active trust and its continuance is necessary to carry out a ***material purpose*** of the settlor.

   Example: T leaves his estate in trust to provide an education to the children of H and W. When that purpose is accomplished, income and, if necessary, part of the principal, are to go to H and W "so that they may live in the style and manner to which they are accustomed." At the death of H and W, the principal is to be divided among their children. When the education of the children is complete, H and W, with the consent of their children, file to terminate the trust. They argue that the sole remaining purpose of the trust is to maintain their lifestyle, and distribution of the assets is necessary for that purpose.

Held, the trust may not be terminated. Besides education of the children, T intended life-long income for H and W through the management and discretion of the trustee. The trustee must use income and part of the principal if necessary for this purpose. That purpose would be defeated if the trust were terminated. *In re Estate of Brown*, 528 A.2d 752 (Vt. 1987). See also *Claflin v. Claflin*, 20 N.E. 454 (Mass. 1889) ("[A] testator has a right to dispose of his own property with such restrictions and limitations, not repugnant to law, as he sees fit, and . . . his intentions ought to be carried out, unless they contravene public policy and are not 'altogether useless.' ")

2. **Minority rule:** In England and in a ***minority*** of United States jurisdictions, the rule is that when all beneficiaries agree, the trust will be terminated even if its purposes have not been accomplished. This view "is based on the theory that the owners of the entire equitable property interest under the trust are sole owners of the trust *res* and should be allowed to enjoy the property as they choose—in trust or not in trust." Ritchie, pp. 643-44. The nature of the beneficiary's interest is emphasized under this view, whereas the intention of the settlor is key under the majority rule.

F. **Need to obtain consent of beneficiaries:** If all of the beneficiaries do not or cannot consent to its termination, the trust will not be terminated.

1. **Partial termination:** In such case a court may decree a partial termination if the interests of the non-consenting beneficiaries or the fulfillment of a material purpose will not be affected.

2. **Effect of unborn beneficiaries on right to terminate trust:** The problem of obtaining the consent of unborn beneficiaries presents special difficulties for settlors wishing to terminate trusts that leave the trust res to ***"issue," "next of kin,"*** or ***"heirs."***

a. **Various solutions applied:** Some jurisdictions apply the ***doctrine of worthier title*** to hold that the grant of trust corpus to the heirs of a settlor creates a reversion in the settlor rather than a remainder in the heirs. See, e.g., *Stewart v. Merchants National Bank*, 278 N.E.2d 10 (Ill. App. 1972). Other jurisdictions have enacted ***statutes*** that make it possible to terminate a trust with the consent of the settlor and all living beneficiaries. A third solution (illustrated by the following Example) is to have a guardian ad litem appointed with authority to consent on behalf of the unborn beneficiaries.

Example: S creates a spendthrift trust that directs the trustees to pay to S for life all the income from the trust estate " for her own use and benefit, without the power to anticipate, alienate or charge the same." Upon S's death the trustees are to distribute the trust corpus in accordance with S's will, or if no such testamentary provisions are made, to her heirs in intestacy. The declaration of trust characterizes the trust as irrevocable. S starts an action to modify the terms of the trust so as to receive additional funds each year out of the corpus to accomodate her lifestyle.

In support of her position she invokes the doctrine of worthier title, which provides that a grant of trust corpus to the heirs of a settlor creates a reversion in the settlor rather than a remainder in his heirs. Applying such doctrine, S would be the sole beneficiary as well as settlor and thus capable of modifying or revoking the trust. Without such a doctrine, S argues, an injustice would result: it would be impossible ever to revoke the trust as the consent of unborn beneficiaries could not be obtained.

Held, S's requested relief is denied. The doctrine of worthier title should not be retained as it rarely reflects the settlor's true intent and leads to confusion and uncertainty in the law. Any act or words of the settlor of a trust which would validly create a remainder interest in a named third party may create a valid remainder interest in the settlor's heirs. S's present action must thus be denied as it is based on the theory that she is the sole heir. S must get the consent of the heirs alive at the time. With respect to unborn beneficiaries, a guardian ad litem may be appointed with the power to consent on behalf of such a class. *Hatch v. Riggs National Bank,* 361 F.2d 559 (D.C.Cir. 1966).

Note: In the states that apply the first of the three solutions cited above — use of the doctrine of worthier title — there is disagreement about how that doctrine is to be applied. Some jurisdictions hold that a disposition in favor of a settlor's heirs automatically and as a matter of law creates a reversion in the settlor and no interest in the heirs. Others hold that a reversion is *presumed* to be created, but that the presumption may be rebutted based on the actual intent of the settlor in creating the interest (so that if the settlor is shown to have intended a remainder in the heirs, that is what will be decreed).

LIMITATIONS ON THE CREATION AND DURATION OF INTERESTS IN TRUSTS

I. THE RULE AGAINST PERPETUITIES

A. Statement of the rule: The common law Rule may be stated as follows: "No interest is good unless it must vest, if at all, not later than twenty-one years after some life in being at the date of the creation of the interest." Gray, *Rule against Perpetuities*, p. 191 (4th Ed. 1942).

B. Rule against remoteness of vesting: The Rule is directed entirely against ***remoteness of vesting***. The sole test is whether the interest must ***vest (or fail)*** within the period of the Rule.

1. **All possibilities must be excluded:** It is not sufficient that the interest does in fact vest or fail within the time requirements. It must be ascertainable at the time of the creation of the interest that there is ***not even the remotest possibility*** that it will not vest or fail within such time.

 Example 1: T devises his estate to such of B's children as attain the age of 30 years. B dies three months after T's death. The gift is invalid even though the interest does in fact vest within the lives of B's children and B's children were lives in being at T's death. As B was alive at the time of T's death, there was the possibility that B would have more children. If B had predeceased T, the gift would have been valid.

 Example 2: T's will provides: "1000 pounds shall be placed out at interest during the life of my wife, which interest I give her during her life, and upon her death I give the said 1000 pounds unto my niece Mary Hall and the issue of her body lawfully begotten, and to be begotten, and in default of such issue I give the said amount to be equally divided between the daughters then living of my kinsman John Jee and his wife Elizabeth Jee." At T's death John and Elizabeth Jee are 70 years old and have four daughters. Mary Hall is approximately 40 years old and unmarried. At issue is whether the gift to the daughters of Jee is void.

 Held, the gift is void by reason of the Rule against Perpetuities as being too remote. The gift will vest upon a general (or indefinite) failure (or non-existence) of the issue of Mary Hall. This means that the gift vests whenever Mary Hall has no more descendants. Such an event could presumably occur more than 21 years after her death. Similarly, it cannot be said that the gift must vest or fail within 21 years after the death of the Jee daughters living (or in being) at the time of the creation of the interest (i.e., T's death). The gift may vest during the life of a daughter not yet in being. John and Elizabeth Jee, though advanced in age, were alive at the time of T's death. It was thus impossible to be sure at the time of T's death that the Jees would not have another daughter who would be a potential beneficiary of the gift. Thus, neither Mary Hall, nor the four living daughters, nor anyone else mentioned or implied in the will can be used as the "measuring" or "validating" life or lives. *Jee v. Audley*, 1 Cox 324, 29 Eng. Rep. 1186 (Chancery 1787).

Note: The court in *Jee* could have found that the Rule against Perpetuities had not been violated if it had construed the will differently. First, it chose to interpret the beneficiaries of the gift as including any after-born Jee daughters even though Elizabeth Jee was already 70 years old at T's death and thus incapable, in practical terms, of bearing any more children. If the court had not so construed such language, it could be said that the gift would necessarily vest or fail during lives in being, i.e., the four daughters living at T's death. Second, the court construed the words "in default of such issue" as meaning that the gift would take effect upon a general or indefinite failure of issue, rather than upon a definite failure. The latter construction, not adopted by the court, is the construction favored by the majority of jurisdictions in the United States and means that the gift would take effect only if Mary Hall's issue were non-existent at a specific date. In a case such as the present one, since no date is specified, the key time would be interpreted to be Mary Hall's death. Thus, under such a construction, the gift would necessarily vest or fail before or upon the death of Mary Hall, a life in being at the time of T's death. See Clark, pp. 763-66.

C. **Lives in being:** Lives in being are those of any person(s) identifiable with the disposition. Their lives must span both the creation of the interest and the vesting thereof. For the purposes of the Rule such lives are called ***"measuring" or "validating" lives***.

1. **Determining whose is the life in being:** The ***measuring life*** may be the donee, or someone else mentioned in the instrument or someone not mentioned but determined by implication.

   Example: T devises his estate to all of his grandchildren as attain the age of 21 years. T's children are by implication the measuring lives. Except for posthumous children (who are included as lives in being), T's children will all be in being at the time of T's death. The gift must vest within 21 years after the death of T's children as the grandchildren must necessarily be born by the time all of T's children die. Simes, pp. 265-66.

2. **Ascertainable group:** It is not necessary to choose which one of an ascertainable group of living persons is the life in being, but it must be possible at the creation of the interest to say that the interest will vest not later than 21 years after the death of ***all*** of these persons. Simes, p. 265.

    Example: By will A leaves property in trust to T to hold for the benefit of A's children during their lives and on the death of the last survivor of A's children, to distribute the principal to A's grandchildren then living. At A's death he has three children living, C1, C2 and C3. It is certain that the remainder to the grandchildren will vest at the death of one of the three whose life will span both the times of the creation of the interest (A's death) and the vesting of the interest (his own death). It is unnecessary to determine whether it will be C1, C2 or C3.

3. **Class gifts and the doctrine of "infectious invalidity":** If gifts to some members of a class are valid and gifts to others in the class are invalid, a court may use the doctrine of ***infectious invalidity*** to invalidate an otherwise valid interest, if the court believes this would effectuate the testator's intent by allowing all in the class to take equally through intestacy.

    Example: T leaves his estate in trust, the income to be shared equally among T's three children (A, B and C) "until my youngest grandchild reaches the age of 25." At that time, 1/3 of the corpus is to be split among A and her children, 1/3 is to be split among B and her children, and 1/3 is to continue in trust for C (who has no children). There is no residuary provision in the will, if the above bequest fails for any reason.

    The gift of corpus to A and B and their children is clearly invalid as a violation of the Rule against Perpetuities (since T's "youngest grandchild" might not yet be born at the moment of T's death, and we might have to wait more than 21 years after all measuring lives have ended for the gift of corpus to vest on that grandchild's 25th birthday.) Therefore, clearly 2/3ds of the estate must pass by intestacy (to be shared equally by A, B and C). The question is what should happen to the last 1/3, which by the terms of the will is to continue in trust, income to C.

    Held, even if the continuation of the last 1/3 in trust, income to C, satisfies the Rule against Perpetuities, the court hereby declares it void. Allowing that income interest to be continued will over-compensate C at the expense of A and B — C will have this income plus a 1/3 share of the 2/3's corpus that passes in intestacy. This would thwart T's clear desire to treat A, B and C equally. Instead, the entire trust corpus should now pass by intestacy. *Merrill v. Wimmer*, 481 N.E.2d 1294 (Ind. 1985).

a. **Gifts to separate sub-classes:** Suppose that there are gifts to two or more distinct ***sub-classes***, and one sub-class receives a gift that doesn't violate the Rule while the other sub-class gets a gift that does violate the Rule. If the court is convinced that the testator intended to treat the two sub-classes differently, the court may apply the doctrine of ***"severed shares"*** to validate the one class' interest while invalidating that of the other class — the valid shares are "severed" from the invalid shares.

Example: T leaves his estate in trust to his wife for life, remainder to his only child, Hannah, for life. At Hannah's death income goes to her children (T's grandchildren) for life. At the death of each grandchild, that child's share goes absolutely to his or her heirs. When T died Hannah had two children, and she subsequently had two more children. The trustee brings this action for instructions concerning the validity of the remainders to Hannah's children and the gifts to their heirs.

Held, as to the two children born after T's death, the remainder over at their deaths is invalid as violative of the Rule against Perpetuities. This is so because they were not lives in being when T died. By contrast, the heirs of Hannah's children who were alive at T's death can be determined within the Rule, so those gifts are valid. The two invalid remainders do not affect the two valid remainders because these are to separate sub-classes and each stands or falls separately. *American Security & Trust Co. v. Cramer*, 175 F.Supp. 367 (D.D.C.1959).

Note: Valid gifts are distributed to a sub-class when the testator intends a separate share for each to ***vest independently*** of others or, when the gift is a ***fixed amount*** of money to each. McGovern, p. 520.

D. **Creation of interest:** Generally, the interest is created ***when the instrument takes effect***. A will, for example, takes effect at the testator's death; a deed, at the time the deed is delivered. Simes, p. 267.

E. **Invalidity:** Any interest which may remain contingent beyond the period of the Rule is ***invalid***.

Example: T's will creates a trust. Income is to go to T's son, S, for life, then to S's wife for life, then the corpus of the trust is to be divided among T's descendants. S has died leaving W as his widow. W seeks to have the trust terminated and the corpus given to her in fee simple. T's descendants assert that the trust should be continued so they can receive their remainder when he dies.

Held, for W. The remainder following W's death violates the Rule against Perpetuities because as of T's death there was a possibility that S's widow had not yet been born. Therefore, W receives the entire trust fund at the S's death. The gift of the remainder to T's descendants is invalid. *Pound v. Shorter*, 377 S.E.2d 854 (Ga. 1989).

F. Applicability: The Rule against Perpetuities applies to both ***legal and equitable interests*** created in trust.

1. **Contingent interests in transferees:** The Rule only applies to ***contingent interests*** created in ***transferees***, i.e. contingent remainders and executory interests.

2. **Interests in transferors:** The Rule does not apply to interests created in ***transferors***, i.e. a reversion, a possibility of reverter, or a reentry right for condition broken.

G. Charitable trusts: In a ***charitable trust***, a gift over from a ***first charity*** to a ***second charity*** on a condition precedent is not void by reason of the fact that the condition may not occur without the period of the Rule. This is an ***exception*** to the Rule against Perpetuities.

Example: A leaves property to T in trust to pay the income therefrom to St. Paul's Church so long as it conducts its regular services in accordance with the Book of Common Prayer, 1789 Version; and if at any time it should discontinue to so conduct its services, then to St. James Church. This is valid.

1. **Charitable interests subject to Rule:** All other charitable interests are subject to the Rule.

   a. **Non-charity to charity:** Property transferred to a non-charity and then to a charity on a remote contingency.

Example: A leaves property in trust to hold for Mary's children for life and on the death of Mary's last surviving child to Mary's female grandchildren then living; if no female grandchild is living then to the Cathedral School for Girls. Mary is living at the time of A's death. The gift to the Cathedral School is void because it may not vest within the Rule.

b. **Charity to non-charity:** Property transferred to a charity and then to a non-charity on a remote contingency.

Example: A leaves property to T in trust to pay the income to St. Paul's Church so long as it conducts its regular services in accordance with the Book of Common Prayer, 1789 Version; and if at any time it should discontinue to so conduct its services, then to Robert or Robert's heirs then living. The gift over is void because it may remain contingent for a period longer than the Rule against Perpetuities. It makes no difference that it is preceded by a gift to charity.

c. **To a charity without prior gift:** Property transferred to a charity on a remote contingency without a prior gift.

Example: A leaves property to T in trust to hold for the benefit of St. Paul's Church if it should adopt a new liturgy proposed by the convention of 1970. The gift is void. The contigency may not occur within the period of the Rule. There is no exception for a gift to charity under such circumstances.

H. **Legislative reform:** In recent years many states have adopted legislation designed to ***eliminate the harsh effect*** of the common law Rule against Perpetuities. These are generally of two types.

1. **Wait-and-see:** Under the ***"wait-and-see"*** approach, the court will not rule a future interest invalid ***until the moment the prior estate terminates;*** if at that moment the future interest has vested within lives in being at the interest's creation plust 21 years, the interest is valid. This approach thus examines the events that have ***actually happened*** rather than the possibilities existing at the time the interest was created.

Example: T, who is without children, dies in 1984. His will sets up a testamentary trust that will, for the next 25 years, meet the educational needs of all descendants of T's father (i.e., all of T's nieces and nephews, and their descendants). At the end of 25 years, the corpus is to go to P, T's favorite nephew. In 1989, the court hears P's suit to have the trust ruled invalid as a violation of the Rule against Perpetuities. P argues (correctly) that viewed as of the moment the trust was created in 1984, it was possible that all of T's father's descendants then living might have died within 4 years (i.e., before 1989); in that event, P points out, the trust would have continued (and made payments, each of which would be a "vesting" of an interest) for more than lives in being in 1984 plus 21 years.

Held, the trust is valid. Mississippi has adopted a "wait and see" statute, under which the only thing that matters is what has actually happened, not what might possibly have happened but didn't happen. As of today (1989), we know that some of T's father's descendants who were living in 1984 are still living, so any of these can be a measuring life. Since the trust will expire less than 21 years from today, the trust will not expire later than the last of the measuring lives plus 21 years. Therefore, we have already waited long enough to know that the trust is valid under the "wait and see" approach. *Estate of Anderson*, 541 So.2d 423 (Miss. 1989).

2. **Cy pres:** The doctrine of ***"cy pres"*** was developed initially to apply to charitable trusts (see *supra*, p. 114), but some states apply it to Perpetuities violations. Cy pres allows the court to ***reform*** the interest within the limits of the Rule to approximate most closely the ***intention*** of the creator of the interest.

   Example: T establishes a testamentary trust which terminates upon the death of W or thirty years from the date of T's death, whichever occurs *last*. Since W might die within nine years of T's death, the trust violates the Rule against Perpetuities: it might not vest within W's life plus 21 years. *Held*, the court will use the doctrine of cy pres or "equitable approximation" to reduce the 30-year period to 21 years so that it will conform to the Rule. *Estate of Chun Quan Yee Hop*, 469 P.2d 183 (Haw. 1970).

II. RULE AGAINST THE SUSPENSION OF THE POWER OF ALIENATION

A. Generally: Some states have adopted provisions ***invalidating any attempt to suspend the power to alienate property for more than a specified period*** (e.g., two lives in being). The purpose of such provisions is to facilitate the transfer of property.

B. Violations of rule: ***A trust may offend the rule*** against suspending alienation if:

1. the ***trustee is prohibited from selling*** the property, either by reason of the terms of the trust instrument or by reason of having no implied power to sell the property, for a specified period longer than the period of the rule; or

2. the ***beneficiary*** of a spendthrift trust is ***restrained from alienating his interest*** for a period longer than the period of the rule.

III. RULES GOVERNING DURATION OF TRUSTS AND ACCUMULATIONS

A. **Duration of trusts:** Rules governing the duration of trusts are to be distinguished from the Rule against Perpetuities, which governs only the vesting of interests, not their duration.

> **Example:** A leaves property in trust to pay the income to B and his successors for fifty years and then to distribute the remainder to St. Paul's Church. All interests are vested so there is no violation of the Rule Against Perpetuities, but the trust may last longer than allowed by a statute restricting the duration to lives in being plus twenty-one years.

1. **Types of limitations imposed by statute:** Some states have statutes limiting the duration of either:

   a. all private trusts; or

   b. certain types of trusts (e.g., voting trusts for corporate stock).

2. **General rule:** Where no statute is in effect, the general rule is that ***private trusts are not limited in duration***.

   a. **Rule in older cases:** Some older cases have held that the private trust is limited in duration as in the Rule against Perpetuities. This has been rejected in the more recent cases.

   b. **Modern view:** Most states today allow private trusts to continue beyond the Perpetuities period so long as all interests under and following it are ***vested***. In some jurisdictions the beneficiaries may terminate the trust after the Perpetuities period. Thus where a trust provides that it is indestructible, the provision will be enforced only for the period of the Rule against Perpetuities. Bogert, p. 191.

3. **Honorary trusts:** In most jurisdictions ***honorary trusts*** are ***restricted*** in duration to the period of the Rule against Perpetuities.

4. **Charitable trusts:** Charitable trusts are ***not limited*** to the period of the Rule; they may last forever.

B. **Accumulations:** An ***accumulation trust*** is one in which the trustee is directed to ***retain all or part of the trust income*** and add it to the trust principal for distribution at some future time. Bogert, p. 195.

1. **Common law rule:** The common law rule is that an ***accumulation of income for a private trust is valid***, but ownership in the accumulation must vest within the period of the Rule against Perpetuities.

Example: T directs by will that the remainder of his estate be put in trust until 21 years after the death of the survivor of T's nieces, A and B. Trust income is to be invested and the income used to pay several annuities. The trust is to cease 21 years after the death of A and B, the principal to be divided into five parts and distributed to the issue of A and B and to three named relatives. The question is whether the trust provision directing the accumulation, through reinvestment, of a large amount of income for a period of "lives in being" plus 21 years is valid.

Held, the provision is valid. The common law rule is that accumulations may be permitted for as long as the period of the Rule against Perpetuities. It is argued that the instant trust is so big and lasts for so long that it would be repugnant to public policy to simply apply the common law rule to this case. Despite such arguments, however, the accumulation provision, which complies with the common law rule, should be upheld. To declare this trust invalid merely because it is too long or too big or both, without setting guidelines for future trusts, would create uncertainty. To change the common law rule by imposing new limitations on accumulations would be inappropriate in this forum. As the question involves far reaching public policy considerations (such as the effect on the country's purchasing power and tax revenues) and requires good facilities for adequate study, such reform is better left to the legislature. Moreover, it is not clear that reform is indicated. Only a few states have changed the common law rule and it remains to be seen whether the changes are an improvement. *Gertman v. Burdick*, 75 U.S. App. D.C. 48, 123 F. 2d 924 (1941).

Note: The modern trend is for states that have adopted special statutes concerning accumulation, to abandon them in favor of the period allowed for the vesting of estates.

2. **Statutory limitations:** A few states have statutes with special rules limiting the duration of provisions for accumulations in private trusts. Some of these statutes forbid accumulations which exceed the period of the Rule against Perpetuties; others are more restrictive. Legislation passed by English Parliament in 1800, for example, restricted accumulations to one of four periods: (1) the life of the donor; (2) twenty-one years after the donor's death; (3) the minorities of persons living at the donor's death; or (4) minorities of persons entitled to income in the absence of a provision for accumulation.

3. **Invalidity:** Accumulation provisions that are valid except for the fact that they exceed the permissible period of accumulation

(usually the Perpetuities period), are generally struck down ***only to the extent that they extend beyond such period***. See Bogert, p. 198. *Walliser v. Northern Trust Co. of Chicago*, 263 87 N.E.2d 129 (Ill. App. 1949).

4. **Accumulation provisions in charitable trusts:** Accumulations in ***charitable*** trusts may continue beyond the Perpetuities period, but not longer that the court regards as reasonable. Accumulations for charities are governed by statute in some states. Bogert, p. 257.

JURISDICTION OVER ADMINISTRATION

I. TRUSTS

A. **Court having jurisdiction:** The court having jurisdiction over matters pertaining to the establishment and enforcement of trusts ***varies*** from state to state depending upon local statutes or practice. In some jurisdictions the ***probate court*** has jurisdiction over testamentary trusts. In others the ***court of general jurisdiction*** has jurisdiction over all trusts.

1. **Concurrent or exclusive jurisdiction:** In many states statutory provisions confer either concurrent or exclusive jurisdiction over testamentary trusts on the ***probate court***.

2. **Equity and plenary jurisdiction:** In the absence of a statute to the contrary, the court having equity jurisdiction has plenary jurisdiction of all questions concerning the establishment, construction, enforcement and preservation of trusts.

   a. **Extent of equity's jurisdiction:** Equity's jurisdiction is not limited to express trusts but extends to resulting and constructive trusts.

B. **Law governing validity of trusts concerning land:** The ***law of the place where the land is situated*** determines the validity and effect of a trust concerning land.

C. **Law governing validity of testamentary trusts of chattels:** The validity of a testamentary trust of chattels (including movables, specialties and nonspecialties) is determined by the ***law of the domicile of the testator***, the lex domicilii, unless to apply such rule would defeat the intent of the testator, in which case it may be determined by the law of the place in which the chattels are situated.

> **Example:** T has lived many years and has accumulated much property in the state of Washington. T moves to California leaving chattels in Washington. He retires, and dies domiciled in California. His will disposes of his chattels in Washington to B in trust, the trust to be administered in Washington. The trust is invalid under the California Rule Against Perpetuities, but is valid under the law of Washington. T's heirs sue in Washington to invalidate the trust.
>
> *Held*, the trust is valid. Under the general rule T's heirs would prevail as the law of the testator's domicile at the time of his death usually governs the testamentary trust of

chattels. When, however, application of the general rule results in invalidity of the trust and runs contrary to the testator's intent, the law that governs is that which makes the trust valid and carries out the testator's intention. See *Matter of Chappell*, 124 Wash. 128, 213 P. 684 (1923).

D. **Law governing validity of inter vivos trust of chattels:** The validity of an inter vivos trust of chattels is governed by the ***law of the place in which the chattels are situated*** at the time of the creation of the trust.

Example: S, a resident of Louisiana, takes securities and cash worth $100,000 to the state of New York and delivers them to T to hold in trust for specific persons and purposes. Under the law of Louisiana, the domicile of the settlor, the trust is invalid, but by the law of New York the trust is valid and enforceable. *Held*, the law of New York governs and the trust is valid. See *Hutchison v. Ross*, 262 N.Y. 381, 187 N.E. 65 (1933).

E. **Law governing administration of trust of chattels:** The administration of a trust of chattels is governed by the ***law of the place*** designated by ***the settlor***.

F. **Uniform Probate Code approach:** In the Uniform Probate Code, the distinction between testamentary and inter vivos trusts is eliminated. Article 7 contains the concept of ***registration*** of testamentary and inter vivos trusts in the probate court. The ***court of registration*** is where the primary administration of the trust is to occur. So the place where the trust was created loses its significance. UPC §7-101.

1. **Information disclosed:** The registration must identify the ***trustee*** and the ***settlor***. There is no judicial action or determination required for registration. UPC §7-102.

2. **Jurisdiction:** The court of registration has complete jurisdiction over trust proceedings. By registering a trust, the trustee submits to the jurisdiction of the court. UPC §§7-103; 7-201.

3. **Failure to register:** If a trust is not properly registered, the trustee is subject to court sanctions. UPC §7-104.

4. **Advantage:** Registration assures that a particular court will be available to the parties on a permissive basis without subjecting the trust to compulsory, continuing supervision by the court.

   a. **Annual accounting:** ***Annual accounting*** to the court is ***eliminated*** under the UPC. This may lower trustee fees, and it eliminates the public nature of the financial affairs of the beneficiaries. Beneficiaries are still entitled to an annual accounting, but that does not have to be filed with the court.

McGovern, p. 702.

II. DECEDENT'S ESTATES

A. **Courts having jurisdiction:** Most states have special courts, usually called the ***probate courts***, which have sole and exclusive jurisdiction over probate of wills, the granting of administration, and the appointment and supervision of the personal representative. Under the English law, various matters with respect to probate were vested in different courts, depending upon the type of property, nature of interest in the property, and status of the decedent. Probate courts were developed to consolidate all such matters in one court.

1. **When jurisdiction arises:** No probate court has jurisdiction to administer the estate of a person unless and until that ***person*** is actually ***dead*** and any proceeding which attempts to do so is a nullity and void.

2. **Venue:** The ***county*** in which decedent was domiciled at the time of his death is usually the proper venue for estate proceedings. See, e.g., UPC §3-201.

   a. **Property outside domicile:** If there is property outside the state of domicile, venue is usually proper in the county where such property is located. See, e.g., UPC §3-201.

3. **Time limitation:** Most states have a statute of limitations for proceedings to probate a will. For instance, under the UPC there is a basic limitation period of ***three years*** to begin the administration of a decedent's estate — if a will is not produced within three years from the death, a conclusive presumption arises that the decedent died intestate. UPC §3-108.

B. **Domiciliary and ancillary administration:** The primary place for the probate of a will and the appointment of an administrator is the state in which the decedent was ***domiciled*** at the time of his death (primary or domiciliary administration). Estate administration may also take place in states in which the decedent left ***property*** (ancillary administration).

1. **Separate administration:** If a decedent dies domiciled in State X and leaves property in States X and Y, usually a ***separate administration*** is ***necessary*** in each state.

2. **Limitations on power of personal representatives:** An executor or administrator as such can exercise no powers beyond the boundaries of the state in which he is appointed.

   a. **Statutory extension of authority:** If a personal representative is appointed in State X he can act as such in State Y only by virtue of a statute in State Y.

b. **Domiciliary administrator as ancillary administrator:** Many states permit the domiciliary personal representative to act also as ancillary administrator. Other states require that the ancillary administrator be a resident thereby precluding the domiciliary administrator from acting.

3. **Law governing duties of administrators:** The ***duties*** of the administrator, domicilary or ancillary, are determined by the ***law of the place of his appointment***.

4. **Principal purpose of ancillary administration:** The principal purpose of ancillary administration is to gather local assets and to assure the payment of the debts of the decedent to the local creditors.

   a. **Insolvent estate:** When a decedent's estate is insolvent, local creditors may not be paid a larger percentage of their claims than is paid to all other creditors of the same class.

      Example: Domiciliary administration of T's estate is pending in the state of Washington. Ancillary administration is pending in Michigan. Creditors A and B are residents of Wisconsin and Washington, respectively. T's estate as a whole is insolvent. The appraised value of property in Michigan exceeds the amount of claims allowed to Michigan creditors. Michigan creditors assert that the assets of the ancillary estate should be applied to paying Michigan creditors in full before allowing non-resident creditors to participate in the assets. A and B claim that they have a right to present their claims for allowance in the ancillary administration and to participate pro rata in the Michigan assets. They also contend that Michigan creditors should not be paid a larger percentage of their claims than is paid to all other creditors of the same class.

      Held, for A and B. Non-resident creditors have a right to present their claims in ancillary administration proceedings. Furthermore, resident creditors of insolvent estates are entitled to receive only pro rata payment of their claims. Any attempt to provide by statute or judicial determination that resident creditors are entitled to a larger percentage of their claim than nonresident creditors would violate Article 4, §2 of the United States Constitution, which guarantees equal privileges and immunities to the citizens of the several states, as well as the Fourteenth Amendment, which prohibits states from denying any person equal protection of the law. However, as the primary purpose of ancillary administration is to spare local creditors the expense and inconvenience of presenting their claims in foreign jurisdictions, resident creditors in the instant case should be paid their ***pro rata*** share to the full extent that other creditors will be paid out of T's estate before nonresident creditors are permitted to participate in Michigan assets. *In re Estate of Brauns*, 276 Mich. 598, 268 N.W. 890, (1936).

5. **Duties of ancillary administrator:** The ancillary administrator's duties are to:
   a. ***collect*** the decedent's assets;
   b. ***pay*** the local creditors; and
   c. ***distribute*** the remaining assets to the domiciliary personal representative.

6. **Law of domiciliary state governs on matters pertaining to personalty:** The state of ancillary administration usually defers to the state of domiciliary administration on matters pertaining to the personal estate of the decedent. Thus, if a will is admitted to probate at the decedent's last domicile the validity of the will is conclusive as to personalty in all jurisdictions.
   a. **Matters pertaining to realty:** The validity of a will concerning realty is determined by the state in which the land is located.

III. DOMICILE

A. **Definition:** The word "domicile" comes from the Latin "domus," which means home; domicile is the legal conception of home. A person's domicile is defined as his ***usual and permanent dwelling place***, as distinguished from any ***temporary*** residence that he might have. If a person has more than one residence, his domicile is usually the residence at which he spends the ***most time***.

1. **Only one domicile:** At ***common law*** it is said that no person has more than one domicile—he always has one and never none. Under certain circumstances, however, ***more than one state*** may claim to be the domicile of a decedent.
   a. **Traditional view:** Under the traditional view, a finding of domicile by the courts of one state is ***not binding*** upon courts of other states — so a second state may also find domicile and grant domiciliary letters. As a result, each court administers the property within its own jurisdiction.

      Example: Georgia executors, E's, and a New York administrator, A, of T's estate each claims the right to stock in the Coca Cola Corporation. Delaware is the situs of the stock. The Georgia courts determine that Georgia was T's domicile at her death. The Supreme Court of Delaware reverses this finding of fact, holding that T was domiciled in New York. The question presented is whether the Georgia judgment on T's domicile conclusively establishes the right of E's to demand delivery to them of the personal assets of T situated in another state (Delaware), when another representative (A) appointed by a third state (New York) asserts a similar domiciliary right. The answer to the question lies in the extent to which the full faith and credit clause of the United States Constitution controls Delaware's action, assuming T was in fact a domiciliary of New York.

Held, Delaware was not bound by Georgia's determination as to T's domicile. Georgia's jurisdiction over property within its borders is *in rem*. Its jurisdiction over property outside of the state, however, is *in personam*. As Georgia had no *in personam* jurisdiction over A, it would be a denial of A's rights to procedural due process to bind A by Georgia's ruling and prevent A from filing a claim in Delaware for assets in that state. Moreover, every state has a legitimate interest in the administration of the property of its citizens which may not be readily frustrated. Although conflicting decisions on domicile may result, both Georgia and New York were entitled to protect their sovereign interests by asserting their right to administer the estates of their domiciliaries. Delaware was free to decide for itself which claiment was entitled to receive the personalty within its borders. *Riley v. New York Trust Co.*, 315 U.S. 343 (1942).

i. *Dorrance* cases: Similarly, in the famous *Dorrance* cases, two different states each found that Dorrance, heir to the Campbell Soup fortune was domiciled there at his death for inheritance tax purposes, and thus each was able to impose an inheritance tax of approximately $17 million dollars. These cases are seen by some as "irreconcilable" and as holding that Dorrance had two domiciles at the same time—one in New Jersey and one in Pennsylvania, in contravention of the traditional theory that one may have only one domicile. Under a more modern view, however, these cases are seen as reconcilable for the following reasons: (i) the facts in evidence were such that reasonable people could differ as to the conclusions to be drawn from them; (ii) the standards applied in determining change of domicile were different in the two states, which is constitutionally permissible; (iii) the first action was not *res judicata* in the second litigation because the parties were not the same; and (iv) the cases may be reconciled on the "avarice" or "pig" theory — both states wanted the $17 million dollars. See *In re Dorrance's Estate*, 163 A. 303 (Pa. 1932), and 170 A. 601

(N.J. Eq. 1934).

ii. ***Texas v. Florida:*** And in *Texas v. Florida*, 306 U.S. 398, (1939) the United States Supreme Court did not make a determination of domicile where four states had made tax claims based on domicile. The claims exceeded the total of the $42 million dollar estate.

b. **Modern view:** Modern statutes often attempt to reduce the possibility that different states may render conflicting findings of domicile. For instance, the Uniform Probate Code provides that the ***determination of domicile*** is to be made by the ***first state*** in which proceedings are commenced. Courts in other states will then stay or dismiss proceedings until the finding of domicile is made by that first state. So long as all parties are given notice and an opportunity to participate, that finding ***must be accepted as determinative*** of domicile. UPC §3-202.

2. **Variety of functions:** The term ***"domicile"*** has a variety of functions. It may have as many meanings as it has fields of application. The concept, for example, is relevant to questions involving inheritance taxes (*Dorrance* and *Texas*, *supra*); the right to administer estates (*Riley*, *supra*, p. 159); and the validity of testamentary transfers of personalty.

3. **Types of domicile:** There are three types of domicile: ***domicile of origin, domicile of choice***, and ***domicile by operation of law***.

   a. **Domicile of origin:** Domicile of origin is that which is ***assigned by law*** to a person at ***birth***.

   b. **Domicile of choice:** Domicile of choice is an ***acquired domicile***, acquired by one having capacity to make a selection of a new domicile. It is a change from one domicile to another. Two essential elements must concur in point of time to establish a domicile of choice:

      i. the person exercising the choice must maintain a ***physical presence*** at the place selected as his new home, and

      ii. he must have the ***intent*** to make that place his home.

      Example: D's domicile is New York. He moves to Arizona and takes up residence in a rented stationary house trailer either with the intention to live there indefinitely or without any present intention to live elsewhere. D is domiciled in Arizona. While D was en route from New York to Arizona his domicile was still New York. When he arrived within the borders of Arizona his domicile was still New York. When he selected the trailer as his home and formulated his intent to remain there, his domicile was changed from New York to Arizona.

c. **Domicile by operation of law:** Domicile by ***operation of law*** occurs when the ***law assigns one a domicile*** by reason of legal status.

   i. **Illegitimate child:** An illegitimate child takes the domicile of its ***mother***.

   ii. **Wife:** A wife's domicile is generally that of her ***husband***. A wife living separately and apart from her husband has the power to establish her ***separate domicile*** regardless of whether she has a cause of action for divorce or is guilty of desertion.

4. **Administration-in-chief:** As noted, the administration-in-chief of an estate should be in the county and state in which the decedent was domiciled at his death.

PROBATE, ADMINISTRATION OF THE PERSONAL REPRESENTATIVE AND MANAGEMENT OF THE ESTATE

Introductory Note: In this chapter, the life cycle of estate administration is examined. The discussion includes the probate process, the appointment of a personal representative, and the management of the estate. Chart IX, *infra*, p. 163 outlines the entire course of estate administration and should thus serve as an effective study aid for this chapter.

I. PROBATE

A. Introduction: Probate is the process under which a document is judicially established as the duly executed last will of a competent testator or the estate of a decedent dying intestate is admitted to administration.

1. **Meaning of the word "probate":** ***Probate*** comes from the Latin word *probatio* which means "to prove"; the ***probate of a will thus means the proving thereof*** in the probate court.

2. **The probate proceeding generally:** The probate proceeding consists of either: (1) in the case of ***intestacy***, the appointment of a personal representative; or (2) in the case of ***testacy***, the probate of the will and the appointment of a personal representative.

   a. **Personal representative:** The personal representative is the official whose duty it is to wind up the affairs of the decedent.

   b. **Purpose of the probate proceeding:** Probate proceedings are necessary in order to achieve: (1) the orderly transfer of assets on the death of their owner; (2) protection of creditors; and (3) identification of successors.

   c. **Concerned with external validity:** The probate proceeding is not concerned with the construction of the will, but with the will's ***external validity***. Relevant issues include: (1) genuineness; (2) due execution; (3) capacity of the testator; and (4) chronology (whether the document is the last formal expression of the testator's intent).

3. **Admissibility of will in other courts:** Every will must be admitted to probate in the probate court before it is admissible in evidence for any purpose in any other court.

CHART IX.

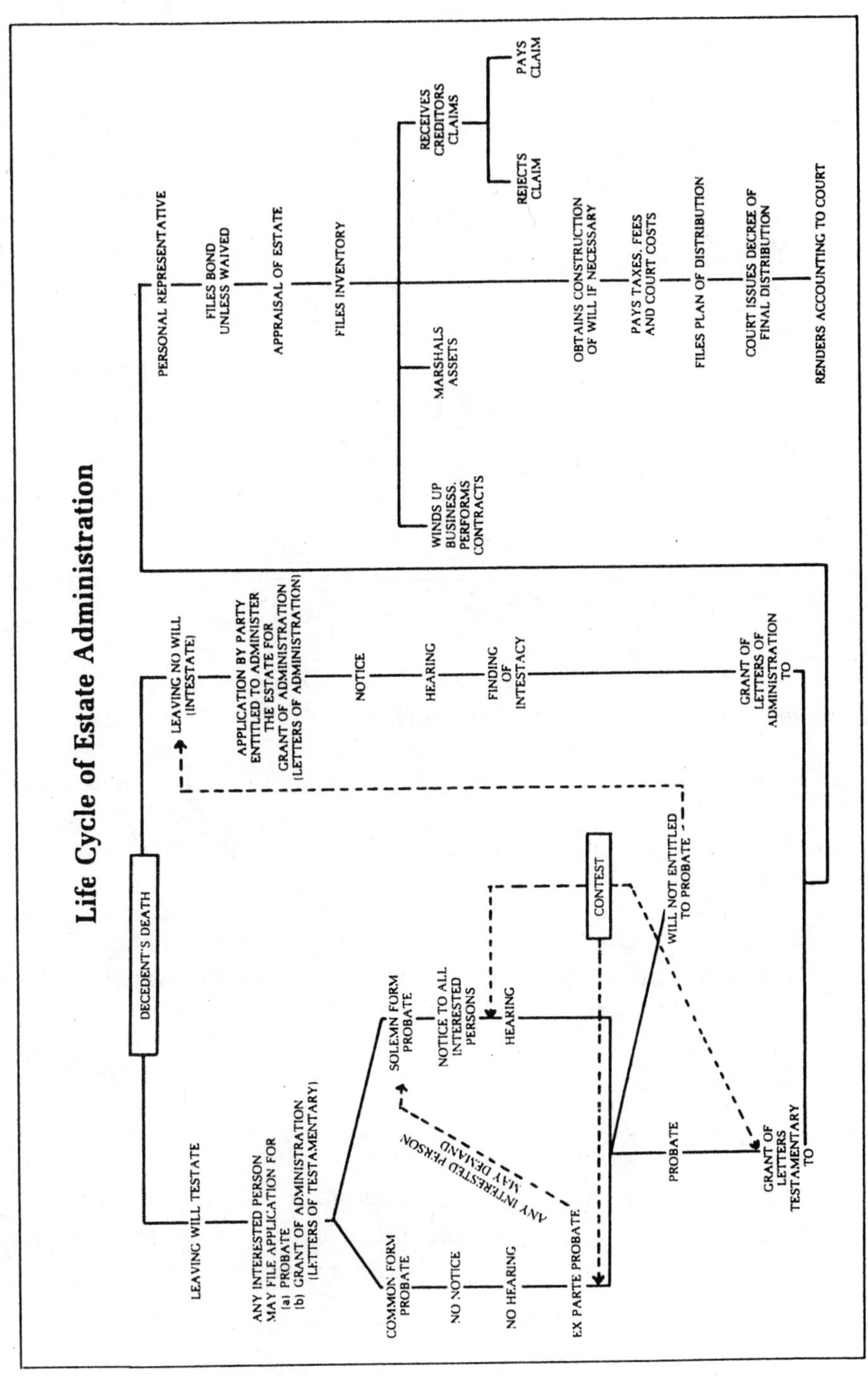
Life Cycle of Estate Administration
DECEDENT'S DEATH
LEAVING WILL TESTATE
ANY INTERESTED PERSON MAY FILE APPLICATION FOR (a) PROBATE (b) GRANT OF ADMINISTRATION (LETTERS OF TESTAMENTARY)
COMMON FORM PROBATE
NO NOTICE
NO HEARING
EX PARTE PROBATE
ANY INTERESTED PERSON MAY DEMAND
SOLEMN FORM PROBATE
NOTICE TO ALL INTERESTED PERSONS
HEARING
CONTEST
PROBATE
GRANT OF LETTERS TESTAMENTARY TO
WILL NOT ENTITLED TO PROBATE
LEAVING NO WILL (INTESTATE)
APPLICATION BY PARTY ENTITLED TO ADMINISTER THE ESTATE FOR GRANT OF ADMINISTRATION (LETTERS OF ADMINISTRATION)
NOTICE
HEARING
FINDING OF INTESTACY
GRANT OF LETTERS OF ADMINISTRATION TO
PERSONAL REPRESENTATIVE
FILES BOND UNLESS WAIVED
APPRAISAL OF ESTATE
FILES INVENTORY
WINDS UP BUSINESS, PERFORMS CONTRACTS
MARSHALS ASSETS
RECEIVES CREDITORS CLAIMS
REJECTS CLAIM
PAYS CLAIM
OBTAINS CONSTRUCTION OF WILL IF NECESSARY
PAYS TAXES, FEES AND COURT COSTS
FILES PLAN OF DISTRIBUTION
COURT ISSUES DECREE OF FINAL DISTRIBUTION
RENDERS ACCOUNTING TO COURT

4. **Early English law:** In 1540 the Statute of Wills made devises of land possible. English law then developed ***two kinds of probate***:

   a. **common form** — the proponent of the will was permitted to prove it by his oath and testimony of other witnesses without notice to other parties. If this procedure was used, an interested party at any time within thirty years could question the grant of probate and require that the solemn form procedure be followed.

   b. **solemn form or *per testes* (through witnesses)** — the interested parties were given notice and an opportunity to be heard and testimony of witnesses was at greater length. Probate by this form could only be questioned on appeal.

   Note: This dual system of probate, "common" and "solemn," is still used in most states today. For example, the Uniform Probate Code provides a similar system, but substitutes the terms "informal" and "formal." See *infra*. UPC §§3-301 and 3-401.

B. **Time for probate:** Probate cannot begin until after the testator's death. In some jurisdictions there is ***no time limit*** after testator's death within which a will may be probated. Other jurisdictions have a time limit. For example, UPC §3-108 requires that probate proceedings be started within ***three years*** from the date of death.

1. **Initial steps:** The person having custody of a will is under a ***duty to produce it***. Many states have statutes imposing penalties for concealing or destroying a will, or for failing to produce it within a given time.

   a. **Filing:** To begin the probate process, the will must be filed in the appropriate court with a ***petition to admit it to probate and to grant letters testamentary to a fiduciary***.

   b. **Who may file:** A petition to admit to probate may be filed by the ***executor*** named in the will, or by any interested person.

2. **Hearing:** At the ***hearing*** on probate, the proponent of the will must prove (1) the death of the testator; (2) his domicile; (3) genuineness of the will; (4) compliance with statutory requirements for the execution of wills; and (5) testamentary capacity.

   a. **Execution and capacity:** ***Execution and mental capacity*** are usually shown by the attesting witnesses.

   b. **Number of witnesses required to testify:** Some states permit probate on the testimony of less than all witnesses to the execution; others require all witnesses if they are available.

c. **Unavailability of witnesses:** When some or all the witnesses to a will are ***unavailable:***

i. If the required witnesses are located outside the jurisdiction, a commission may be sent to the foreign jurisdiction to take their testimony under oath and return it to the court.

ii. If the required witnesses have predeceased the testator, the proponent offers proof of such fact, plus evidence of the genuineness of the signatures and any other proof of execution available.

iii. If required witnessess cannot be located, proof must be offered of a diligent search with tracing to last known whereabouts, plus evidence of the genuineness of the signatures and other proof of due execution.

d. **Foreign language:** If the will of the testator is written in a foreign language in most states it may be admitted to probate, in the same way as if written in English. A translation is usually required to accompany the will.

e. **Lost or destroyed wills:** ***Lost or destroyed wills*** generally may be admitted to probate in the ***same manner*** as those in existence, upon full and satisfactory proof of contents and due execution.

i. **Special statutes:** Some states have special statutes relating to lost and destroyed wills.

f. **Uncontested:** If ***no objection*** is made at the time of the hearing, the will, on a prima facie case of due execution, will be admitted to probate.

3. **Will contests:** Statutory provisions in all states govern the methods by which either a will may be contested, or a will denied probate may be established. Such methods include: (1) ***contest*** (or caveat) in the court having jurisdiction over probate; (2) ***appeal*** from the order granting or denying probate; and (3) separate ***actions to set aside*** the order granting or denying probate.

a. **Without notice:** In states in which wills may be ***probated ex parte without notice***, contest is usually after probate and is either:

i. in the ***probate court*** upon notice filed by the interested parties after probate; or

ii. in a ***higher court on appeal*** with trial ***de novo*** or by separate action.

b. **Notice:** In jurisdictions that ***require notice prior to probate***, the procedures for contest ***vary***.

  i. In some states contest is permitted ***only prior*** to probate; i.e., the probate proceeding is the forum for the contest when objections have been filed by interested parties.

  ii. Some states allow contest ***both before and after*** probate; the former takes place in the probate court, the latter in some higher court.

  iii. Some states allow contest only in a higher court ***after*** probate.

  iv. Some states allow contest ***prior*** to probate and an ***appeal*** to a higher court on a trial de novo.

c. **Right to jury trial:** There is ***no constitutional right*** to trial by jury in probate or will contest proceedings as these were not common law proceedings. Most states, however, have ***statutes giving the right*** to trial by jury in a will contest.

d. **Time limitations:** Statutes usually set time limitations for the commencement of will contests.

e. ***In rem* proceeding:** A will contest is usually considered a proceeding ***in rem*** that is binding on all parties having interests in the property, whether or not they are parties to the proceeding (as the question is ***"will or no will"***), but statutes usually require notice to interested parties.

f. **External validity issues:** Will contests are concerned only with ***external validity issues***, such as failure of due execution, fraud, undue influence, mistake, lack of testamentary capacity, revocation, or lack of intent to make a will. Issues of ***internal*** validity, such as violation of the Rule Against Perpetuities or Statutes of Mortmain, must be raised in other proceedings at a later stage of administration.

g. **Who may contest a will:** The general rule is that only ***"persons interested"*** may contest a will; i.e., persons who would derive pecuniary advantage from having the will set aside. These may include:

  i. ***next-of-kin*** who will receive property if the will is set aside and intestacy results;

  ii. ***beneficiaries*** under prior wills;

  iii. ***purchasers*** of property from heirs;

  iv. ***the state***, if there is a question of escheat; and

v. ***administrators or executors*** under ***prior wills***, but only to insure that bequests to beneficiaries are not impaired by probate of an invalid will.

Example: P is named a contingent trustee in the codicil of a will. A later codicil removes P as contingent trustee. P contests the later codicil's validity. The challenged codicil eliminates the prior codicil's trust scheme, under which the estate was placed in a trust with income going to a museum. Instead, the estate now is to go directly to museum trustees. Proponents of the later codicil contend that P is not an interested person with standing to contest that codicil.

Held, P is not an interested person. A trustee takes legal title to the trust res, with equitable title in the beneficiary. The naked title of the trustee, without more, is not a pecuniary interest. The rights of the trustee to control the trust res and receive fees for the administration of the trust are not the same as rights to the trust res. Under the new codicil the beneficiary will receive more money by receiving the property directly and having fees of the intermediate trust eliminated. Thus it is to the benefit of the beneficiary to uphold the codicil. P is not an interested person because, if P is successful, the beneficiary will receive less income. *In re Estate of Getty*, 149 Cal.Rptr. 656 (Cal. App. 1978).

h. **Estoppel:** A party may be ***estopped to contest a will*** if he has accepted benefits under the will, failed to object to probate proceedings or taken action regarding the will that has been relied on by a third party.

i. **Rules of evidence:** The same ***general rules of evidence*** relating to ***competency*** of witnesses and ***admissibility*** applied to other actions, are also applied to will contests.

j. **Burden of proof:** The general rules as to burden of proof in will contest cases are:

i. The person seeking to establish the validity of the will, the proponent, has the burden of proof on the issues of: (1) due execution and (2) mental capacity.

ii. The contestants have the burden of proof on the issues of undue (1) influence, (2) fraud and (3) revocation.

Note: Some states have passed statutes placing the burden of proof on all issues on the contestant.

4. **Proceedings after probate: *Collateral attack*** of a will will not be allowed on matters of external validity. Such matters may only be questioned in direct proceedings to set aside the probate or

contest the will.

a. **Grounds for setting aside probate:** A decree of probate may be set aside on grounds of ***fraud or collusion*** upon the court, failure to comply with the provisions of the ***Soldiers' and Sailors' Relief Act***, ***new evidence*** or ***failure of notice***.

b. **Protection after reliance on probate:** When a decree of probate or intestacy is set aside, bona fide purchasers and others who relied on the earlier decree, are usually protected.

c. **Discovery of later will:** If a ***later will is discovered*** after either an earlier will has been admitted to probate or a decree of intestacy has been entered, it is generally held that the later will may be probated in the same manner as if no other proceeding has occurred.

C. **No-contest clauses in wills:** Many wills contain a ***"no-contest"*** clause. Such a clause provides that a gift shall be void if the beneficiary disputes or contests the will. The validity of a no-contest clause usually depends on the ***nature of the contest*** and the ***construction of the particular condition***.

1. **Condition fails with will:** If a beneficiary contests the will and the will is declared invalid, the no-contest condition of course fails with the remaining parts of the will.

2. **No probable cause:** Courts will generally ***uphold*** the no-contest condition if the contest is ***without probable cause***.

3. **Probable cause exists:** If the person opposing the will has ***probable cause*** to believe that the will is invalid, there is disagreement among jurisdictions about the effect of a no-contest clause. Some courts ***uphold*** the forfeiture even though the will contest is based on probable cause. However, most courts and UPC §3-905 ***refuse to enforce*** the no-contest condition if there is probable cause. They reason that public policy requires the protection of the family and the exposure of frauds.

4. **Realty/personalty distinction:** ***Early cases*** distinguished between gifts of realty and personal property when there was a no-contest clause and no gift over. If the no-contest clause affected a gift of personalty, it was void. If the no-contest clause affected a gift of realty, it was valid even in the absence of a gift over. ***Modern cases*** make no distinction based on either the nature of the property or the presence of a gift over.

5. **Construction of clause:** Whether or not there is in fact a breach of a no-contest clause depends upon the ***construction of the clause***. Thus, a provision for forfeiture in case of contest may be construed as requiring a forfeiture against beneficiaries who do not

as well as those who do participate in the will contest.

a. **Is action a contest?** When the provision requires forfeiture in the case of a contest, it must be decided whether a given action is a "contest" under the particular clause.

Examples: Claiming title in property given to another is generally held to be a contest. Filing a creditor's claim is generally not a contest. Bringing suit to *construe a provision* in a will, such as a contention that a gift is void because of a violation of the Rule against Perpetuities, is not a contest.

b. **Strict construction:** Courts generally construe no-contest provisions ***strictly*** on the theory that ***forfeitures*** should be ***discouraged***.

D. **Agreement not to contest:** A ***testator*** may enter into a ***contract*** with his ***heir at law*** not to contest his will. If the contract is supported by ***good consideration*** and the agreement is otherwise valid, the heir will be estopped to contest the will. The ***beneficiaries*** under a will and the ***heirs at law*** may enter into a valid contract not to contest a will.

1. **Remedies for breach:** States vary with respect to the remedies a party to an agreement not to contest a will may have on its breach. Remedies include injunction against the prosecution of the contest, action at law for damages, and defense to contest.

2. **To support agreement:** In order to support an agreement not to contest, it is usually held that the heir must have either a ***reasonable ground for contest*** or a ***good faith intention to contest***.

E. **Settlement of will contest action:** The settlement of a will contest action is valid if all interested parties ***agree*** even though it may defeat the intention of the testator.

1. **Effect given to settlement:** The ***states vary as to the effect*** that a probate court will give to a settlement of a contest action. Some states will admit or reject a will and order distribution in accordance with the stipulation. Others require that the settlement be carried out among the parties and that any remedy be sought on the contract in courts of general jurisdiction.

II. THE PERSONAL REPRESENTATIVE

A. **Definition:** One who is authorized by the probate court to administer the estate of a deceased person is called a ***personal representative***. Non-residence, lack of mental capacity, infancy, conviction of crime or other causes are usually ***statutory disqualifications*** for serving as a personal representative.

1. **Executor:** A personal representative ***nominated by the decedent's will*** is called an ***executor***.

2. **Administrator:** A personal representative ***appointed by the court*** when the decedent dies ***intestate*** is called an ***administrator***.

3. **Adminstrator with the will annexed:** A personal representative appointed by the court to administer the estate according to the ***terms of the will*** of the decedent is called an ***adminstrator with the will annexed*** (in Latin, *cum testamento annexo*, or c.t.a.). *Supra*, p. 34.

4. **Administrator de bonis non:** A personal administrator appointed by the court to administer an estate that a prior executor or administrator has ***not completed*** is called an ***administrator de bonis non*** or d.b.n., which means ***"administrator of goods not administered."***

5. **Special administrators:** A special administrator is one appointed by the court to preserve the estate while regular proceedings get under way. The proceeding of appointment is usually ex parte. His authority ceases automatically when a regular personal representative is appointed and qualifies.

   Example: A special administrator is appointed to sell perishables in the grocery store of the deceased.

B. **Appointment and qualification:** If there is a ***will*** the petition for probate is usually accompanied by an application for the ***court appointment of the executor named in the will***. The court usually appointes the executor named in the will.

1. **Intestacy:** In an ***intestate*** estate the administration is usually initiated by filing a petition for the grant of ***letters of administration*** by the person entitled to appointment under the applicable statute.

   a. **Priorities:** State statutes generally provide guidelines for the determination of who is to be appointed adminstrator and the order of preference to be followed. The "most usual order is to (1) surviving spouse; (2) next of kin; (3) creditors; (4) public administrator."

2. **Authority:** Executors and administrators ***derive their authority from court appointments***. They are responsible to the court and must account to it at specified periods. Their principal duties include:

   a. ***Inventory and collect*** the assets of the estate;

   b. ***Manage*** the assets during administration;

c. ***Pay claims*** of creditors; and

d. ***Distribute*** assets to those entitled to them.

3. **Notice and hearing:** The ***majority of states require notice***, usually by publication, ***and a hearing*** with respect to the application for appointment of the personal representative. Some jurisdictions ***allow appointment without notice*** and anyone who desires to object must bring a motion to set the appointment aside.

4. **Filing of a bond:** The administrator, and in some cases the executor, ***must file a bond*** for the protection of those interested in the estate against losses due to improper administration. Statutes generally set the ***amount of the bond*** at twice the estimated value of the personalty in the estate. The value of real estate is, generally, not included for purposes of setting a bond because of the comparative difficulty in dissipating the realty and because title passes directly to the heirs. See *infra*, p. 172, for further discussion of title matters. Statutes also prescribe rules concerning the ***sureties*** required as well as the ***terms*** of the bond.

   a. **Waiver:** Many states allow the ***testator*** to ***waive bond from the executor(s)*** named in the will, but the court still has authority to require a bond if it finds it necessary for protection of the estate.

5. **Certificate of appointment:** When a bond satisfactory to the court is filed, the court under its seal issues a ***certificate of appointment*** to the personal representative. This is called:

   a. in the case of a will, ***letters testamentary***;

   b. in the case of ***intestacy, letters of adminstration.*** These letters are evidence that the personal representative has been made an officer of the court ***authorized*** to carry out the administration of the estate as prescribed by law.

C. **Revocation of administration:** Once properly appointed and qualified as executor or administrator, the acts of a personal representative within the scope of his authority are valid and binding until his letters are ***revoked***.

1. **Revocation when letters should not have been granted:** The court may ***revoke*** the letters of appointment of the personal representative on the ***grounds*** that, at the time of appointment, the ***letters should not have been granted*** in that:

   a. the supposed ***decedent*** is ***not dead***;

   b. a ***will*** is ***found naming an executor*** after an administrator is appointed;

c. a ***later will*** is ***found***;

d. the appointment was obtained by ***fraud***;

e. decedent was ***not domiciled*** in the state and did not have any property there;

f. another person had ***priority*** for appointment; or

g. there was ***lack of qualification*** at the time of appointment.

2. **Revocation due to subsequent events:** the court may remove or revoke the letters of the personal representative on the ground that subsequent to his appointment:

   a. he became ***incapacitated***; or

   b. he ***failed to administer*** the estate ***properly***.

3. **Purchaser protected:** If the personal representative sells property of the estate to a purchaser (before revocation of his letters), the purchaser is protected in his purchase.

4. **Debtor protected:** If one who owed a debt to the decedent pays the debt to the personal representative (before revocation of his letters), the ***debtor is protected*** in such payment.

5. **Cannot undo acts:** If the letters testamentary or of administration are revoked and a new representative is appointed and qualifies, the new representative ***cannot undo the acts of his predecessor*** in good faith either as to sales or as to the collection of debts owed the decedent.

6. **Resignation:** A personal representative is usually allowed to ***resign***, either by the terms of applicable statutes or of the will. To be effective, however, the ***resignation must be accepted by the court***.

D. **Title of personal representative:** When a person dies (testate or intestate) the title to his ***personal property*** vests in the personal representative when appointed and qualified and relates back to the instant of death. When the personal representative distributes the personal property, after payment of decedent's debts, to the legatees in case of testacy and to the next of kin or statutory heirs in case of intestacy, title vests in the legatees and statutory heirs respectively.

1. **Real property:** When a person dies ***testate*** the title to his ***real property*** vests in his devisees, subject to the right and duty of the personal representative to take possession and use for the purpose of paying debts. When a person dies ***intestate*** the title to his ***real property*** vests in his heirs subject to the right and duty of the personal representative to take possession and use for the purpose of paying debts.

E. Personal liability for torts: The personal representative is personally liable for his ***torts*** committed in the course of administering the estate.

F. Personal liability on contracts: The personal representative is personally liable on his contracts in the course of administration although made to benefit the estate. He may, however, attempt to protect himself by express stipulation.

> **Example:** Such a stipulation may provide. "This note is given by X, as the executor of the estate of D, and not individually; it constitutes a promise to pay only to the extent that the assets of the estate are sufficient for such purpose and it is expressly agreed that any judgment will only be satisfied out of the assets of the estate and not out of X's individual assets."
>
> **Note:** To obtain limited liability, it is not sufficient to sign "X, Executor of Estate of D."

III. MANAGEMENT OF THE ESTATE

A. Generally: Once appointed, the personal representative is responsible for ***managing the decedent's estate***. Estate management consists of identifying and collecting the decedent's assets; paying administrative expenses, taxes and decedent's debts; and distributing the remainder to the heirs in intestacy or under the will. See Haskell, pp. 162-65.

1. **Duties compared to those of trustee:** As in the case of a trustee, the personal representative is a ***fiduciary*** and owes certain duties to the decedent's beneficiaries. For further discussion of the duties of a fiduciary, see *infra*, pp. 185-96. In contrast to the trustee, who is a long-term manager of investments, the personal representative's role is ***short-term*** and is basically to ***wind up the financial affairs of the decedent***. See Haskell, p. 163.

   a. **Standards:** Consequently, the personal representative's performance is to be judged by somewhat ***different standards*** than those applied to trustees. A question may arise as to what standard is to be applied when judging the acts of an ***executor who is also the trustee***. In the case below the court held that an executor's duties are not altered by the fact that he is also the trustee and that the applicable standard is thus that of an executor.

   > **Example:** T places the bulk of his estate in a testamentary trust for the benefit of his four children. In his will he names Bank both executor and trustee. T's estate includes 27,700 shares of oil and gas stock. As executor, Bank sells 3,000 shares of the stock for approximately $16.00 per share (which is above the appraised value of the stock at T's death) for the

payment of claims, taxes and administrative expenses. A decision is made to retain the remaining shares for distribution into the trust, based on the determination that the oil and gas company was not deteriorating, that no further cash was needed to administer the estate and that the stock was a suitable asset for inclusion in the estate. The decision is also a product of state imposed restrictions on the power of an executor to reinvest. At the time the stock is distributed to the trust it is worth little more than $6.00 per share. The residuary trust beneficiaries claim that they are entitled to damages arising from the executor's alleged negligence in failing to sell the stock while its market price was above its appraised value at the date of death. They allege that as the Bank was both executor and trustee, the proper standard to be used in judging Bank's actions was that of a trustee and that Bank, by retaining the stock, violated the diversification of investments rule imposed on trustees.

Held, for Bank. The fact that Bank was named as both executor and trustee is immaterial. The executor's duty in handling estate assets does not vary according to whether the executor and trustee are the same or different entities. As opposed to a testamentary trustee, whose primary responsibility is to serve the beneficiaries under the terms of the trust, the executor's management of estate assets "concern[s] the interests of the trust beneficiaries only through its effect on the nature and value of the property distributed to the trustee and the timing of such distributions. . . ." In this regard, Bank as executor applied the skill, knowledge and competence ordinarily possessed of professional (as opposed to lay) executors. *Estate of Beach*, 125 Cal.Rptr. 570, 542 P.2d 994 (1975).

Note: In clearing Bank of any negligence in its duty to preserve estate assets, the court in *Beach* noted that the decline in the stock was due to the stock market's general decline and that an executor "normally is not held to account for failure to anticipate fluctuations in the price of a publicly traded stock arising from general market conditions, as distinct from conditions peculiar to the company in which the stock is held."

B. Inventory and appraisal: The personal representative is required to ***prepare and file with the court an inventory of the assets*** of the estate. The inventory usually contains an ***itemization and description*** of all property in the estate. This serves as ***prima facie evidence*** of the extent of the assets of the estate. Either prior to or after the filing of the inventory, the court appoints ***appraisers***, disinterested persons who value the items in the inventory. The appraisers' valuations are presumptively correct but not binding on anyone.

1. **Objection to inventory:** Some states have procedures under which an interested party's objections to the inventory may be heard and determined by the court.

C. **Collection of assets:** After identifying the estate's assets, the personal representative is required to collect such property so that it may be disposed of in accordance with the decedent's obligations and wishes.

1. **Commencing actions and compromising claims:** The personal representative may ***commence actions and compromise claims***. Some jurisdictions, however, require ***court approval of compromises***.

   a. **Substitution as party:** The personal representative must have himself substituted as a party with respect to all pending actions to which the decedent was a party during his lifetime.

D. **Preservation of assets:** After collecting the estate assets, the personal representative, while not a long-time manager of investments, must make certain decisions relating to the ***preservation*** of such property. He must decide which assets to ***liquidate*** and which to ***retain*** for distribution. See *Estate of Beach, supra*, p. 174.

1. **Sale of personal property:** Sometimes it is necessary to sell ***personal property*** to satisfy obligations of the estate.

   a. **Without court authority:** The personal representative may usually sell personal property ***without court authority*** if:

      i. there is no statute providing otherwise; or

      ii. the testator has given him a power of sale in the will.

   b. **By court order:** But some jurisdictions absolutely require court authority for the sale to be valid.

2. **Sale of real property:** Although the general rule is that real property passes directly to the heirs or devisees, the personal representative may have authority to sell realty if:

   a. he is given authority by the will to do so; or

   b. the personal assets are insufficient to pay the debts and the court orders the sale.

3. **Report of sale:** In most jurisdictions where either realty or personalty is sold by court order, the personal representative is required ***to report the sale to the court*** and obtain a confirmation of the sale.

4. **Business of decedent:** The personal representative must wind up a business conducted by decedent at his death unless he is given

authority to continue its operation by:

a. the court;

b. the testator's will; or

c. consent of all interested parties.

E. Claims against the estate: Immediately following appointment, the personal representative must ***publish notice*** of his appointment for a stated period of time in a newspaper of general circulation in the area. The notice serves to notify ***unknown creditors*** that claims against the estate must be presented within a statutory period of limitation. Due process requires actual notice to ***known creditors***; see *Tulsa Professional Collection Services, Inc. v. Pope, infra*, p.177.

1. Survival of claims: At common law contract claims generally survived the death of the debtor and could be enforced against and by the personal representative. Tort claims did not. Most jurisdictions have extended survival to various tort claims. Statutes dealing with this problem are of several types. They may provide:

a. that ***enumerated causes*** of action survive in addition to those that survived at common law;

b. that ***all causes*** of action survive ***except*** enumerated actions; or

c. that ***all causes*** of action survive.

2. Statutes barring claims not presented: Virtually all states have statutes called ***statutes of "nonclaim,"*** which provide that all claims, against an estate must be presented to the personal representative or filed with the probate court by a certain time or be ***"forever barred."*** A claim not presented within the period provided is not only barred procedurally, but ***ceases to exist legally*** — neither the personal representative nor the court has the power to allow such a claim after the nonclaim statutory period has elapsed.

a. Two types: There are two distinct types of nonclaim statute. One type provides a relatively short period — usually 2 to 6 months — that begins to run when ***probate proceedings are commenced***. (We'll refer to these as ***"shorter-type"*** statutes.) The other type provides a longer period — usually 1 to 5 years — that begins to run at the decedent's ***death***. (We'll call these ***"longer-type"*** statutes.)

i. Both types on books: Most states have ***both types*** on their books, and provide that a claim must ***satisfy both standards*** in order to be valid. This means, for instance, that even if probate proceedings are *never* commenced (so that the shorter-type statute never starts to run), the claim will be barred if not filed within the period set by the longer-type statute.

b. Direct notice required where feasible: The statutes on the books of most states require only ***publication notice*** to potential creditors that they should file claims with the probate court. But as the result of a 1988 Supreme Court decision, publication notice will now ***not*** usually be sufficient — in the usual situation where a state has a shorter-type statute (i.e., one triggered by the commencement of probate proceedings), the ***due process clause*** of the U.S. Constitution requires that known or reasonably-indentifiable creditors be given ***individualized notice*** (i.e., by ***mail***).

Example: Oklahoma law requires that creditors present certain claims to the executor of an estate within two months after publication of a notice advising of the commencement of probate proceedings. This provision is challenged as violative of the Due Process Clause. *Held* (by the U.S. Supreme Court), this provision violates due process. A fundamental requirement of due process is notice reasonably calculated to apprise interested parties of the action and afford them the opportunity to present their objections. Creditors may not know of the death or institution of probate proceedings, so publication of notice may not benefit them. As a result their claims would be extinguished. While the state has a legitimate interest in prompt resolution of probate proceedings, a requirement of actual notice does not hinder that goal. Therefore, *actual notice to known or reasonably ascertainable creditors* is required. *Tulsa Professional Collection Services, Inc. v. Pope*, 485 U.S. 478 (1988).

Note: The court in *Tulsa* hinted (though it did not explicitly hold) that a "longer-type" statute (one running from the date of death) does ***not*** trigger a due process requirement of personalized notice to creditors. The reason is that such a statute is a "self-executing" statute involving no meaningful state action, and the due process clause applies only to state action. (By contrast, the state is heavily involved in the operation of a "shorter-type" statute, since the statute doesn't start to run until the state appoints the personal representative.) Therefore, if a state were willing to rely solely on a longer-type statute, it could probably, even after *Tulsa*, rely solely on publication notice to creditors.

3. Contingent claims: A claim is called ***"contingent"*** if no one can ascertain at the decendent's death whether the claim will ever become due. (Example: The decedent before his death guaranteed to pay a third person's debt, and at death we don't know yet whether the third person will pay.) Nonclaim statutes vary with respect to the treatment of contingent claims.

a. **Presentment required:** Some require that the claim be presented before the nonclaim period runs, or else be barred. This type of statute generally requires either that the personal representative put aside assets to pay the filed contingent claims, or that the distributees file a bond requiring them to pay if the claim later becomes absolute.

b. **Presentment not required:** Other statutes do not require any action by the contingent creditor during the nonclaim period. If, after the period has run, the contingent claim becomes absolute, the creditor can sue the ***distributees***.

4. **General statute of limitations:** If the ***general statute of limitations*** has run on a debt of the decedent before his death the personal representative should not pay such claim. If he does he cannot charge the estate with it.

5. **Time limits concerning rejection of claims:** Statutes usually fix a period within which the personal representative can reject claims. Rejection must usually be in writing. Statutes usually require a creditor to file suit upon any rejected claim within a certain time after rejection or his claim will be forever barred.

6. **Secured creditors:** A secured creditor ***may collect the value of the security without presenting his claim*** to the personal representative but will lose the excess of the claim, if any, over the value of the security if he does not present his claim within the required period.

7. **General rule of exoneration:** Under the traditional common-law approach, an heir, legatee or devisee who receives mortgaged property is ***entitled to have the personal representative pay the mortgage debt***, if owed by the decedent, out of the general assets, and to take the property free of the mortgage, unless the will or statute indicates otherwise. This is the doctrine of ***exoneration of liens***.

   a. **Not always followed today:** Many states, and the UPC, ***no longer follow*** the doctrine of exoneration of liens. Thus UPC §2-607 provides that "a ***specific devise*** passes ***subject to any mortgage interest*** existing at the date of death, ***without right of exoneration***, regardless of a general directive in the will to pay debts."

8. **Priorities for payment of claims in insolvent estates:** Various statutes establish special procedures and ***priorities for the***

payment of claims in insolvent estates. The usual order of priority is:

- **a.** family allowances;
- **b.** funeral expenses;
- **c.** costs of administration;
- **d.** federal taxes;
- **e.** state taxes;
- **f.** wages, rents and judgment debts; and
- **g.** all other debts.

9. Protection for personal representatives in cases of insolvency: Under most modern statutes the ***personal representative pays debts only on court order which will not be made until after the period for proving claims is over***. In this way he receives protection against pitfalls often encountered at common law. Personal representatives of insolvent estates in the past faced the possibility of either: (1) exhausting the estate in payment of claims of an inferior class and therefore facing personal liability for late claims of a superior class or (2) pleading insufficiency of assets and thereby being held liable to a creditor under a procedural penalty.

10. Overpayment: ***Overpayment*** made to creditors, legatees or distributees ***may be recovered*** by the personal representative on the ground of mistake of fact.

11. Expenses of administration: As opposed to debts of the estate, which are obligations owed by the decedent while alive, ***expenses of administration*** are obligations undertaken by the personal representative for the estate after the death of the decedent. In most jurisdictions expenses of administration are paid out of the estate's assets prior to the satisfaction of decedent's debts.

- **a. Reasonable expenditures:** ***Reasonable amounts*** for decedent's funeral, for preservation of estate assets, for attorney's fees and other costs of administration ***may be deducted from the estate*** by the personal representative. Similarly, the personal representative is entitled to reimburse himself from the assets of the estate for reasonable expenditures made for the estate. The reasonableness of expenditures by the personal representative is determined by the discretion of the probate court.

12. Taxes: The personal representative has a duty to ***file*** all appropriate federal and state ***returns*** concerning taxes on the estate and to

pay the ***taxes*** due.

13. **Obligation to perform contracts:** The personal representative is ***bound to perform an impersonal contract*** of the decedent, such as a promissory note to pay money, but need not perform a purely personal contract, such as to try a lawsuit or paint a portrait.

F. **Accounting:** Statutes generally require that the personal representative render an ***accounting*** (showing the receipts and expenditures of the administration) to the court at stated intervals and upon the completion of the administration. Statutory ***penalties*** for failure to render accounts include: an action on the personal representative's ***bond***, ***revocation of letters***, ***attachment*** or ***imprisonment***.

1. **Conclusive adjudication:** When notice is given to interested parties with an opportunity for them to object to the accounts, acceptance by the court after a hearing on the objections, if any, constitutes a ***conclusive adjudication*** of the correctness and propriety of the accounts.

G. **Distribution:** Upon final settlement of the estate, the court gives a ***decree of final distribution*** finding the persons entitled to share in the estate and their respective shares under the will, or the statutes of descent and distribution in an intestate estate. The decree of final distribution is a ***judgment*** and is ***conclusive*** of the rights of the legatees, devisees and heirs, subject only to the right of appeal or relief for fraud.

1. ***Res judicata:*** The decree is ***res judicata*** both as to persons to take and the shares of each even if there is obvious error.
2. **Collateral attack:** The decree is not subject to ***collateral attack***.
3. **Manner of distribution:** The ***manner of distribution*** is:

    a. **specific legacies:** delivery of chattel to legatee;

    b. ***pecuniary legacies:*** payment in cash;

    c. ***residuary legacies and intestate distributions:*** personal representatives may have duty to convert personalty to cash, but statutes in many states provide that the court may order distribution in kind, in whole or in part.

    Note: The ***order*** of distribution in contrast to the ***manner***, is governed by the rules of ***abatement***. For a discussion of abatement, see *supra*, pp. 58-59.

H. **Construction proceedings:** ***Construction proceedings*** are usually brought after the will has been admitted to probate: (1) upon the initiative of the ***personal representative*** in order to carry out his duties without incurring personal liability; (2) by ***parties to an action at law*** such as ejectment or trespass in which the outcome may be affected by the interpretation of the will; or (3) at the time the personal representative files his plan of distribution, by persons who oppose it.

1. **Purpose:** Construction proceedings usually are ***necessary to:***
   a. clear up ambiguities in the will;
   b. provide for situations which the testator did not foresee;
   c. determine meanings of words used by testator; or
   d. determine which is controlling when two or more terms of a will are contradictory.
2. **Jurisdiction:** The jurisdiction of probate courts to construe wills is usually limited to matters necessary to the administrative process, such as matters determining to whom the executor should pay funds. Will construction proceedings other than those ancillary to the administration process, are usually conducted in the courts of general jurisdiction.
3. **Power to make binding interpretation:** Testamentary ***provisions giving the executor power to make a binding interpretation*** of the instrument are usually upheld.
4. **Maxims of construction:** For cases in which the court is unable to ascertain the testator's intention from the language of the will and surrounding circumstances but the will does not fail for indefiniteness, the courts have developed a series of ***maxims of construction*** to be applied. These have developed from what it is thought most testators would desire if they had considered the matter. See miscellaneous rules of construction, *supra* p. 61-62.
5. **Notice:** In any construction proceeding all interested parties must have ***notice*** of the proceeding and an ***opportunity to participate***.

IV. INFORMAL ADMINISTATION

A. **Minimum court supervision and formality:** In response to widespread criticism regarding the expense and time involved in formal estate administration, a number of states have adopted ***provisions for administering estates of limited size*** (which qualify under the statute) with a ***minimum of court supervision and a minimum of formality***.

B. **Non-intervention administration:** A few states permit ***non-intervention administration***, which allows the executor to administer the estate without court supervision if:

1. testator so provides in the ***will***; or
2. the residuary legatees and the executor ***consent*** to such administration.

C. Summary procedure: Many states, and UPC §§3-1201 and 1202, have statutes which provide a ***summary procedure for releasing the small estate from formal administration***. Such statutes usually are based on the estate's having total assets less than a statutory maximum, such as $5,000, or on the fact that assets are not in excess of statutory exemptions and allowances. Such statutes vary in detail, but in general contain these features:

1. **Affidavit:** The surviving spouse or children prepare an affidavit stating that they are entitled to payment of any obligations due decedent and that the value of the estate is less than the statutory amount;
2. **Time:** At least thirty days must have elapsed from the death of the decedent;
3. **Representative:** No personal representative is appointed; and
4. **Debtors:** Persons who deliver property or who pay debts due decedent (e.g., wages due or money in a bank account) based on the affidavit, are protected.

D. Payments without court supervision: Some states have statutory provisions allowing (in limited amounts) the ***payment of bank accounts, wage claims and insurance without administration***.

> **Example:** The Uniform Probate Code provides that if it appears from the inventory and appraisal that the value of the entire estate, less liens and encumbrances, does not exceed homestead allowance, exempt property, family allowance, cost and expenses of administration, reasonable funeral expenses, and reasonable and necessary medical and hospital expenses of the last illness of the decedent, the personal representative may immediately disburse and distribute the estate to the persons entitled thereto. The representative then files a closing statement with the court, and sends the statement to all distributees. That statement must also be sent to all creditors who are not paid. UPC §§3-1203 and 3-1204.

V. THE UNIFORM PROBATE CODE

A. Introduction: In 1962 the American Bar Association and The National Conference of Commissioners on Uniform State Laws began a study of the various probate laws. This study resulted in the promulgation of the Uniform Probate Code (UPC) in 1969. The UPC has since been amended several times. Among the UPC's more significant changes from the traditional rules of probate law are in the procedures for the administration of estates. The UPC has had a profound impact on American law, and is being adopted in an increasing number of states.

B. Administration under the UPC: The Uniform Probate Code adopts a ***"flexible system"*** of adminstration of decedent's estates. In general, it provides procedures under which: (1) procedural and adjudicative safeguards are adapted to the particular circumstances and; (2) the court's role in the administration of the estate remains passive until an interested party invokes its power to secure resolution of problem, at which time the role is limited to the relief sought. See UPC, Article 3, General Comment.

1. **Necessity of probate and court appointment of personal representative:** The Uniform Probate Code contemplates that: (1) some form of probate must occur to make a will effective to provide for the transfer of property and (2) court appointment of a personal representative is necessary in order to create the powers and duties of such office. See UPC §§3-102 and 3-103.

   a. **Informal distributions may be valid:** The Uniform Probate Code ***does not require any type of probate or administration proceeding***. It is within the discretion of persons claiming an interest in the estate to ask either for probate of a will or the appointment of an administrator. If no proceeding is brought within a three- year period, ***informal distributions*** of the decedent's property become ***final***.

2. **Two methods for probating wills:** The Uniform Probate Code provides ***two methods for probating wills:***

   a. **Informal:** "Informal" proceedings are nonadjudicative proceedings, and do not require advance notice to interested persons, a hearing, or the taking of testimony. This method resembles common-form probate. UPC §3-301.

   b. **Formal:** The other type is "formal" or "adjudicated" proceedings. Interested persons may request adjudicated proceedings instead of informal probate to determine whether the decedent left a valid will. A request for formal proceedings may also, but need not, request appointment of a personal representative. Notice is given to all interested persons. UPC §3-401.

3. **Two methods for appointing personal representative:** The Uniform Probate Code provides ***two methods of appointment of a personal representative:***

   a. **Informal:** Appointment by a non-judicial officer without notice or final adjudication of matters with respect to priority of appointment, see UPC §3-301;

   b. **Formal:** Appointment by judicial officer with notice to interested persons. See UPC §§3-402 and 3-414.

4. **Two schemes of estate settlement:** The Uniform Probate Code comtemplates two schemes of estate settlement: (1) fully supervised administration, and (2) "in and out" supervision.

   a. **Fully supervised administration:** Fully supervised administration is little different from the administration scheme in effect in most states. It requires:

      i. ***formal probate*** of a will or a judicial finding of intestacy;

      ii. ***court appointment*** of a personal representative; and

      iii. ***settlement*** of the estate under the continuing supervision of the court.

   b. **"In and out" supervision:** The "in and out" type of administration allows persons interested in the estate to obtain an adjudication on a particular matter without subjecting the whole administration process to supervision.

      Example: It is possible under this system to determine the status of a decedent as testate or intestate without subjecting the estate to court supervised administration.

5. **Powers of personal representatives:** Personal representatives are given statutory powers to collect and manage the assets of the estate and to distribute the estate. See UPC §3-704.

6. **Statutes of limitation:**

   a. **UPC §3-108:** ***Informal probate*** is final if no formal proceeding is begun within ***three years*** after death or within one year from informal probate, whichever is later;

   b. **UPC §3-108:** ***Intestate*** status is final if there is ***no probate*** within ***three years***; and

   c. **UPC §§3-802 and 3-803:** All claims are barred which arose before the death of decedent unless presented within ***one year after the decedent's death***. The defense of limitations may be ***waived*** by the personal representative and successors.

7. **Protection for purchasers:** ***Bona fide purchasers*** for value from personal representatives and distributees are protected in the event that an improper or unauthorized distribution is made. See UPC §§3-714 and 3-910.

THE TRUSTEE AS FIDUCIARY

Introductory Note: While the functions and powers of personal representatives differ from those of trustees, both are fiduciaries. Both have control over property in which others have rights of enjoyment. Consequently, they share the same basic fiduciary duties toward the beneficial owners of the property. Some of the material below, therefore, (see in particular the discusson of the fiduciary duty of loyalty), applies to personal representatives as well as trustees. See the preceding chapter for a more in depth coverage of the personal representative.

I. APPOINTMENT AND QUALIFICATION

A. **Basis for authority:** The ***trustee of an inter vivos trust*** derives his authority from the ***trust instrument***, and he administers the trust without supervision of the court. ***Testamentary trustees*** derive their authority from ***court appointments***. The court usually appoints the trustee named in the will. He is responsible to the court and must account to it at specified periods.

B. **Bond:** A bond is usually required before a person may qualify as a testamentary trustee. Wills often waive such requirements with respect to the trustee named.

II. DUTIES

A. **Duty to take possession of trust property:** It is the duty of the trustee to take possession without delay and maintain control of the trust property; he must use every reasonable means, such as litigation, to ***recover trust property*** in the hands of a third party, including the executor. He has a duty to take reasonable action to ***enforce claims*** which are held in trust and to ***defend***, to the extent reasonable, ***actions*** which may result in a loss to the trust estate.

Example 1: T holds in trust for C a $1000 promissory note signed by the maker, D. The note becomes due and is collectible. T negligently permits the statute of limitations to run. T sues D who sets up the statute of limitations in defense. The defense is good and the trust estate loses the note and the interest due thereon. T is liable to C for the loss.

Example 2: S's will names Bank as both executor and trustee of a testamentary trust. As executor, Bank retains counsel to prepare D's inheritance tax return. Counsel makes a judgmental error in the preparation resulting in a non-refundable overpayment by S's estate. The account of Bank as executor is nonetheless approved. A beneficiary of the trust files an objection to the account of Bank as trustee claiming that the trustee breached its duty to the beneficiaries when it failed to recover the overpayment from itself as executor.

Held, for the trust beneficiaries. A successor fiduciary is obliged to compel its predecessors to turn over trust property that they are under a duty to turn over and "to redress any breach of duty committed by them." Bank as trustee was thus under an unqualified duty "to take action to recover for the benefit of the beneficiaries that portion of the trust property [that] had been wrongfully disbursed by [Bank] while acting as executor." Moreover, inasmuch as Bank's liability stems from its failure to carry out responsibilities as trustee, the failure of the objecting beneficiary to file exceptions to the account of the executor does not preclude her from filing exceptions to Bank's account in its capacity as trustee. *In re First National Bank of Mansfield*, 37 Ohio St.2d 60, 307 N.E.2d 23 (1974).

Note: The dissent in *Mansfield* argued that the majority had erred in its basic premise that the executor was personally liable for the overpayment. According to the dissent an executor who reasonably relies on the advice of counsel, particularly in an area requiring legal expertise, is not personally responsible for its attorney's mistakes. As the executor was thus not negligent, the trustee breached no fiduciary duty in failing to recover the overpayment.

B. Duty of loyalty to the beneficiary: The trustee owes an absolute ***duty of loyalty to the beneficiary to administer the property solely in the interest of the beneficiary***. He may not:

1. ***sell to or buy from himself personally*** on behalf of the trust without the approval of a court regardless of the fairness and good faith of the transaction;

2. sell trust property to a ***third party*** with the understanding that the third party will ***convey to the trustee individually*** or hold it for him (what he may not do directly he may not do indirectly);

3. **purchase for himself trust property** or a claim against the trust at a ***private or judicial sale***;

4. ***purchase for himself*** individually property which it is his ***duty to purchase for the trust***;

5. ***use*** trust property for his ***own purposes***;

6. enter into ***competition*** with the beneficiary; or
7. ***disclose information*** to third persons where the disclosure would be detrimental to the trust.

Example: T holds $20,000 and Blackacre, worth $10,000, in trust for C. T personally owns 10,000 shares of stock in X corporation which are worth $4,000. T transfers these shares of stock to himself as trustee and pays himself $10,000 from the trust money causing a loss to the trust estate of $6,000. He then buys Blackacre from himself as trustee for $8,000 and sells it for $12,000 making $4,000 profit for himself. Both of these transactions constitute breaches of T's fiduciary duty to use the trust property wholly and solely for the benefit of the cestui. T is liable to C to account for the $4,000 profit made on Blackacre and for the $6,000 loss caused by the stock transaction. In no event has a trustee any right to deal with himself respecting the trust property unless he discloses all the facts to the beneficiary and the beneficiary is sui juris and consents thereto.

C. **Duty to preserve property:** It is the duty of the trustee to use ***due care to preserve the trust property.***

Example: T holds a dwelling house and lot in trust for C. T negligently permits the roof to deteriorate and leak so that rain causes the plaster to fall from the ceilings, the hardwood floors to warp, and the house to become unrentable. T is liable to C for the loss and damage to the trust property.

D. **Duty to disclose:** Although a trustee may deal with the beneficiary in the trustee's individual capacity, if the transaction concerns the interest of the beneficiary under the trust he must ***disclose*** to the beneficiary all relevant facts, including the legal rights of the beneficiary. The trustee must also, of course, ***deal fairly*** in the matter. See Rest. of Trusts, 2d. §170(2).

Example: A commercial building in downtown Seattle is left in trust. The bank trustee sells the property in a private sale without notice to the trust beneficiaries. *Held,* the trustee violated its fiduciary duty to the beneficiaries. Although the trustee had power to sell, it had the duty to inform the beneficiaries prior to the sale of all material facts of this nonroutine transaction, so that they could, for instance, have bid on the property themselves. Furthermore, the trustee did not obtain an independent appraisal of the property or offer it for sale on the open market, thus failing to obtain the best possible price for the property, a second breach of its duty. *Allard v. Pacific National Bank*, 663 P.2d 104 (Wash. 1983).

E. **Delegation of duties:** Except as otherwise permitted by the terms of the trust, the trustee ***cannot delegate*** his duty to administer the trust ***personally***. That is, he cannot delegate to another person duties the performance of which a person of ordinary prudence, in the management of his own affairs, would not employ an agent to do.

1. **Ministerial acts:** A trustee may, however, delegate the performance of ***purely ministerial acts***. For instance, the act of hiring an attorney, accountant or real estate agent may be found to be ministerial, so that the trustee may turn the hiring process over to another person. In determining the acts which a trustee may properly delegate, some of the relevant factors are:

   a. the amount of ***discretion*** involved;

   b. ***value*** of the property;

   c. whether the act is related to ***principal or income***;

   d. the ***remoteness*** of the subject matter of the trust; and

   e. whether the act involves ***professional skill*** or facilities possessed by the trustee himself. See Rest. of Trusts, 2d. §171, Comment d.

2. **Advice:** A trustee may take advice from others as to matters concerning the trust that he can not delegate, but he ***must personally decide*** the matter based on the advice.

3. **Supervision:** A trustee generally must ***supervise acts and conduct of agents and co-trustees*** to whom he has properly delegated duties in connection with trust matters. See Rest. of Trusts, 2d. §171, Comment k.

4. **Liability:** If the trustee does delegate where a person of ordinary prudence wouldn't, the trustee is personally liable for ***any loss***, not merely loss due to negligence. Dukeminier, p. 874; *Shriners' Hospitals for Crippled Children v. Gardiner*, 733 P.2d 1110 (Ariz. 1987).

F. **Duty to keep accounts:** The trustee has the ***duty to keep clear and accurate accounts*** with respect to the trust. He may be compelled to render an account of his administration.

1. **Regular accounting:** In many states testamentary trustees must submit accounts to the court at regular intervals for approval.

2. **Furnish information to beneficiary:** At the ***reasonable demand of the beneficiary***, the trustee is under a duty to ***furnish complete information*** as to the trust property and to permit him to ***inspect the property and records*** of the trust.

G. **Duty not to commingle:** The trustee ***may not commingle*** the trust property with his own or with other property not subject to the trust.

When he makes deposits of trust property in a bank he must use reasonable care to select a bank in sound condition and have the deposit earmarked as a deposit by him as trustee.

> **Example:** T has $20,000 in trust for C. T has an account in B bank entitled merely "T." T deposits the $20,000 trust money in that account. B bank has a claim against T and sets off the money in the account on such a claim. T committed a breach of trust when he intermingled the trust funds with his own and is liable to C for breach of trust.

H. Duty to invest trust property: The trustee has a ***duty to invest*** trust property and make it productive.

1. **Standards governing investments:** In making investments the trustee may be bound by: (1) directions by the ***settlor*** with respect to the investments to be made; (2) ***statutes*** governing investments by trustees; and (3) the standards which would govern a ***prudent investor*** in making investments of his own property with respect to the preservation of the estate and income to be earned.

   > **Note:** "Prudence" is judged from the ***trustee's perspective at the time the investment decision was made***, not with the benefit of hindsight or with the benefit of facts that the trustee could not reasonably have known.

   a. **Restrictions imposed by settlor:** The ***settlor often specifies*** in the will or trust instrument the ***types of investments*** the trustee is to make. The trustee is obligated to follow such directions and is protected against liability in doing so.

      i. **Changes in circumstances:** If the settlor directs the trustee to make or retain certain investments and, because of ***changes in circumstances*** not known to or anticipated by the settlor, compliance will result in loss to the trust or defeat of the trust purposes, the trustee may petition the court for ***permission to deviate from the terms of the trust***. The court, however, will not authorize a deviation merely for convenience or to produce greater income.

      Example: A testamentary trust is created in 1931 that provides that the trustees are to limit investments to certain types of bonds. In 1951, the life beneficiaries request the court to authorize the trustees to deviate from such terms and invest in accordance with the state's statutory "prudent man rule." All interested parties except one trustee and unlikely unborn contingent remaindermen support the application for modification. The argument behind the request is that world events and changes in the economy since the creation of the trust have rendered the restrictions ill-advised, and that the proposed deviation from the testator's specific intent concerning the nature of investments, would further his general intent to secure as large an income for the beneficiaries as possible commensurate with reasonable safety.

Held, the deviation from the trust terms concerning investments should *not* be authorized. When the main purpose of a trust is threatened, the courts can and should grant permission to deviate from restrictive administrative provisions. However, the settlor's expressed wishes regarding what constitutes appropriate investments cannot be lightly disregarded. The settlor managed to preserve a large fortune during the depression. He was determined to protect his heirs from the unpredictability of the economy and decided this could be best accomplished by limiting the reinvestment powers of the trustees. His restrictions have not proved devastating. No emergency exists and the main trust purpose is not being defeated. The value of the trust assets has increased throughout the years and the income has proved sufficient to support the reasonable needs of the beneficiaries. *Stanton v. Wells Fargo Bank & Union Trust Co.*, 150 Cal.App.2d 763, 310 P.2d 1010 (1957).

Note: The power to permit deviation from the terms of private trusts is analogous to the ***cy pres*** doctrine applicable to charitable trusts. For further discussion of ***cy pres*** see *supra*, pp. 114-17, 120-150.

ii. **Discretion often granted:** The settlor will often grant to the trustee discretion in making investments. In such cases he does not have to select from the ***"legal list"*** (*infra*). However, he does not have the right to exercise his discretion recklessly. He must use good faith and prudence.

Note: In some legal-list states such clauses in wills and trusts as ***"invest as he deems proper"*** may be narrowly construed to mean ***"within the legal list"*** (*infra*).

b. **The "prudent person" rule for investments:** Nearly all states regulate, either by statute or by common-law doctrines, the ***investment practices*** of trustees. Most states follow the ***"prudent person"*** (formerly the "prudent man") standard: the trustee, in making investment decisions, is "to observe how men of prudence, discretion and intelligence manage their own affairs, not in regard to ***speculation***, but in regard to the permanent disposition of their funds, considering the ***probable income***, as well as the ***probable safety*** of the capital to be invested." *Harvard College v. Amory*, 26 Mass. 446 (1830).

Example: D, a bank acting as trustee, buys stocks for a series of trusts whose beneficiaries are the Ps. D has previously adopted internal standards requiring that stocks bought for trust accounts (1) be rated at least B-plus or better by a particular rating service and (2) be issued by companies having at least $100 million in annual sales. Certain stocks bought by D for the Ps' trusts fail to satisfy one or both of these requirements. Also, the stocks fail to satisfy certain other safety standards urged by leading commentators (e.g., a good dividend record). D then sells the stocks at a loss, at a time when the market is extremely depressed. The Ps' bring a class action against D seeking damages equal to the difference between the money paid by the trust for the stocks and the money received when the stocks were sold (plus the interest that would have been received on this difference during the interim).

Held, for the Ps. D failed to act as a prudent investor would have acted. The fact that D failed to meet its own preannounced safety standards is not dispositive. But this factor, together with the fact that the purchases violated safety rules urged by other experts, and the fact that D's own experts at trial never recommended the purchase of these stocks, made D's purchases a violation of its duty of prudence. Also, when D acted prudently in buying some stocks, but sold them when the market was very depressed, the sales were a failure of prudence. A judgment of $1.4 million is affirmed. *First Alabama Bank of Montgomery v. Martin*, 425 So.2d (Ala. 1982).

i. **Uniform Probate Code:** The Uniform Probate Code similarly follows the prudent person rule. See UPC §7-302, setting the standard as that of "a prudent man dealing with the property of another . . . " Observe that this provision requires the trustee to invest as a prudent person would invest ***another person's*** money, which is probably a more demanding standard than the traditional *Harvard College* "manage one's own affairs" standard.

ii. **"Legal list" states:** A few states have statutes containing a ***list*** of the types of investments which a trustee may legally make. These statutes are of two types: (1) ***"permissive"*** statutes, under which the trustee may invest outside the list, but has the burden of justifying any investment not on the list (so that the list functions as a sort of "safe harbor"); and (2) ***"mandatory"*** statutes, under which the trustee is automatically liable for losses due to making of any investment not on the list.

2. **Investments in participating mortgages, etc.:** Because of the rule against ***commingling***, until recent years it was held that investments in ***participating mortgages, common trust funds and investment trusts*** were improper. The ***modern trend***, however, is to ***allow*** such investments, usually by way of specific legislation subject to restrictions which vary from state to state.

3. **Duty to dispose of improper investments:** Except as the terms of the trust otherwise provide, the trustee has a duty to dispose of investments included in the trust property when the trust is created which are not proper investments for trustees. If investments, although proper when added, subsequently become improper, the trustee has a duty to dispose of them as soon as reasonably possible.

   Example: Securities are given to a bank in trust with directions in the will to invest in "legal securities." That refers to a list of investments approved by state law for fiduciaries. Many of the securities received are not "legal securities." The bank retains them for many years based on a state statute allowing retention of non-legal securities except where the will specifically directs the manner in which the trust fund should be invested. The beneficiaries bring suit for breach of trust. *Held*, the trustee is ordered to sell the securities and pay into the trust the difference between the value of the non-legal securities when accepted and the amount received from their sale, plus the loss of income resulting from their retention. *Dickerson v. Camden Trust Co.*, 64 A.2d 214 (N.J. 1949).

I. **Duty to distribute income and principal properly:** It is the duty of the trustee to ***distribute income and principal in accordance with the terms of the trust***. A settlor may specifically provide for the allocation of receipts and expenses to principal and income.

   1. **Allocation of receipts:** When the trust documents are silent as to allocation of principal and income the ***general rule*** is that ***income*** is the return derived from the principal and ***principal*** is the property received as a substitute for, or change in form of, the original corpus of the trust. Thus, in the case of a business, the net profits are income while increases in good will or the value of assets are principal.

      a. **Delayed sale of unproductive property:** When the trustee is under a duty to sell ***unproductive property*** and ***the sale is delayed***, a portion of the proceeds is to be allocated to income equal to the amount it would have earned had the property been sold at the time the duty to dispose of it arose and the proceeds had been invested in normally productive property. *In* *re Kuehn*, 308 N.W.2d 398 (S.D.1981); Bogert, p. 431; McGovern, p. 681.

b. Wasting assets: A ***"wasting asset"*** is an asset which is ***consumed***, such as mines or oil and gas wells. If a wasting asset is part of the trust property, the common law makes the division between principal and income depend on whether the asset was already being exploited at the moment the trust acquired the asset:

i. Not exploited at time of acquisition: If the asset was ***not*** being exploited at the time the settlor gave it to the trust, the holder of the income interest can receive proceeds from exploitation only if some of the income is put aside into an ***"amortization fund"*** which will eventually go to the holder of the principal interest. For instance, if land has no oil well on it when a trust receives it, and the trust then permits a well to be drilled, some part of the royalties from the well must be put aside for the principal-holder, since the well is being depleted and may have no value by the time the principal is distributed. Bogert, p. 437.

ii. Exploited at time of acquisition: But if the asset ***was*** being exploited at the time the settlor contributed it to the trust, the holder of the income interest gets ***all proceeds*** from exploitation (without any deduction for amortization), under the common-law view. This is because the settlor is viewed as wanting the income beneficiary to receive the same income as the settlor himself was getting.

Example: The owner of certain oil royalty interests is receiving royalty payments when he places them in a trust. Income beneficiaries are paid all income, and no reserve is set up for the benefit of remaindermen of the trust. *Held*, since the oil wells were open when the trust was created, the income beneficiary is entitled to all royalties without deduction for depletion. *First Wyoming Bank v. First National Bank & Trust of Wyoming*, 628 P.2d 1355 (Wyo. 1981).

iii. Revised Uniform Act changes rule: The Revised Uniform Principal and Income Act, in force in nearly 20 states, changes the common-law rule. Under the Uniform Act, it makes no difference whether natural resources were being taken from the land at the time the trust received the land. The trustee gets full discretion in deciding how to allocate royalties, except that no more than 50% of the net receipts in any year may be added to principal. Revised Uniform Principal and Income Act, §9.

c. **Allocation of dividends:** There are a number of views as to proper allocation of ***dividends***:

i. **The Kentucky Rule:** Under the "Kentucky rule," all dividends regardless of form or source are income. In some jurisdictions accepting this view the rule has been modified to regard stock dividends from the declaring corporation as principal.

ii. **The Pennsylvania Rule:** Under the "Pennsylvania rule," ordinary cash dividends are income. Extraordinary cash and stock dividends are examined to determine source and allocated to maintain book value of the stock as of the date of creating the trust.

iii. **The Massachusetts Rule:** Under the "Massachusetts rule," cash dividends of whatever kind are income, as are dividends paid in the stock of a company other than the one declaring the dividend, such as stock in a subsidiary company. Stock dividends in the declaring corporation are principal. This is the most widely used rule. It is also the rule adopted by the Revised Uniform Principal and Income Act, in effect in nearly 20 states. See Revised Uniform Principal and Income Act §6. *In re Arens' Trust*, 197 A.2d. 1 (N.J. 1964); *In re Trust of Warner*, 117 N.W.2d 224 (Minn. 1962).

Example 1: T by will devises to B "during her natural life, all dividends accruing and payable on the fifty shares of capital stock I own in [X Corp.] as well as all dividends on my seventeen shares of capital stock in [Y Corp.]." Since T's death, twenty five and one-half shares of Y Corp. have been issued as a result of successive common stock dividends being declared. At issue is whether title to these shares belongs to the remaindermen or B, the life tenant.

Held, for the remaindermen. With respect to extraordinary corporate dividends, states generally follow one of three approaches known respectively as the Kentucky rule, the Massachusetts rule, and the Pennsylvania rule (see also *supra*). The Kentucky rule awards all such dividends in their entirety to the life tenant. The Masachusetts rule, which is the majority rule, awards to the corpus (or remaindermen) the entire dividend if essentially a stock dividend and to income (or the life tenant) the entire dividend if essentially a cash dividend. The Pennsylvania rule "inquires as to the time covered by the accumulation of earnings embraced by the extraordinary distribution. If earned before the commencement of the life estate, it goes to the corpus; if earned after that time, then to the life estate as income." The Massachusetts rule is the best rule as it is direct, simple and easy to apply. Moreover, it is most likely to conform to the testator's intentions. A stock dividend is not in any true sense a dividend at all. Rather than distributing property it simply dilutes the shares as they existed before. Thus, only ***cash*** dividends declared during B's life on the stock issued as a result of a stock dividend shall be payable to B. *Bowles v. Stilley's Executor*, 267 S.W.2d 707 (1954).

Example 2: A publically traded company declares a stock dividend in shares of another company. *Held*, these shares should be distributed to trust income beneficiaries. *First Wyoming Bank v. First National Bank & Trust of Wyoming*, 628 P.2d 1355 (Wyo.1981).

2. **Allocation of expenses:** When the trust instrument does not provide for allocation of expenses between income and principal, ordinary expenses, such as recurring taxes, accountant's fees, repairs, maintenance and utility charges, are to paid out of income. Expenses which are extraordinary or largely beneficial to persons with a remainder interest should be paid from trust principal. Revised Uniform Principal and Income Act, §13; Bogert, p. 446.

   Note: A trustee is now generally held to be able to establish depreciation reserves and charge them against income.

3. **Duty to act impartially:** The trustee has a duty when there are successive beneficiaries to ***act impartially*** and with due respect for their respective interests. Thus, a trustee may not invest in unproductive property that will produce no income for the life beneficiary but may increase in value and thus unduly benefit those with a remainder interest. Conversely, a trustee may not retain property that is producing current income but depreciating rapidly.

   Example: Three commercial buildings are left in trust. The trustee retains the properties, and distributes rents to the income beneficiaries. The trustee knows (or at least should have known) that the value of the buildings to the remaindermen will be small, considering the decline in property values generally in the area and the fact that the buildings have not been renovated or modernized. The Ps (holders of the interests in the trust's principal) sue the trustee. *Held*, the trustee acted unfairly, as distinguished from imprudently, in retaining the buildings. The trustee must pay $345,000 to the trust principal, to put the Ps in the position they would have been in had the trustee sold the properties at the time (34 years earlier) when the depreciating value and consequent unfairness to the Ps should have become apparent. *Dennis v.*

Rhode Island Hospital Trust National Bank, 744 F.2d 893 (1st Cir.1984).

4. **When income begins:** When the instrument does not specially provide, income usually begins:

   a. in the case of a ***testamentary trust***, on the date of death;

   b. in the case of an ***inter vivos trust***, on the effective date of the trust.

5. **Payment to estate of life beneficiary:** When property is held in trust to pay income to a life beneficiary and then principal to others, income accruing but not paid out prior to death of the life beneficiary is paid to his personal representative.

III. POWERS

A. **Generally:** The trustee has such ***powers as are expressly*** given to him in the ***trust instrument*** and such ***implied powers*** as are necessary to the ***accomplishment of the trust purpose*** and which are not prohibited by the terms of the trust. The trustee must do the things which the trust instrument commands and he may do the things which are left to his discretion provided he does not abuse such discretion. Dukeminier, p. 891.

> **Example:** S conveys Blackacre to T in trust for C and directs T to sell Blackacre and invest the proceeds in Government bonds bearing 4% interest. S reserves no power to revoke the trust. T takes possession of Blackacre and is about to sell it for a very good price for such land, \$50,000. S changes his mind and tells T not to sell Blackacre. T advise S that he is directed in the trust deed to sell Blackacre and feels he must obey such command. S sues T to enjoin such sale. S will fail in his suit. Unless the settlor reserves some power over the trust in the trust instruments, he has no right, power or authority over the trust or the trust property. The rights, duties and powers of the trustee are determined by the trust instrument or terms of the trust at the time of its creation. Therefore, T is bound to sell Blackacre and invest the proceeds in U.S. bonds; the fact that S has changed his mind is quite immaterial.

B. **Power to incur reasonable expenses:** Unless forbidden to do so by the trust instrument a trustee ***may incur reasonable expenses*** to carry out the trust purposes.

> **Example:** S conveys Blackacre, a house and lot to T to hold in trust for C and to pay the income therefrom to C. The house is in a good location and in good repair, but is old and

does not have a modern kitchen. The house is either not rentable at all or must be rented at a very low rent. With a modern kitchen it would be readily rentable for $350.00 per month. T makes a contract to have a new kitchen installed for $2,500. The remodeling is done and he rents the house for a year at $350 per month. T personally pays for the improvements. T is entitled to reimbursement from the fund. Ordinarily a trustee does not have power to expend trust funds for the improvement of the trust property unless the trust instrument so provides; however if such improvements are reasonable in amount and are necessary to carry out the trust purpose or to make the property reasonably productive, the trustee is empowered to make such improvements and to reimburse himself for the expenses incurred in so doing. In this case it might be said that the trust instrument impliedly authorized T to improve the property because he was to pay C the income therefrom, which could not be done if the property could not be rented. The trust purpose requires an income; the improvements are necessary to make the property reasonably productive; and the expenditure of $2500 is reasonable under the circumstances. Hence, the expenses incurred for the improvements are proper and T is entitled to reimbursement.

C. **Power to lease:** Unless forbidden to do so by the trust instrument, the trustee has the power to lease trust property for such periods and on such terms as are reasonable.

D. **Power to sell:** The trustee has a power to sell trust property if: (1) the trust instrument expressly confers such power; or (2) the sale is necessary or proper to carry out the purposes of the trust. Courts almost always find the power of sale implied as to personal property. By contrast, many jurisdictions are likely to find no such implied power with respect to real estate.

E. **Power concerning claims:** The trustee may, if appropriate to the trust purpose, ***compromise, abandon, or submit to arbitration claims*** affecting the trust property.

Example: S bequeaths to T all of his property in trust for C. Among the assets T receives is a promissory note for $1,000 signed by X who is honest but insolvent and judgment proof, and being threatened with involuntary bankruptcy by his other creditors. As a compromise T accepts $500 from X and returns the note to X marked paid in full. This is within T's power as trustee.

F. **Power of shareholder:** The trustee holding securities has the ***power to vote the shares*** and exercise any rights of ordinary shareholders.

G. **Power of predecessor:** A successor trustee or surviving trustee ***may exercise the powers conferred upon his predecessor*** unless it it otherwise provided in the terms of the trust.

H. **No power to mortgage, etc.** Unless expressly provided in the terms of the trust instrument the trustee has ***no power to mortgage or pledge the trust property or to borrow money on the credit of the trust***.

I. **Joint action to be binding:** In a private trust if there are ***several trustees*** they must act jointly unless the terms of the trust provide otherwise. A majority may act in a charitable trust.

IV. LIABILITIES

A. **Liability on contracts:** The trustee is ***personally liable on all contracts made by him in the administration of the trust*** unless it is expressly agreed that the creditor shall look only to the trust property for his compensation. *Vaughan v. Jones*, 179 Okla. 545, 66 P.2d 504 (1937).

> **Example:** T holds Blackacre in trust for C with express authority to sell the land and invest the proceeds in securities. T lists Blackacre for sale with broker B, who sells it and earns the agreed commmission of $2000. T refuses to pay B's commission. B sues T for such. T insists that he should be sued in his representative capacity as "T, trustee for C." T's contention is immaterial, because a suit against "T" as defendant has the same legal effect as a suit against "T, trustee for C." In both cases T is personally liable and a judgment against him can be satisfied out of T's individual property. Furthermore, there is no right on the part of the judgment creditor to satisfy such judgment out of the trust property in the absense of an equity decree permitting such. In this case when T listed Blackacre for sale with B and agreed to pay the commission for B's sale of the property, it was T's promise to pay and he alone is liable personally on the obligation. If it is an expense properly incurred in the administration of the trust, as this one is, the trustee may reimburse himself out of the trust property. If it is not a proper expense the trustee has no right to reimburse himself.
>
> **Note:** Had T, when he gave the listing to B, told B that he, T, would not be personally liable on the contract for B's commission, and that B would have to look to the trust fund solely for his pay, B's sole remedy would have been against the trust property. See Rest. of Trusts, 2d §§262-263.

B. **Liability for torts:** A trustee is ***personally liable for all torts committed in the course of the administration of the trust assets*** to the same extent as if he had held them free of trust. Thus if the trust holds an unincorporated business, the trustee will be liable under *respondeat superior* for torts committed by the business' employees.

> **Example:** L, as co-executor of an estate, continues to operate the deceased's automobile agency. J is injured at the agency because of the negligence of an employee. *Held*, L is personally liable to J for his injury, based on the doctrine of *respondeat superior*. However, L may seek indemnification from the estate, because L is not personally at fault. *Johnston v. Long*, 181 P.2d 645 (Cal. 1947). See also Rest. of Trusts, 2d §264.

C. **Liability for breach of trust:** The trustee is ***liable to the beneficiary for any injury caused by a breach of trust***. (The phrase "breach of trust" refers to the breach of *any* duty owed to the beneficiary).

1. **Loss in value of trust property:** The trustee is ***not liable*** to the beneficiary ***for loss or decrease in value*** of trust property ***unless there is a breach of trust***.

> **Example:** T holds negotiable securities in trust for C and has them in the safe deposit box in B bank. Burglars break into the bank and steal the securities. As there is no negligence or breach of duty on T's part, he is not liable for the loss to C.

2. **Loss of interest:** The trustee is liable to the beneficiary for ***loss of interest*** if he ***holds trust money an unreasonable time without investing it***, when such investments are readily available.

> **Example:** T has $10,000 which he holds in trust for C. T deposits the money in a commercial bank which does not pay any interest on deposits. Reasonable diligence on T's part would disclose many sound investments for the money at 6% interest within 90 days after deposit. T leaves the $10,000 in the bank for more than a year without investing it. T is liable to C for interest on the money after the 90 day period.

3. **Payments to persons other than beneficiary:** The trustee is liable for ***payment of trust funds or income to anyone other than the beneficiary***.

> **Example:** T is trustee of $60,000 for C for life and then for D, which T has invested at 5% interest. For many years T, who lives in Chicago, has been sending a regular monthly check for $200 to C, who lives in Seattle. C dies but T does not learn of the death. T continues to send the checks which are returned in T's regular monthly vouchers, having been paid out of the trust estate. T does not examine the monthly vouchers; if he did so, he would discover that the endorsements are forgeries. This continues for 2 years after C's death. T is liable

to D for the loss of $200 per month for 2 years, or $4800. See Rest. of Trusts, 2d §226.

4. **Breach of trust by co-trustee:** The trustee is liable to the beneficiary for ***loss caused by a breach of trust by a co-trustee*** if he participates in such breach or delegates the administration of the trust to a co-trustee improperly.

   Example: T and X are trustees of a $100,000 trust estate for C which is in the form of negotiable securities readily reduced to cash. T tells X to make such investments and do with the trust property as he wishes without consulting T (as T knows nothing about investments). T makes no inspection of the trust accounts and does not even inquire of X about the trust property. He simply relies on X to administer the trust. This goes on for several years. X embezzles $60,000 of the trust property and dies insolvent. T is liable to C for the loss. He has breached his duty to exercise due and constant diligence concerning the administration of the trust property; it was T's personal duty to supervise the administration by his co-trustee. He had no right to delegate or divide the powers of administration. See Rest. of Trusts, 2d §4.

5. **Losses and profits**: The trustee, in the event of a ***breach*** of trust, is chargeable with: (1) any ***loss*** resulting from the breach of trust; (2) any ***profit*** resulting from the breach of trust; and (3) any ***profit*** the trust would have made in the absence of the breach of trust.

   a. **No offset:** In measuring damages caused by breach of trust, courts do ***not*** allow ***"netting"*** or ***"offset"***. That is, the court will not allow gains on some investments to offset losses on other (imprudent) investments — each investment is separately evaluated for whether it caused losses.

      Example: The trust corpus is $200,000. The trustee invests $100,000 in speculative gold stocks and realizes a profit of $9,000. He also invests $100,000 in speculative oil stock and sustains a loss of $50,000. He is accountable for the $59,000 total of loss and profit. The trustee may not set off the $9,000 profit against the $50,000 loss. See Rest. of Trusts, 2d §205. See also *In Re Accounting of the Bank of New York*, 323 N.E.2d 700 (N.Y. 1974).

   b. **Profits:** The trustee is accountable to the beneficiary ***for any profit*** arising out of a transaction involving the trust property ***even though he has not committed a breach of trust***.

      Example: A devises Blackacre to T in trust for C. Blackacre is subject to a first mortgage of $10,000 and a second mortgage of $5,000. To prevent the foreclosure of the second mortgage, T purchases it with his own funds for $3,000. Later the full amount of the second mortgage is realized. T is only entitled to $3,000. See Rest. of Trusts, 2d §203.

6. **Appreciation damages:** In some situations, the trustee may be liable for ***"appreciation"*** damages. These are the damages attributable to the ***increase in value*** of estate assets between the date that they were sold and the date of the court decree finding that the sale violated a fiduciary duty.

   a. **Duty to retain property:** Where the trustee has a duty to ***retain*** the property and instead sells it, appreciation damages are allowed. The reason is that the beneficiaries are entitled to be placed in the same position they would have been in had the trustee obeyed her duty.

   b. **Duty to sell property:** Where a trustee has a duty to sell assets, beneficiaries are only entitled to a fair price on the date of sale. If assets are sold at an inadequate price, damages are the difference between the sale price and the fair market value on the date of sale.

      i. **Exception for misfeasance:** But where the breach of duty consists of a serious ***conflict of interest***, as well as in selling for too little, appreciation damages are usually allowed.

      Example: A famous artist (Mark Rothko) leaves paintings to A, B and C in trust, and directs that they be sold. The trustees contract with an art gallery for the gallery to sell the paintings at a 50% commission. This gallery had previously sold the artist's works for a 10% commission. A is an officer and director of the gallery. B is a "not-too-successful artist, financially", who finds it to his advantage to curry favor with A and agree to the contracts. C does not act in his own self-interest, but knows of A's conflict of interest and agrees to the contracts without investigation or consultation with disinterested appraisers. The paintings appreciate between the time some are sold to the public and the date of the court decree. Beneficiaries sue to cancel the contracts, replace the trustees, return unsold paintings and obtain damages for paintings sold to bona fide purchasers.

      Held, for the beneficiaries on all counts. On the question of damages, A and B transferred the property in breach of trust, and that fact was known to the galleries. A, B and the galleries must therefore pay appreciation damages, measured by the difference between the price the estate received for the paintings and their value at the date of the court decree. This is because, had the paintings not been sold in breach of the fiduciary relationship, they would still be part of the estate.

The sales were not merely below market value, but were "inherently wrongful transfers which should allow the owner to be made whole." C is liable only for the difference between the value of the paintings and their selling price — he is not responsible for appreciation damages because he was not in a dual position acting for his own interests. *In re Rothko*, 372 N.E.2d 291 (N.Y. 1977).

7. **Remedies for breach of trust:** Besides money damages for breach of trust, certain ***equitable remedies*** may be available to a beneficiary. The question of the fiduciary's conduct of the trust may be raised in the following proceedings:

   a. a request by fiduciary for ***instructions***;

   b. an ***injunction*** action by beneficiaries against a threatened breach of trust;

   c. an action by beneficiaries for ***specific performance*** of trust obligations;

   d. objections filed to fiduciary's ***accounts*** with request to surcharge;

   e. an action to ***appoint a receiver***; or

   f. an action to ***waive the fiduciary's compensation***. See Rest. of Trusts, 2d §§197-198.

8. **Right to sue for breach:** No one except the beneficiary (not even the settlor) has a right to enforce the trust or maintain an action for breach of trust, unless the settlor has retained an interest which would be affected by the breach, such as the power to revoke. See Rest. of Trusts, 2d §200.

   a. **Action by beneficiary:** A beneficiary may maintain an action:

      i. to compel the trustee to perform his duties;

      ii. to enjoin a breach of trust;

      iii. to compel the trustee to redress a breach of trust; or

      iv. to appoint a receiver to administer the trust. See Rest. of Trusts, 2d §199.

   b. **Estoppel:** Even where a trustee commits an act which would otherwise be a breach of duty, if the beneficiary is found to have ***approved*** the act, the beneficiary will be***"estopped"*** from later suing for the breach. Successors in interest to the beneficiary will also be estopped. Estoppel frequently occurs when the beneficiary approves a good-faith action made by a trustee under a conflict of interest.

Example: S creates an inter vivos trust with Bank T as trustee. The income is to be paid to S for life, and then to certain of S's relatives. S reserves the right to cancel the trust at any time. The corpus consists of 3,000 shares of stock in Bank B. Later, Bank T merges with Bank B. S is aware of the merger, and is aware that Bank T is now in effect acting as trustee over stock in itself. Nonetheless, S asks that the shares be kept. Later, the value of the stock declines from $400 per share to $18 per share. S dies. A guardian is appointed for P, a minor who is one of the remaindermen following S's life interest. The guardian aserts that Bank T, by keeping the stock after the merger, had a conflict of interest, and should therefore be liable to P and the other beneficiaries for the decline in value.

Held, for Bank T. After the merger, Bank T was indeed serving as trustee of stock in itself, a conflict of interest. Therefore, Bank T would normally be automatically liable for the decline in value. But because S knew of the conflict, and consented to keeping the shares, she was estopped from later objecting. Furthermore, this estoppel also now binds P and the other beneficiaries, whose interest derived from S. *City Bank Farmers Trust Co. v. Cannon*, 51 N.E.2d 674 (1943).

9. **Effect of exculpatory clauses:** A ***settlor***, by the express provisions of the trust, ***may relieve the trustee from liability for breach of trust***. Such provisions are strictly construed by the courts and are generally ***limited*** to cases of ***errors in judgment and mistakes committed in good faith***. An exculpatory provision which attempts to relieve the trustee of liability for ***willful wrongdoings or gross negligence*** is against public policy and ***void***.

   a. **Ineffective if obtained by breach of fiduciary relationship:** An exculpatory provision is ineffective if it is made part of a trust agreement by reason of the ***trustee's breach of a fiduciary or confidential relationship***.

   Example: The trustee, an attorney, draws the trust document for his client, who is not a person with business experience, and inserts the exculpatory clause without discussing it with the client. The client obtains no independent advice. The exculpatory provision would be held to be of no effect. See Rest. of Trusts, 2d §222.

V. TRUSTEE'S COMPENSATION AND RIGHT OF INDEMNITY

A. **Compensation:** A trustee is entitled to ***reasonable compensation*** for his services. This amount may be: (1) stipulated in the ***trust***

agreement; (2) ***fixed by the court*** after considering the value of the trust assets, cost of comparable services, amount of responsibility, time consumed, skill of the trustee and other relevant factors; or (3) ***fixed by state statute or court rule*** usually on the basis of capital or income and capital. Bogert, p. 505.

1. **May waive compensation:** A trustee may ***waive compensation*** by paying out all net income to the beneficiary or making an accounting without asserting the right to compensation.
2. **Liens:** The trustee has a ***lien*** on the trust property to the extent of any amount properly due him for services.
3. **Denial of compensation:** The court may ***reduce or deny*** compensation to a trustee guilty of a breach of trust. This is up to the court's discretion, so if the trustee acts by mistake or in ignorance and damages are slight, compensation may still be allowed. *In re Johnston's Estate*, 18 A.2d 274 (N.J. 1941).

B. Indemnity: The trustee is entitled to ***indemnity*** out of the trust property for:

1. expenses properly incurred in the administration of the trust;
2. expenses not properly incurred in the administration of the trust if such expenses were incurred:
   - **a.** conferring a benefit on the trust to the extent of the benefit incurred; or
   - **b.** with the consent of beneficiary.

The trustee is entitled to ***exoneration*** for liabilities incurred by him either on contracts or in tort if such liabilities were incurred by him in the proper administration of the trust.

VI. TRACING TRUST FUNDS

A. May trace property or its product: If a trustee wrongfully disposes of trust property, the beneficiary ***may trace either the property or its product*** into the hands of third parties (except a purchaser for value without notice) or the trustee, and secure its return to the trust. The beneficiary in each instance must elect whether to trace the original trust property or the product. If the product is more valuable than the trust property used in its acquisition, the beneficiary may, by tracing, obtain any profit derived from the disposition. Bogert, p. 577.

> **Example:** The trust res consists of standing timber. The trustee wrongfully cuts down the trees and has them made into lumber. The beneficiary is entitled to recover the "product," which is the lumber, from the trustee.

B. **Priority:** Tracing of trust property or product wrongfully disposed of places the beneficiary in a position of ***priority over general creditors*** if the trustee is bankrupt or insolvent. The beneficiary's right is based on a ***property right*** in the trust res or its product.

C. **Identification:** In order to trace trust property the beneficiary must be ***able to identify the trust property or its product***. In making identification of the trust property, the beneficiary is entitled to the benefit of certain ***presumptions***. Bogert, p. 580.

1. If the trustee mingles trust property with his own property and exchanges the mingled property for other property, the beneficiary may enforce a constructive trust on the property for which it is exchanged, proportionate to his share of the mingled fund.

2. If the trustee mingles trust funds with his own funds in an account or fund, it is presumed that any withdrawals from the fund were of trust moneys proportionate to the total of the fund.

> **Example:** A is trustee of $5,000 which he deposits in his bank account where he has personal funds of $5,000. T withdraws $5,000 and purchases stock which increases in value to $50,000. B is entitled to one-half of the stock as well as one-half of the money remaining in the bank.

D. **Withdrawal and dissipations:** If the trustee mingles trust funds with his own personal funds and then ***withdraws and dissipates the withdrawn commingled funds***, subsequent additions from his personal funds to the commingled deposit may not be claimed by the beneficiary unless the trustee makes subsequent deposits ***intending restitution***.

> **Note:** The additions may be claimed by the beneficiary when the amounts withdrawn are ***not*** dissipated and are redeposited.

E. **Equitable lien:** In any case in which a beneficiary may trace the trust funds or product wrongfully disposed of, he may elect instead to enforce an ***equitable lien*** upon the product in the hands of the trustee to secure payment of damages for breach of trust.

F. **Bona fide purchaser:** The beneficiary may ***not*** enforce a constructive trust against a bona fide purchaser for value who takes without actual or constructive notice of the trust.

ESSAY EXAM QUESTIONS AND ANSWERS

The following Essay Questions are taken from the Wills & Trusts volume of *Siegel's Essay & Multiple Choice*, a series written by Brian Siegel and now published by Emanuel Law Outlines, Inc. The full volume contains 25 essays (with model answers), as well as 91 multiple choice questions. (The essay questions were originally asked on the California Bar Exam, and are copyright the California Board of Bar Examiners, reprinted by permission.) The book is available from your bookstore, or from us directly.

ESSAY QUESTIONS

QUESTION 1

Tom's first will, properly executed on July 1, 1983, created a $50,000 trust for Lil, the 65-year-old widow of Tom's deceased brother Bob. The Trustee was directed to pay to Lil "as much of the income and, if income be insufficient, as much of the principal, as may be required for her proper support and maintenance, for so long as she lives." After providing for the remainder interest in this trust to go to the American Red Cross on Lil's death, Tom gave "the rest and residue of my estate to the surviving issue of my brothers, per stirpes."

On July 1, 1986, while Tom was confined to the hospital for major surgery, a new will was delivered to Tom in a sealed envelope by two secretaries from his attorney's office. One of them told Tom, "We have a will here that Attorney Smith has asked us to deliver to you for your signature which we are to witness." Tom opened the envelope, signed it at the end in front of the secretaries, and handed it to them. The secretaries then walked to a small table in the hallway around the corner from Tom's room, signed the paper on the lines provided therefor, and then immediately returned the paper to Tom. In accordance with Tom's instructions, the new will was identical to the 1983 will, except that nephew E was now the sole residuary beneficiary.

Tom died in an automobile accident one month ago. He had never been married and left no issue. He was survived by:

1) A and B, grandchildren of his deceased brother Sam and children of Sam's deceased son James;

2) C, son of his deceased brother John; and

3) D and E, children of his deceased brother Frank.

The original of the 1983 will was found in Tom's safe deposit box. It bears no evidence of acts of revocation. The 1986 will, which contained no express revocation clause, cannot be found, but an unsigned copy is in

Attorney Smith's possession. The $50,000 trust produces a net annual income of $5,000.

1. Which will, if either, should be admitted to probate? Discuss.

2. Except for the $50,000 trust, what difference, if any, does it make to the family whether they take under the 1983 will or under the laws of intestacy? Discuss.

3. Lil's support needs are approximately $1,000 per month; she has pension and other income of $500 per month and has been making up the difference by withdrawals from savings. If either will is admited to probate, should the trustee pay Lil $1,000 per month or $500 per month? Discuss.

QUESTION 2

Bill, a widower had one child, his daughter June. Bill purchased a $100,000 farm (Blackacre), bought a single payment life insurance policy on his own life (face amount $50,000), and maintained a large balance in a checking account (usually $100,000). Title to the farm and the account was always in Bill's name only. June was named originally as beneficiary of the insurance policy, but Bill reserved the power to change the designation of his beneficiary.

A few years before his death, Bill asked the insurance company to make Joe, his neighbor, sole policy beneficiary. After the company informed Bill that the change had been made, Bill wrote Joe: "I have named you my life insurance beneficiary. You collect the proceeds and divide them three ways. You are one; the others I shall name later." Joe replied: "Sure, I'll do what you want."

In July 1986, Bill executed a deed conveying Blackacre to an old friend, Pete. The day of this execution, Bill mailed a signed letter to Pete directing him to "rent my farm, pay the net income to June yearly, and when she dies, convey the farm to my church." Pete received and read the letter.

A few days later, Bill attempted to deliver the deed to Pete, but learned from Pete's housekeeper that Pete had just left on a three-month sailing trip in the South Pacific. Bill gave the housekeeper the deed and told her to give it to Pete when he returned.

Recently, Bill suffered a heart attack and while hospitalized, executed a valid will which left "all property I own to my daughter, June, and I recommend that she look after my 90-year-old Aunt Selma, as long as she lives, making such gifts and provisions for her as she, June, thinks best."

The day after executing this will, Bill wrote the following on a separate piece of paper: "To Joe: the other two beneficiaries are Tom Allen and his wife." This note was ***not*** signed by Bill.

Bill died the following day. Two days after Bill's death, Pete returned from his trip and his housekeeper handed Pete the deed.

Who is entitled to Bill's assets and why? Discuss.

QUESTION 3

Leonard and Fay Woods had two children, Michael and Linda. Michael was married to Wanda, and they had one adopted child, Roberta. On March 25, 1985, Fay executed a will, with the necessary legal formalities, which contained the following dispository provisions:

"To my daughter, Linda, I give $10,000 in cash, my business property at 1125 Main Street, and such of my jewelry as is enumerated on the list which will be found in my jewel box. To my son, Michael, I give my 1000 shares of XYZ Class A stock. To my husband, Leonard, I give the rest and residue of my estate."

In November, 1986, Leonard and Fay were divorced, without entering into a property settlement agreement. In January, 1987, Michael was killed. In April, 1987, Fay sold the business property at 1125 Main Street for $20,000 and deposited one-half the proceeds in her commercial account and the other one-half in a savings account in the name of "Fay Woods, Trustee for Linda Woods." In May, 1987, XYZ Corporation declared a stock dividend and issued to the holders of Class A stock one-half share of Class A stock and one-half share of Class B stock for each share of Class A stock held.

Fay recently died. The following ***typed*** note was discovered in her jewel box;

"In accordance with the provisions of my will of March 25, 1984, I want my daughter, Linda, to have the following jewelry found herein: Grandmother Barnes' diamond ring, my wedding rings, and my pearl necklace and earrings."

The note was signed and dated March 25, 1985.

All the above events took place, and all property was located, in the State of Franklin. Fay's estate, after payment of all taxes, expenses, and debts, consists of 1500 shares of XYZ Class A stock, 500 shares of XYZ Class B stock, the jewelry described in the March 25, 1984 note, $10,000 in the savings account in the name of "Fay Woods, Trustee for Linda Woods" and $15,000 in her commercial account. All property was Fay's separate property.

Assume (1) the applicable statutory law of Franklin is the same as comparable provisions of the Uniform Probate Code, and (2) Fay's parents are no longer living.

How should Fay's estate be distributed? Discuss.

ESSAY ANSWERS

ANSWER TO QUESTION 1

Was the 1986 will valid?

An attested will is valid if it is witnessed by at least two persons, who are both present at the same time and witness the testator's signing of the will or the testator's acknowledgment of (1) his signature, or (2) the will; U.P.C. Section 2-502. Since (1) Tom ("T") executed the will in front of the two secretaries, and (2) they signed the document almost immediately thereafter, the 1986 will appears to be valid.

Was the 1986 will revoked by operation of law?

If a will which was last seen in the testator's possession or control, cannot be found upon his/her death, there is ordinarily a rebuttable presumption that the testator destroyed the will with the intent to revoke it.

E could attempt to rebut this presumption by contending that T had enlisted the assistance of an attorney when he desired to make a new will in 1986. He would argue that T would have retained legal counsel if he had actually desired to revoke the 1986 will. However, this fact would probably ***not*** be sufficient to rebut the presumption that the 1986 will had been revoked. The fact that T retained the 1983 will in his safe deposit box (where, presumably, the 1986 document would have been found if T had desired that document to be probated) supports the presumption in this instance.

Thus, the copy of the 1986 will would probably ***not*** be admitted to probate.

If, however, the 1986 will was not revoked by operation of law, its contents could be proved by the unsigned copy in Attorney Smith's possession. Attorney Smith could testify that (1) he gave the original to the two secretaries who visited T, and (2) the latter individuals could verify that T had signed the document in their presence.

If the 1986 will is valid, is the 1983 will revoked?

Revocation can ordinarily occur as a result of inconsistency. Since the 1986 will purports to dispose of T's entire estate, it would supersede the 1983 instrument. Therefore, if the 1986 will is valid, it (and not the 1983 will) would be admitted to probate.

If the 1986 will was revoked by law, is the 1983 will revived?

In some states, where a second will, if effective, would revoke an earlier will, but is thereafter revoked, the initial will is revived. Since the 1986 will was revoked by operation of law, the 1983 will could possibly be reinstated.

However, there is no direct evidence that T intended or desired the 1983 will to be reinstated. T could simply have inadvertently neglected to dispose of the 1983 will after the 1986 document was created. However, the other beneficiaries would probably prevail, ***if*** it could be shown that T was ordinarily a careful person (i.e., one who recognized that a will is an important document which should be retained in a safe place). In this instance, T's retention of the 1983 will would arguably manifest his desire to have that document constitute his testamentary scheme.

The doctrine of dependent relative revocation ("DDRR"') would ***not*** be applicable in this instance because (as discussed above) the 1986 will was probably valid when originally created. (Even if the 1986 will was ***not*** valid, DDRR would probably not be applied, since there is a substantial difference in the residuary clauses of the two wills.)

Summary

If the court finds that T desired to revive the 1983 will, that document will be probated. If not, T would be deemed to have died intestate.

What is the difference between the 1983 will and intestacy?

Under the 1983 will, the surviving issue of T's brothers take per stirpes (i.e., through the roots of each brother). Thus, D and E would each receive 1/6 of T's estate, A and D would each receive 1/6 of T's estate, and C would receive the balance of 1/3.

Under testacy, T's heirs would take "per capita, by right of representation." Thus, D, E and C would each receive 1/4 of T's estate, while A and B would divide the balance equally (i.e., each would receive 1/8).

Should Lil receive $1,000 per month, or $500 per month?

Ambiguous provisions in a will are construed to effectuate the testator's intent. Lil could argue that T would naturally prefer depletion of the trust res, rather than requiring her (his brother's widow) to live on the minimal amount possible.

However, since T presumably knew that Lil was receiving funds from other sources, he arguably would have requested Attorney Smith to use the language, "exclusive of Lil's present income" if he did not want her other income taken into account. Additionally, since (1) the principal would be exhausted in a relatively short period of time if Lil received $12,000 per year, and (2) the trust was apparently to last for her entire life (i.e., the trust language states, "for so long as she lives"), T probably intended that Lil draw only $500 per month from the trust. Thus, the trustee should pay Lil only $500 per month.

ANSWER TO QUESTION 2

The Insurance Policy

The proceeds of an insurance policy are ***not*** part of the insured's estate, so June would have no interest in this asset except as designated by Bill.

Joe ("J") might contend that no trust was created by the letter to him; and therefore he is entitled to all of the proceeds from the policy. J could contend that (1) Bill ("B") had no immediate trust intent, as evidenced by the fact that at the time of the initial letter, two-third's of the beneficiaries were not ascertainable, and (2) there was no delivery of the trust res (the insurance proceeds) to J at that time. Additionally, since Bill could still change the policy beneficiary, no constructive delivery had occurred.

J could also contend that even if a trust were created by the letter to him from B, the policy proceeds became his sole property, since a merger occurs when trustee and the sole beneficiary are the same party (which was the case until B later attempted to name two additional beneficiaries).

However, Tom Allen and his wife (collectively, the "Other Beneficiaries") could argue in rebuttal that, while J is probably correct in asserting that no trust arose by reason of B's initial letter to J, all of the elements of a trust relationship were concurrently satisfied on the day before B's death. At that time (1) the requisite intent to create a trust was renewed by reason of B's writing which contained the names of the Other Beneficiaries (this memo was obviously written with reference to the earlier letter to J), (2) all of the beneficiaries were ascertainable, and (3) there was sufficient constructive delivery of the trust res to J (as trustee) by naming him as the beneficiary of the policy, since this is all that could be done (i.e., the insurance company was not legally obliged to deliver the proceeds to the beneficiaries prior to B's death).

(However, assuming B still had the right to change the beneficiaries under the policy, it is likely that no delivery occurred.)

If no valid trust was found to exist, the Other Beneficiaries could probably successfully impose a constructive trust upon two-thirds of the insurance proceeds. Under the constructive trust doctrine, one is under an equitable duty to convey property to another where the former would be unjustly enriched at the latter's expense by retention of that asset. Because J had advised B that he would do whatever the latter requested (upon which statement B presumably relied), J would be unjustly enriched to the extent that he retained more than one-third of the insurance proceeds.

Blackacre (the "Farm")

If a valid trust was ***not*** created, the farm would still be part of B's estate. It would therefore pass to June under B's will. However, if a valid trust was created, the Farm would ***not*** pass to June.

We'll assume that B's "my church" can be identified (i.e., the entity with which he was affiliated could be shown by extrinsic evidence).

June could conceivably contend that no valid trust arose because: (1) there was no delivery of the trust res (the deed) to Pete ("P"), since P had embarked on a trip prior to the time the deed arrived, (2) P never explicitly agreed to act as trustee (in fact, leaving on an extended trip despite receipt of B's letter indicates his unwillingness to serve as trustee), and (3) P never signed a writing indicating his acceptance of the Farm as trustee, and therefore the Statute of Frauds (applicable to transfers of real property) was not satisfied.

However, P (who presumably would like to observe the trust) and the church could probably successfully contend in rebuttal that: (1) there was a constructive delivery of the deed to P's housekeeper (i.e., when the deed was unconditionally given to P's housekeeper, it was irrevocably placed beyond Bill's control); (2) it is not necessary that a trustee specifically acknowledge acceptance (or even be aware) of his/her appointment as trustee (as B's old friend, P would have objected immediately to his appointment as trustee if he had not desired to act in that capacity); and (3) since only parties to the alleged trust can assert the Statute of Frauds, June cannot complain about the lack of a writing signed by the trustee of P is willing to observe a trust relationship. Thus, the Farm was ***not*** part of B's estate.

Did the reference to Aunt Selma create a testamentary trust?

Selma might contend that the language in B's will created a trust, whereby June was obliged to support her for life from B's estate (with the remainder then passing to June). However, June could probably successfully argue in rebuttal that B's language was merely precatory in nature (it was a mere request, rather than a clear directive). This is evidenced by utilization of the word "recommend". While Selma's argument would be strengthened if B had supported her during his lifetime, the language in the will is still probably too weak to support a finding that a trust was intended. Thus, June is ***not*** obliged to provide any type of support to Selma.

ANSWER TO QUESTION 3

What is the effect of the sale of the business property and the deposit of the funds in bank accounts?

Ademption

A ***specific*** devise of property which is no longer in the decedent's estate at his/her death is adeemed. A specific devise is a gift which can be identified as against all other assets of the estate. Since the business property was described in a detailed manner, it will likely be considered a specific devise. Thus, as a result of the sale, this devise was extinguished.

Totten Trust

The $10,000 deposited into a bank account designated "Fay Woods, Trustee for Linda Woods" is probably a Totten trust (i.e., the trust relationship is evidenced only by the designation upon the trust account). Under this type of arrangement, the trust res is owned by the trustee during his/her lifetime, and by the beneficiary at the death of the trustee. Thus, Linda should be entitled to the $10,000. The remainder of the funds derived from the sale of the business property would pass into the residue of the estate.

What disposition would be made of the jewelry described in the typed note?

The note designating the specific jewelry to pass to Linda was (apparently) not executed with the requisite testamentary formalities. It was not witnessed, and so does not qualify as an attested will. The material portions were not in the testator's handwriting, and so it was not a valid holographic will. Linda, however, can made two arguments in support of her right to the jewelry.

First, U.P.C. Section 2-513 states that a will may refer to a written list to dispose of specific items of tangible personal property, provided the writing is in the testator's handwriting ***or*** signed by him. Since Fay signed the note in question, it should be effective (even though it may have been prepared ***after*** the will).

Second, under the incorporation by reference doctrine, a writing which was (1) in existence when the will was created, and (2) referred to in the will, is incorporated into the will (even though the included writing was not executed with the requisite testamentary formalities). Although it is unclear whether the note was made before or after the will was executed (both documents were dated March 25, 1985), a court would probably presume that the note was made simultaneously with the will. This presumption would effectuate the testator's intentions.

Thus, the jewelry described on the list should pass to Linda.

What is the effect of Michael's death upon the gift of stock in the will?

Since Michael was a lineal descendant of Fay, the gift of stock to him (which would otherwise lapse because of his failure to survive Fay) will pass to Roberta, his issue; U.P.C. Section 2-605. Adopted children are treated in the same way as natural children; U.P.C. Section 2-109.

What is the effect of the stock dividend upon the testamentary gift to Michael?

The phrase "***my*** 1000 shares . . . " is sometimes viewed as being a specific bequest of the stock (especially where this is of all of the shares owned by the testator). While the general rule is to the contrary, under the Uniform Probate Code the beneficiary of a ***specific*** devise of stock is entitled to additional securities of the same corporate entity owned by the testator by reason of action initiated by that corporation; U.P.C. Section 2-607. This would include stock dividends. Thus, the original stock and dividends would pass to Roberta by reason of the antilapse provision.

If, however, the gift of stock to Roberta was deemed to be a ***general*** devise, the additional shares would pass via the residuary clause.

What is the effect of the divorce upon the gift to Leonard

A divorce has the effect of revoking a testamentary gift to the former spouse. Leonard would therefore ***not*** be entitled to participate in the estate. The result is that Fay died intestate as to the residuary portion of her estate. Thus, the $15,000 in the commercial account should be distributed according to the laws of intestate succession.

The U.P.C. provides that, where the testator dies leaving issue (but no spouse), the estate passes to the issue per capita if all of them are related in the same degree of kinship. Otherwise, the estate passes to the issue by right of representation (commencing at the earliest level at which there are living descendants); U.P.C. Section 2-103(1). Since Fay was survived by Linda and Roberta (the adopted daughter of Michael), the residuary portion of Fay's estate will be divided equally between Linda and Roberta.

MULTISTATE-STYLE QUESTIONS

Here are 25 multiple-choice questions, in a Multistate-Bar-Exam style. These questions are taken from *"Siegel's Wills and Trusts"*, a compilation of questions edited by Professor Brian Siegel, published by us. *Siegel's Wills & Trusts* is available at your bookstore or from Emanuel Law Outlines, Inc., along with similar compilations by Professor Siegel in nine other subjects.

1. Ellen Morris recently died intestate. Her husband, Ed, had predeceased her. Ellen and Ed had adopted a daughter, Lisa, and also had a natural-born son, Tom. One year ago, Ellen gave Tom $10,000 to invest in a fast-food franchise, telling him orally that it would be deducted from his share of her estate, unless it was repaid prior to her death. A friend of Ellen's who was present when the conversation with Tom took place is prepared to testify to Ellen's statement. Ellen's net estate available for distribution is separate property of $150,000. How should her estate be distributed?

   (A) $75,000 each to Lisa and Tom.

   (B) $80,000 to Lisa; $70,000 to Tom.

   (C) $150,000 to Tom; nothing to Lisa.

   (D) $150,000 to Lisa; nothing to Tom.

2. Ann executed a valid will which contained the following bequest:

   "I leave the sum of $100,000 to those persons who are the income beneficiaries, at the date of my death, under an inter vivos trust created by my brother, John."

   Prior to the time Ann executed her will, John had created an inter vivos trust naming his children as income beneficiaries and his grandchildren as beneficiaries of the corpus. At Ann's death, John had two children, Adrian and Kimberly. Ann was survived by her mother, Rita, by her brother, John, and by a sister, Lisa. How should Ann's estate be distributed?

   (A) To Adrian and Kimberly, in equal shares.

   (B) To the trustee of the trust created by John with the income to be paid to Adrian and Kimberly and, at their death, the $100,000 to be paid to John's grandchildren.

   (C) To Rita.

   (D) One-half to Rita; one-fourth each to John and Lisa.

3. Bill executed a valid will which contained the following bequest:

   "I leave the sum of $500,000 to those persons who are the residuary legatees under my mother's last will and testament."

   At the time Bill executed his will, his mother had executed a valid will which left her residuary estate to Bill's uncles, Tom and Tim. Thereafter, she revoked that will and executed a new one, naming State University as her residuary legatee. When Bill's mother died, her residuary estate was paid to State University. When Bill died, he was survived by his wife, Ann, and by one child, Emily, both of whom were provided for in his will. Bill's residuary estate was left to The American Red Cross. To whom should the $500,000 bequest be paid?

   (A) To Tim and Tom, in equal shares.

   (B) To State University.

   (C) To the American Red Cross.

   (D) To Ann and Emily as intestate property.

4. Kathy executed a valid will disposing of her entire estate. One of the dispositive provisions is as follows:

   "I give all of my 100 shares of ABC Corp. stock to my good friend, Edna. The remainder of my stocks, I give to my mother, Kay."

   Five years prior to Kathy's death, the stock of ABC Corp. split, two for one. After that split,

Kathy owned 300 shares of ABC Corp. stock. One year later, ABC Corp. declared a ten per cent stock dividend so that Kathy received 30 additional shares of stock. One year before Kathy's death, XYZ Corp. made a "2 for 1" tender offer for all of the outstanding shares of ABC Corp., and Kathy received 660 shares of XYZ Corp. in exchange for her ABC Corp. stock. One month later, she purchased 40 shares of XYZ Corp. for cash. Thus, at her death, Kathy owned 700 shares of XYZ Corp. stock. Kathy was survived by her son (who was alive when her will was made), Bill, her friend, Edna, and by her mother, Kay. What disposition should be made of the XYZ Corp. stock owned by Kathy at her death, assuming that the residue of the estate is devised to Bill?

(A) The XYZ Corp. stock should be distributed to Edna.

(B) One hundred shares of the XYZ Corp. stock should be distributed to Edna and the balance should be distributed to Kay.

(C) Six hundred and sixty shares of the XYZ Corp. stock should be distributed to Edna, and the balance should be distributed to Kay.

(D) All of the XYZ Corp. stock should be distributed to Bill as part of the residue of the estate.

5. Jamir executed a valid will disposing of his entire estate to his father. One year later, Jamir executed a second will which revoked the first will, and disposed of his entire estate to his mother. Six months later, Jamir tore up the second will, stating to his friend, Steve, who was present at the time, "this will take care of my estate so that my father gets it under the other will which I executed." At Jamir's death, the first will was found among his papers. He was survived by his parents and two sisters. How should Jamir's estate be distributed?

(A) To his father under the first will.

(B) To his mother under the second will.

(C) Equally, to his mother and father by intestate succession.

(D) Equally, to his sisters by intestate succession.

6. Edgar validly executed Will 1, which disposed of his entire estate to his brother, Tom. One year later, Edgar validly executed Will 2, which disposed of his entire estate to his sister, Wilma. Will 2 did ***not*** contain a revocation clause. Six months later Edgar validly executed Will 3, which expressly revoked Will 2 and left Edgar's estate to The American Red Cross. One year later, Edgar revoked Will 3 by physical act. At Edgar's death, Will 1 is found among his important papers with an unsigned note on it which read "This is my will." Edgar was survived only by his brother, Tom, and his sister, Wilma. How should Edgar's estate be distributed? You may assume that no mortmain statute exists in this jurisdiction.

(A) To Tom under the terms of Will 1.

(B) To Wilma under the terms of Will 2.

(C) To The American Red Cross under the terms of Will 3.

(D) To Tom and Wilma by intestate succession.

7. Tim executed a valid will disposing of his real estate to "my nephew, Albert" and devising the remainder of his estate "to my brothers and sisters, share and share alike." Tim specifically disinherited his own children. After Tim's death, Albert filed a valid, written statement renouncing his interest in Tim's estate. Tim was survived by Albert, two brothers, one sister, and his (Tim's) three children. Albert has one child. How should Tim's estate be distributed?

(A) Real estate to Albert; residue to Tim's brothers and sister.

(B) The entire estate to Tim's brothers and sister.

(C) The entire estate to Tim's children.

(D) The real estate to Albert's child; residue to Tim's two brothers and sister.

8. John and Betty met in Hawaii, where both were vacationing. They spent much of their time together and, after returning to their homes, Betty discovered that she was pregnant. After her child, Jennifer, was born, Betty sued John to establish paternity.

Although John denied that Jennifer was his child, the jury found by clear and convincing evidence that John was the father. The court entered judgment accordingly. Thereafter, John refused to acknowledge Jennifer as his child or to spend any time with her, but did pay the support ordered by the court. When John died, his will (executed prior to the birth of Jennifer) left his entire estate to ABC Charity. John was survived by Betty, Jennifer and his parents. How should his estate be distributed?

(A) To Jennifer.

(B) To ABC Charity.

(C) Half to Jennifer, and the remainder to ABC Charity.

(D) Half to Jennifer, and the remainder to John's parents, in equal shares.

9. Arnold and his father, Clay, entered into an oral agreement by which Arnold agreed that Clay could live in Arnold's house, that Arnold would provide Clay with food and clothing, and that Clay would devise his entire estate to Arnold at Clay's death. When Clay died, he left a valid will which (1) made no reference to the agreement with Arnold, and (2) disposed of his entire estate to Anne. How should Clay's estate be distributed, assuming (1) Clay was survived by Arnold and Arnold's brother, Tom, and (2) Anne also wishes to take the estate?

(A) Anne.

(B) Arnold.

(C) Arnold and Tom, equally.

(D) One-half to Anne and one-half to Arnold and Tom, equally.

10. Parker, a widower, executed a valid will which disposed of his entire estate to "the children of my best friend, Sam Riley." At that time the will was executed and at Parker's death, Sam Riley had no children. However, prior to Sam's death, three children, Bob, Sally, and Ellen were born to him. Parker was survived by his (1) sister, Ann, and (2) parents. To whom should Parker's estate be distributed?

(A) To Bob, as Sam's first born child.

(B) To Bob, Sally and Ellen, at Sam's death.

(C) To Ann.

(D) To Parker's parents.

11. Bill executed a last will and testament. It made two bequests, as follows:

1. $10,000 to my son, Jim.

2. All the rest, residue and remainder of my estate to my daughter, Elizabeth.

The will also explicitly revoked a prior valid will which had expressly disinherited Jim and left everything to Elizabeth. Bill was survived by his two children (Jim and Elizabeth) and parents. It is admitted by all parties that Bill's first will was valid. Assuming that there are grounds for opposing probate of Bill's will, who may contest probate of the will?

(A) Jim only.

(B) Jim or Elizabeth.

(C) Jim or Elizabeth or Bill's parents.

(D) Elizabeth only.

12. John and Beth Askew were married for many years. During the course of their marriage, a son, Clay, was born. Although he had no rational basis for his suspicions, John believed that Clay was conceived as the result of a relationship between Beth and another man. Although Beth denied this, John persisted in his belief. Several tests showed that Clay had the same blood type as John. When Clay was six, John executed a holographic will, as follows:

"My wife has betrayed me. She gave birth to a child by another man. The child is not mine, although I have provided a home for him. I therefore disinherit Clay. I leave everything to my aunt, Matilda Askew.

/s/John Askew"

John died without changing his belief or the will. Should the will be admitted to probate?

(A) No, if John was suffering from an insane delusion.

(B) Yes, if the will was validly executed.

(C) No, since John had been unduly

influenced in his beliefs.

(D) Yes, since John has the absolute right to disinherit his son.

13. John executed a will giving his friend, Ted, a power of appointment over the residuary of John's estate. The residuary clause reads as follows:

"I give, devise and bequeath the rest, residue and remainder of my estate to such person or persons as my friend, Ted, may appoint either by deed during Ted's lifetime or by his will; if my friend, Ted, does not exercise this power of appointment, at Ted's death the residue of my estate shall be distributed to my heirs."

The power of appointment given to Ted is classified as a:

(A) General power presently exercisable.

(B) Special power presently exercisable.

(C) General testamentary power.

(D) Special testamentary power.

14. Stephanie executed a will which disposed of all her property to her son, Rick. Thereafter, she wrote and delivered to her brother, Sam, a letter which reads as follows:

"Dear Sam: As you know, I am leaving for Europe in two weeks. When I return, it is my intent that my farm, on which you now reside, shall be placed in trust for the benefit of your children. I have given the rest of my estate to Rick. All my love, Stephanie".

Stephanie died while on her European trip. She was survived by Sam, Sam's daughter, Tina, her mother Ann, and by Rick. What disposition should the court make of the farm?

(A) Since a valid trust was created upon delivery of the letter to Sam, the farm should be distributed to Sam as trustee for Tina.

(B) No valid trust was created, and so the farm should be distributed to Rick pursuant to the will.

(C) Although no valid trust was created at the time of delivery of the letter, a trust came into being upon Stephanie's death, and so the property should be distributed to Sam as trustee for Tina.

(D) No valid trust was created, and so the farm should be distributed to Rick under intestacy principles.

15. T was feeling very weak. After he signed his typed will in front of X and Y, Y left the room to obtain a glass of water for T. While Y was away, X signed the will as a witness. When Y returned, she signed the will in front of X and T. Which of the following statements is correct?

(A) T has a valid holographic will.

(B) T has a valid formal will.

(C) T's will is invalid, because the witnesses did not sign in each other's presence.

(D) T's will is invalid, if the will was undated.

16. Elaine made the following bequest in her will:

"I give, devise and bequeath the sum of $1,000,000 to my husband, Will, if he survives me, as trustee, the income from such trust to be paid to my husband so long as he remains unmarried. In the event that my husband shall remarry, or upon his death, whichever shall first occur, I appoint my brother, Tom, as successor trustee, to pay the income to my children, so long as they remain unmarried, and, in the event they marry, or upon their death, whichever first occurs, to pay all accrued income and principal to my alma mater, State College."

Elaine was survived by her husband, Will, her brother, Tom, and her children, Bob and Ellen. Will and the children, Bob and Ellen, have petitioned the court to strike the conditions that they not marry and distribute the property otherwise in accordance with the trust. How should the court distribute Elaine's estate?

(A) The court should strike the conditions as to all beneficiaries and distribute $1,000,000 to Will, as trustee.

(B) The court should strike the conditions as to Will, but not as to Bob and Ellen and distribute $1,000,000 to Will, as trustee.

(C) The court should strike the conditions as to Bob and Ellen, but not as to Will, and distribute $1,000,000 to Will as trustee.

(D) The court should declare the trust invalid and distribute the property pursuant to the residuary clause of the will, or by intestate succession, whichever is appropriate.

17. Amy Jones deposited $10,000 in a bank account at First Bank. The account was created as "Amy Jones, Trustee for Karen Smith." Karen Smith is Amy's sister. Amy used this account as her checking account, depositing her monthly paychecks into the account and paying her bills from it. Karen Jones had no knowledge of the account. After creating this account, Amy executed a will in which she left all of her property to her brother, Ed Jones. Amy recently died and was survived by her parents, her sister, Karen, and her brothers, Ed and Warren Jones. The balance in the account at Amy's death was $35,000. How should the bank account be distributed?

(A) To Karen Smith.

(B) To Ed Jones.

(C) To Karen, Ed and Warren Jones, in equal shares.

(D) To Amy's parents, in equal shares.

18. Alice created a trust in her will which provides that the income shall be paid to her children during their lifetimes, and upon the death of her last child, the principal shall be divided among her grandchildren. The trust contains the following clause:

"My children shall not, by way of present or future anticipation, assign their interest in this trust under any circumstances. The income interest of my children shall not be subject to the claims of their creditors, whether by voluntary or involuntary transfer."

After Alice's death, one of her children, Beatrix, transferred her income interest to her sister, Karen, in satisfaction of a debt which Beatrix owed to Karen. Under these circumstances:

(A) The transfer of Beatrix's interest is void.

(B) The transfer of Beatrix's interest is valid, and the trustee must pay Beatrix's income interest to Karen.

(C) The transfer of Beatrix's interest is valid, but revocable by Beatrix; and so the trustee may pay the income to Karen until Beatrix revokes the assignment.

(D) Although the transfer of Beatrix's interest is void, the debt owned to Karen by Beatrix is deemed to be satisfied, since Karen knew the transfer was void.

19. Maura created a testamentary trust which provides as follows:

"I give, devise and bequeath the sum of $1,000,000 in trust to First National Bank, trustee; the income therefrom to be paid to International University to provide scholarships for children of low-income families."

International University is a privately-owned, profit-making corporation which educates persons for technical jobs in industry. It has an outstanding reputation.

Maura was survived by her son, Will, to whom she devised the remainder of her estate. Under these circumstances:

(A) The trust is a valid charitable trust for education.

(B) The trust is a valid charitable trust to mitigate poverty.

(C) The trust is a valid charitable trust, only if the recipients of the scholarships are indigent.

(D) The trust is invalid as a charitable trust, and so the trust property should be distributed to Will.

20. Edward is the trustee of an inter vivos trust created by his father. The trust res consists of an office building which produces revenue that is equivalent to a 4.5% return on investment. In order to increase income resulting from the trust, Edward purchased the office building from the trust for $200,000 and invested the proceeds in higher-yield assets. The trust instrument made no mention of a power to sell trust assets. Under these circumstances:

(A) Edward violated his fiduciary duties by selling the trust asset.

(B) Edward violated his fiduciary duty in purchasing the trust asset for himself.

(C) Edward violated his fiduciary duty in purchasing the trust asset for himself, but only if he paid less than the fair market value to this asset.

(D) Edward did not violate his fiduciary duty.

21. Ted is the trustee of an inter vivos trust. The trust res is comprised of $300,000 in cash, and the beneficiaries are Ted's nephews and nieces. Ted recently located a parcel of unimproved property that is available for sale. The price of the property is $300,000, and Ted projects that the property will increase in value to $500,000 within two years. Under these circumstances, Ted may:

(A) Invest in this property, if a prudent investor would do so.

(B) Invests in this property, if he obtains an appraisal showing that the value of the property is now at least $300,000.

(C) Not invest in this property, regardless of what the trust instrument authorizes.

(D) Not invest in this property, unless the trust instrument specifically authorizes real estate investments.

22. Karl, a college professor, is the trustee of a trust created by his father-in-law for the benefit of Karl's children. Karl accepted a visiting professorship at Cambridge University for an academic year. Since he was going to be out of the country, Karl retained Edward, a stockbroker, to be the substitute trustee for that year. Karl executed a document authorizing Edward to "exercise all powers and fulfill all duties which I now possess as trustee." Under these circumstances:

(A) Karl is effectively relieved of his duties as trustee during the year, and is not liable for any breach of fiduciary duties which might occur.

(B) Karl is not relieved of liability for any breach of fiduciary duty, but properly delegated the powers of the trustee to Edward.

(C) Karl is not relieved of liability for any breach of fiduciary duties, but Edward may exercise all discretionary powers of the trustee under the trust.

(D) Karl has breached his fiduciary duty and is liable for all damages resulting from Edward's acts or omissions.

23. Laura is the trustee of an inter vivos trust. She entered into a contract with a third party for the purchase of trust assets. A bona fide dispute arose concerning performance of the agreement. The third party sued Laura for breach of contract, when the latter refused to pay the former for goods delivered to her. Assuming the third party prevails:

(A) Laura is personally liable for breach of contract, but may indemnify herself from trust assets (assuming she acted in good faith).

(B) Laura is not personally liable for breach of contract, but may be sued only in her capacity as trustee.

(C) Laura is personally liable for breach of contract, and may not be indemnified from trust assets.

(D) Laura is personally liable for breach of contract, and may not be indemnified from trust assets, unless the trust instrument specifically contains an exculpatory clause.

24. Ben created a testamentary trust by bequeathing 300 shares of Bloomfield, Inc. common stock to Adams National Bank, as trustee. The trustee was instructed to pay the income to his children for life, and the remainder to his grandchildren at the death of the survivor of his children. Bloomfield has a net profit for the current year. However, due to plans to expand its facilities, it does not wish to declare ***cash*** dividends. It has decided to declare a ***stock*** dividend of one share for each four shares of stock currently owned by shareholders. The trust created by Ben will receive 75 shares of Bloomfield, Inc. common stock. Under these circumstances, the trustee should:

(A) Add the stock dividend shares to the corpus of the trust.

(B) Distribute the stock dividend shares to the income beneficiaries.

(C) Distribute half of the stock dividend to the income beneficiaries, and the other half to the corpus of the trust.

(D) Distribute stock, equal in value to the cash dividend which would have been declared but for the expansion plans, to the income beneficiaries and add the remainder of the stock to the trust corpus.

25. Ellen created an inter vivos trust by transferring $100,000 in trust to First National Bank, as trustee, for the benefit of her children for life, with the remainder to her grandchildren. Subsequent to the creation of the trust, Ellen delivered a letter to the trustee, advising it that she wished to revoke the remainder gift to the grandchildren and to substitute her nephews as remaindermen. The trustee rejected Ellen's modification of the trust. Angered by the trustee's response, Ellen delivered a second letter to the trustee, revoking the trust in its entirety. The trustee rejected this letter also. Ellen is entitled to:

(A) Modify the trust by revoking the gift to the remaindermen and substituting her nephews, but cannot revoke the trust in its entirety.

(B) Revoke the trust in its entirety, but cannot modify it.

(C) Modify and revoke the trust.

(D) Neither revoke nor modify the trust.

ANSWERS TO MULTISTATE-STYLE QUESTIONS

1. **A** An adopted child is treated as a natural-born child for purposes of inheritance. Property given by a decedent during his/her lifetime is treated as an advancement against that person's share only if it is (1) so declared in a contemporaneous writing by the decedent, or (2) acknowledged in writing by the recipient. Lisa will inherit equally with Tom, since she was adopted by Ellen. The $10,000 will not be treated as an advancement, since the only evidence of Ellen's intent was oral. Thus, Lisa and Tom will each take $75,000. Choice B is incorrect since it assumes that the $10,000 will be treated as an advancement against Tom's share of the estate. Choice C is incorrect since it assumes that Lisa is not treated as Ellen's child for purposes of inheritance. Choice D is incorrect since it fails to provide for inheritance by Tom.

2. **A** A writing which is in existence when a will is executed may be incorporated by reference, if the language of the will manifests this intent and describes the writing sufficiently to permit its identification. In this case, the will relies upon an extrinsic document to identify the devisees. This document was executed prior to the will and is described sufficiently to allow incorporation. Since Adrian and Kimberly were the only income beneficiaries at the time of Ann's death, they take equally. Answer B is incorrect since (contrary to the facts) it assumes that Ann intended to put the bequest in trust. The trust was incorporated to identify the beneficiaries under Ann's will. The devisees are given Ann's estate free of trust. Answer C is incorrect since the trust document was validly incorporated. Thus, Rita takes nothing. Answer D is incorrect, since Rita, John and Lisa take nothing under Ann's will.

3. **B** A will may dispose of property by reference to acts and events which have significance apart from their effect upon dispositions made by the testator in his will (whether they occur before or after the execution of the will, or before or after the testator's death). The execution or revocation of a will of another person is such an event; U.P.C. Section 2-512. Since Bill's mother's will was executed after Bill's will, it ***cannot*** be said to be incorporated by reference into Bill's will. The will of Bill's mother is an event of independent significance since the statute expressly provides for it and it was made to dispose of her estate (separate and apart from its effect upon Bill's testamentary scheme). Answer A is incorrect since the prior will was revoked. Therefore, Tim and Tom were not residuary devisees under the will of Bill's mother. Answer C would be correct only if the gift to State University had failed. Answer D is incorrect since, if the gift to State University had failed, it would have passed under the residuary clause to The American Red Cross.

4. **C** The specific devisee of stocks is entitled to (1) any additional or other securities of the same entity owned by the testator at death by reason of action initiated by that entity, and (2) any securities ***of another entity*** owned by the testator as a result of a merger, consolidation, reorganization or other similar action ***initiated by the latter entity***; U.P.C. Section 2-607. Use of the words "all of my 100 shares" is ordinarily construed as a specific bequest. When ABC split its stock and declared a stock dividend (actions initiated by ABC), the additional shares became part of the specific bequest of stock to Edna. When XYZ made a tender offer (an action ***initiated by XYZ***), the shares of XYZ stock received by Kathy took the place of the ABC shares. The final 40 shares of XYZ stock were purchased subsequently by Kathy, and so were not part of the original specific bequest of ABC stock. Choice A is incorrect, since the 40 shares of XYZ subsequently purchased by Kathy are not included in the specific devise. Choice B is incorrect, since the shares resulting from the stock split and stock dividend, as well as the XYZ shares received in the merger, pass to Edna. Choice D is incorrect since, even if none of the XYZ shares passed to Edna, they

would be distributed to Kay under the terms of Kathy's will.

5. **A** A will or any part thereof is revoked (1) by a subsequent will which revokes the prior will expressly or by inconsistency, or (2) by being burned, torn, cancelled, obliterated, or destroyed by the testator with the intent of revoking. Where a second will which, had it remained effective at the testator's death, would have revoked the first will, is thereafter revoked by an act, the first will is revived if it is evident from (1) the circumstances of revocation of the second will, or (2) testator's comtemporary or subsequent declarations, that he intended the first will to take effect as executed; U.P.C. Section 2-509. Although the second will expressly revoked the first will, the statements of Jamir that his father should take the estate under the first will evidence an intent to revive the initial instrument. Choice B is incorrect, since the second will was revoked by physical act. Choice C is incorrect, since the first will was revived. If revival of the first will had ***not*** occurred, Choice C would be correct. Choice D is incorrect since Jamir's mother and father would take by intestate succession if no revival occurred.

6. **D** A will is revoked by a subsequent will which is inconsistent with the former instrument; U.P.C. Section 2-507. If a second will which, had it remained effective would have revoked the first will, is thereafter revoked by a third will, the first will is ***not*** revived, unless it appears ***from the terms*** of the third will that the testator intended the first will to be revived; U.P.C. Section 2-509. Will 2 revoked Will 1 by inconsistency. Since Will 3 revoked Will 2, but gives no indication that revival of the first will was intended, revival of Will 1 will ***not*** occur. Thus, Edgar died intestate and his estate should be divided between Tom and Wilma. Choice A is incorrect in that Will 3 indicates no intention by Edgar to reinstate Will 1. Choice B is incorrect since Will 2 was expressly revoked by Will 3. Choice C is incorrect in that it is stipulated that Will 3 was revoked.

7. **D** A person who is a devisee under a testamentary instrument may renounce the right of succession to any property or interest therein by filing a written renunciation; U.P.C. Section 2-801(a). Unless the decedent has otherwise provided, the property or interest renounced devolves as though the person renouncing had predeceased the decedent; U.P.C. Section 2-801(c). If a devisee who is a grandparent or a lineal descendant of a grandparent of the testator predeceases the testator, his/her issue who survive the testator by 120 hours take in place of the deceased devisee; U.P.C. Section 2-605. Since Albert renounced his gift, he is treated as though he predeceased the testator. Since Albert is a descendant of a grandparent of the testator and was survived by issue, Albert's child takes the real estate. The remainder of the estate is divided among Tim's brothers and sisters. Choice A is incorrect since Albert is expressly permitted to renounce by statute. Choice B is incorrect since the antilapse statute applies where a devisee is treated as having predeceased the testator. Choice C is incorrect in that the gift of the real estate, even if it had failed, would have become part of the residuary.

8. **A** A person born out of wedlock is the child of the father, if paternity is established by clear and convincing proof before his death; U.P.C. Section 2-109(2). If a testator fails to provide for a child born or adopted after the execution of his will, the omitted child ordinarily receives an intestate share; U.P.C. Section 2-302. A decedent's estate passes to his/her issue if there is no surviving spouse; U.P.C. 2-103(1). Since paternity was established prior to John's death, Jennifer is treated as his child. As a consequence, she receives the entire estate as her intestate share. Choice B is incorrect since Jennifer's claim to the intestate share as a pretermitted child supersedes the devise to ABC. Choices C and D are incorrect in that Jennifer is entitled to the entire estate.

9. **A** A contract to make a will or devise, or not to revoke a will or devise, or to die intestate, can be established only by: (1) provisions of a will stating material provisions of the contract, (2) an express reference in a will to an agreement and extrinsic evidence proving the terms of that contract, or (3) a writing signed by the decedent evidencing the contract; U.P.C. Section 2-701. Since Arnold will be precluded from proving the oral contract, Anne will take under the will. Choice B is incorrect since, because the agreement is oral and not referred to in Clay's will, it cannot be proved. Choice C is incorrect since, even if the agreement could be proved, Arnold would take to the exclusion of Tom. Choice D is incorrect since the will leaves Clay's entire estate to Anne.

10. **B** Where there are no members of a class in existence when a will is executed or at the testator's death, members of the class (whenever born) ordinarily receive their gifts when the class can be determined. Since Parker must have known that Sam Riley had no children, he presumably would want the determination postponed until all of the class members could be determined. Choice A is incorrect in that it does not include all of Sam's children. Choice C is incorrect because Parker did not have to provide for Ann. Choice D is incorrect because, even if the will was not valid, Parker's estate would not pass to his parents; U.P.C. Section 2-103(2).

11. **D** Only "interested parties" may contest a will. An interested party is one who is adversely affected by the will's admission to probate. If the will is probated, Jim gets $10,000 more than he would have received under the prior will and thus cannot contest. Bill's parents cannot contest, since they take nothing either by will or by intestate succession. Only Elizabeth has standing, since she would take everything under the first will, but suffers a $10,000 reduction under the second will. Answers A and B are incorrect, since Jim's interest is not adversely affected under the second will (i.e., he gets more than he would if the first will remained in effect). Answer C is incorrect since Jim and Bill's parents are not adversely affected by the second will.

12. **A** A person suffering from an insane delusion does not have the capacity to execute a valid will. There is no evidence that Clay was conceived as the consequence of an illicit relationship. In fact, the blood tests proved that Clay had the same blood type as John. Additionally, the will recites that John took the action as a result of his irrational belief. Thus, John's purported will would ***not*** be admitted to probate. Answer B is incorrect, since correct formalities do not entitle a will to probate where the testator lacked the capacity to execute such a document. Answer C is incorrect because there is no indication that anyone unduly influenced John. Answer D is incorrect in that, although John has the legal right to disinherit Clay, his lack of capacity prevented him from executing a valid testamentary document.

13. **A** A general power of appointment is one which is exercisable in favor of the donee, his estate, his creditors or the creditors of his estate. A power is "presently exercisable" if there is no condition precedent to the donee's exercise of it. There are no limits on the persons to whom Ted can appoint, and so the power is a general one. There is no condition precedent, since Ted is authorized to exercise the power during his lifetime by deed. It is therefore presently exercisable. Choice B is incorrect since Ted is not prohibited from appointing the bequest to himself, his estate, his creditors, or the creditors of his estate. Choice C is incorrect since Ted can exercise the power by deed. Choice D is incorrect because (1) Ted can appoint to himself, and (2) there is no condition precedent (i.e., his death) to the exercise of the power of appointment.

14. **B** A trustor must have an immediate trust intent for that type of relationship to be created. Where a trustor manifests an intent that a trust take effect at some future point in time, no trust is immediately operative. Since Stephanie manifested an intent that the trust be created upon her return from Europe, no valid trust was created. Thus, the farm was still part of her estate and passed to Rick pursuant to the will. Choice A is incorrect, since the letter expressed no intent that the trust be effective immediately. Choice C is incorrect because there is insufficient indication that Stephanie, via her letter, intended to create a testamentary trust. Choice D is incorrect in that the farm passed pursuant to Stephanie's will, not by intestacy principles.

15. **B** A formal will must ordinarily be signed by the testator and at least two persons, each of whom witnessed either the signing of the will or the testator's acknowledgment of his signature of the will; U.P.C. Section 2-502. Since X and Y had witnessed T's execution of his will, T had a valid testamentary writing. Choice A is incorrect because the will was typed, and therefore the "material provisions" were not in the testator's handwriting. Choice C is incorrect because there is no requirement under the U.P.C. that the witnesses sign the will in each other's presence. Choice D is incorrect because there is no requirement that an attested will be dated to be valid.

16. **C** A condition in a trust unreasonably restraining marriage is usually not enforced. An impermissible condition in a trust will be stricken from the trust. However, a gift over to an alternate beneficiary upon remarriage of the trustor's surviving spouse is usually not viewed as an unreasonable restraint upon marriage. The condition imposed upon the children that they may not marry is probably unreasonable. Thus, this condition should be stricken, and the gift made without this restraint. The condition imposed upon Will that he may not remarry is generally held to be enforceable. Choice A is incorrect since the condition that Will not remarry is probably enforceable. Choice B is incorrect in that the condition imposed upon Will is usually viewed as being reasonable, and should be enforced. However, the similar condition imposed upon the children is unreasonable, and will probably be stricken. Choice D is incorrect in that, if a condition is deemed to be invalid, it is stricken and the trust otherwise enforced.

17. **A** A bank or savings deposit in the name of "X, in trust for Y" is called a "Totten Trust." This situation is ordinarily viewed as a valid, revocable trust; U.P.C. Section 6-104(c). Withdrawals during the trustor's lifetime constitute a partial revocation, and the balance at the trustor's death passes to the named beneficiary. Since there is no evidence that Amy did not intend to create a trust, the presumption of a Totten Trust would prevail. Therefore, Karen takes the funds in the account. Choice B is incorrect since there was a valid Totten Trust. If no trust had existed, Choice B would be the correct answer. Choice C and D are incorrect since, even if no trust is found, the account would pass to Ed under the residuary clause of Amy's will.

18. **C** A spendthrift trust is one in which the equitable interest of a beneficiary is inalienable. If, despite the existence of a spendthrift clause, a beneficiary voluntarily assigns his interest, the assignment is valid. However, it may be revoked by the beneficiary at any time. The assignment was valid, but revocable by Beatrix. The trustee may thus pay the income to Karen, until such time as Beatrix revokes the transfer. Choice A is incorrect since the assignment is valid (even though revocable). Choice B is incorrect, since it fails to indicate that the assignment is revocable. Choice D is incorrect, since Karen could seek to recover the balance of the debt owed to her if Beatrix revoked the assignment.

19. **D** A charitable trust cannot benefit a profit-making organization. A profit-making organization is non-charitable, even if its purpose is one that is ordinarily viewed as charitable. Although International University is an educational institution, it is a profit-making organization. It is therefore disqualified as a valid charitable beneficiary. Choice A is incorrect because, even though the purpose of the trust is education, a profit-making organization may not be benefitted. Choice B is incorrect since the beneficiary of the trust is a profit-making entity. Choice C is incorrect because, although the students are indigent, the beneficiary cannot be a profit-making organization.

20. **B** The power of sale over trust assets may be implied in circumstances where it is not expressly granted by the trustor. A trustee is ordinarily prohibited from any type of self-dealing. Self-dealing constitutes a breach of fiduciary duty; Rest. 2d., Section 170. Although Edward has an implied right to sell the trust asset, the purchase of trust property ***for himself*** is prohibited. Choice A is incorrect in that Edward does have an implied power to sell trust assets under those circumstances. Choice C is incorrect since a breach of Edward's fiduciary duties occurred, even if fair market value was paid. Choice D is incorrect since self-dealing is prohibited.

21. **D** Investment in unimproved land for resale is ordinarily a violation of a trustee's fiduciary duty. Where, however, the trust instrument expressly authorizes investments not ordinarily permitted, the trust instrument will control. Because property values historically fluctuate greatly, a trustee is generally not authorized to invest in unimproved land for resale or appreciation. However, a trust instrument may authorize the trustee to make such an investment. Choice A is incorrect because, while a trustee is governed by the prudent investor rule, investment in unimproved land for appreciation or resale is generally considered imprudent. Choice B is incorrect in that the applicable rule is not mitigated by the fact that a favorable appraisal has been obtained. Choice C is incorrect, since an otherwise improper investment may be specifically authorized by the trust instrument.

22. **D** A trustee must personally administer the powers of the trust. However, a trustee may employ agents to perform services for the trust, so long as he/she exercises the care of a reasonably prudent person in their selection and continues to oversee the performance of these functions. While Karl is allowed to employ persons to advise him in the exercise of his powers, he cannot delegate administration of the trust to others or disavow his own duty to exercise such powers. Choice A is incorrect in that Karl cannot, even temporarily, completely relieve himself of his duties as trustee. Choice B is incorrect in that the powers of the trustee cannot be delegated to Edward. Edward can only assist Karl in performing the services attendant upon performing Karl's trust duties. Choice C is incorrect in that the exercise of Karl's discretionary powers under the trust cannot be completely delegated to Edward.

23. **A** A trustee is ordinarily personally liable for breach of a contract regarding trust assets. A trustee held liable for breach of contract has a right of indemnification from the trust, so long as he/she acted in good faith. While Laura is personally liable as trustee, she has a right of indemnification from the trust (assuming, of course, she acted in good faith). Choice B is incorrect, since Laura is personally liable for the breach. Choice C is incorrect, since Laura probably has a right to indemnification. Choice D is incorrect since Laura has a right of indemnification, regardless of whether the trust document contains an exculpatory clause.

24. **A** Stock dividends are ordinarily allocated to the corpus of a trust. Stock dividends which are necessary to maintain a trust's ownership proportion of a corporation are allocated to corpus. Choices B, C and D are incorrect because stock dividends are usually allocated exclusively to the corpus of a trust.

25. **D** In most states, a trustor does not retain the power to modify or revoke an inter vivos trust. These powers must be expressly retained at the time the trust is created. Since the facts fail to indicate that Ellen expressly retained a power to modify or revoke, she could do neither. Choices A, B and C are incorrect because Ellen apparently did not explicitly retain the power to modify or revoke the trust.

TABLE OF CASES

RESTATEMENT OF TRUSTS, SECOND

UNIFORM PROBATE CODE

SUBJECT MATTER INDEX

question & answer collections

siegel's
essay & multiple-choice Q & A's

Now published by Emanuel, each of these books contains 20-25 essay questions with model answers plus 90-100 Multistate-format Q & A's. The objective is to acquaint the student with the techniques needed to successfully handle law school exams. Titles are:

Civil Procedure	Criminal Procedure
Constitutional Law	Evidence
Contracts	Real Property
Corporations	Torts
Criminal Law	Wills & Trusts

each title...$15.95

steve finz's
multistate method

967 MBE (Multistate Bar Exam)-style *multiple choice questions and answers covering* all six Multistate subjects - **Plus** a complete 200 question model MBE practice exam—perfect for law school exam review and for the BAR EXAM in all states.

'92-93 Title...$31.95

steve emanuel's
first year Q & A's

1,143 Objective-style questions & answers in first year subjects, as preparation for exams. A single volume covers Contracts, Torts, Civil Procedure, Property, Criminal Law & Procedure.

with

'91-92 Civil Procedure Supplement................$17.95

For any titles not available at your local bookstore call us at (914) 834-7735.
Mastercard and Visa accepted.
Hours: 9-5:30 EST Monday-Friday

flashcards

Civil Procedure 1 (New '94-95 Ed.).........$16.95
Civil Procedure 2 (New '94-95 Ed.)...........16.95
Constitutional Law....................................16.95
Contracts 16.95
Corporations..16.95
Criminal Law 16.95
Criminal Procedure 16.95
Evidence..16.95
Future Interests 16.95
Professional Respon. (2 part set) 29.95
Real Property 16.95
Sales (UCC Art.2) (New '94-95 Ed.).........16.95
Torts 16.95
First Year Law Set.....................................95.00
Multistate Bar Review Set 165.00

software

Civil Procedure 1 (New '94-95 Ed.) $24.95
Civil Procedure 2 (New '94-95 Ed.) 24.95
Constitutional Law....................................24.95
Contracts 24.95
Corporations...24.95
Criminal Law 24.95
Criminal Procedure 24.95
Evidence...24.95
Future Interests 24.95
Professional Respon...................................39.95
Real Property 24.95
Sales (UCC Art. 2) (New '94-95 Ed.).........24.95
Torts 24.95
California Baby Bar Set..............................95.00
First Year Law Set....................................145.00
Multistate Bar Rev. Set 225.00
Multi-Year Set..295.95

strategies & tactics books

Strategies & Tactics for First Year Law $12.95
Strat. & Tact. for the MPRE
(Multistate Prof. Respon. Exam) 19.95
Strat. & Tact. for the MBE
(Multistate Bar Exam) 34.95

*** 1994-95 Academic Year ends May 31, 1995. After that date, editions and prices are subject to change.**